ROME
ENCOUNTER

CRISTIAN BONETTO

Rome Encounter

Published by Lonely Planet Publications Pty Ltd
ABN 36 005 607 983

Australia	Head Office, Locked Bag 1, Footscray, Vic 3011
	☎ 03 8379 8000 fax 03 8379 8111
	talk2us@lonelyplanet.com.au
USA	150 Linden St, Oakland, CA 94607
	☎ 510 250 6400
	toll free 800 275 8555
	fax 510 893 8572
	info@lonelyplanet.com
UK	2nd fl, 186 City Rd
	London EC1V 2NT
	☎ 020 7106 2100 fax 020 7106 2101
	go@lonelyplanet.co.uk

This title was commissioned in Lonely Planet's London office and produced by: **Commissioning Editors** Paula Hardy, Jo Potts **Coordinating Editor** Laura Crawford **Coordinating Cartographer** Amanda Sierp **Layout Designer** Nicholas Colicchia **Assisting Editor** Anne Mulvaney **Assisting Cartographer** Brendan Streager **Managing Editor** Annelies Mertens **Managing Cartographer** Shahara Ahmed **Managing Layout Designer** Indra Kilfoyle **Cover Researcher** Sabrina Dalbesio, lonely planetimages.com **Thanks to** Glenn Beanland, Helen Christinis, Melanie Dankel, Trent Paton, Celia Wood

ISBN 978 1 74179 681 0

Printed by Hang Tai Printing Company, Hong Kong
Printed in China

Mixed Sources
Product group from well-managed forests and other controlled sources
www.fsc.org Cert no. SGS-COC-005002
© 1996 Forest Stewardship Council

HOW TO USE THIS BOOK

Colour-Coding & Maps

Colour-coding is used for symbols on maps and in the text that they relate to (eg all eating venues on the maps and in the text are given a green knife and fork symbol). Each neighbourhood also gets its own colour, and this is used down the edge of the page and throughout that neighbourhood section.

Shaded yellow areas on the maps denote 'areas of interest' – for their historical significance, their attractive architecture or their great bars and restaurants. We encourage you to head to these areas and just start exploring!

Prices

Multiple prices listed with reviews (eg €10/5 or €10/5/20) indicate adult/child, adult/concession or adult/child/family.

Send us your feedback We love to hear from readers — your comments help make our books better. We read every word you send us, and we always guarantee that your feedback goes straight to the appropriate authors. The most useful submissions are rewarded with a free book. To send us your updates and find out about Lonely Planet events, newsletters and travel news visit our award-winning website: ***www.lonelyplanet.com/contact***.

Note: We may edit, reproduce and incorporate your comments in Lonely Planet products such as guidebooks, websites and digital products, so let us know if you don't want your comments reproduced or your name acknowledged. For a copy of our privacy policy visit ***www.lonelyplanet.com/privacy***.

CRISTIAN BONETTO

A self-confessed romantic with a weakness for devious driving and smooth-talking, irresponsibly tanned hedonists, it's not surprising Cristian is a shameless Rome junkie. Since first hitting the city with his rucksack in 1997, the Italo-Australian journalist and playwright has tread both its well-worn and lesser-known streets enough times to know how to charm his way out of parking fines, find the perfect slab of ricotta and spend an afternoon body painting to Roman rap in a suburban piazza. Cristian's musings on Rome and Italy have featured in magazines worldwide, and

his play *Il Cortile* was performed in Rome in 2003. He spends much of his life travelling between Italy, Scandinavia, New York and his home town of Melbourne, where you'll find him hunting down decent zabaglione gelato. Cristian's other Lonely Planet titles include *Naples & the Amalfi Coast*, *Sweden* and *Copenhagen Encounter*.

CRISTIAN'S THANKS

A big thank you to Paula Hardy for the commission, ideas and support. On the ground, *grazie infinite* to Vincenzo Maccarrone for his insights, generosity and passionate critiques of Roman life. Much gratitude also goes to Marco Bernardi, Carla Zaia, Christopher Lenthall, Beatrice Bertini, Valerio Prodomo, Valentina Bacci, Giorgio Maroni, Martina Fiori, and my ever-growing posse of secret-slipping *romani*.

THE PHOTOGRAPHER

Will Salter produces award-winning images of travel, sport and portraits. He sees photography as a privilege, a rare opportunity to become intimately involved in people's lives. See more at www.willsalter.com.

Our readers Many thanks to the travellers who wrote to us with helpful hints, useful advice and interesting anecdotes: Carole Barnabas, Severine Covens, Martin Cumberworth, Laura Dunlop, Gregory Morrison and Mangaia Tofilau.

Cover photograph Spiral staircase, inside Vatican Museums, Kelly Han/Photolibrary. **Internal photographs** p80, p100, p114, p127, p147, p166 by Cristian Bonetto; p14 Look Die Bildagentur der Fotografen Gmbh/Alamy; p15 Ettore Ferrari/EPA/Corbis; p21 Alinari Archives/Corbis; p22 Giovanni Simeone/SIME 4Corners; p24 Franco Origia/Getty Images; p27 Marco Longari/AFP/Getty Images; p28 Vincenzo Pinto/AFP/Getty Images; p111 CuboImages srl/Alamy; p136 Gautier Stephane/sagaphoto.com/Alamy; p178 Alessandro Di Meo/epa/Corbis; p190 Allegra Pazienti/freniefrizioni.com; p198 Andrea Matone/Alamy; p199 Gough Guides/Alamy. All other photographs by Lonely Planet Images and by Will Salter except p4 Glenn Beanland; p6 Krzysztof Dydynski; p11 Russell Mountford; p20, p55, p147, p200, Martin Moos; p32 Ilarian Isachar; p45 Jon Davison; p56 Philip & Karen Smith; p59, p60, p74, p121, p163, p170 Paolo Cordelli; p88 Oliver Cirendini; p184, p201 Greg Elms.

All images are copyright of the photographers unless otherwise indicated. Many of the images in this guide are available for licensing from **Lonely Planet Images**: www.lonelyplanetimages.com.

Jump on board and explore the cobbled laneways of Trastevere (p146), one of Rome's most atmospheric neighbourhoods

CONTENTS

Our authors are independent, dedicated travellers. They don't research using just the internet or phone, and they don't take freebies, so you can rely on their advice being well researched and impartial. They travel widely, visiting thousands of places, taking great pride in getting all the details right and telling it how it is.

THIS IS ROME

It starts off as a casual fling – a date with the Sistine Chapel, a flirt with the Spanish Steps, and (if you're lucky) a steamy session with a creamy carbonara.

Suddenly you can't stop thinking about that electrifying fresco, the sea of spires and domes below a hilltop terrace, and those languid nights of perfect Campari sodas on an intimate, rust-hued piazza. You're intrigued by the contradictions: sophisticated yet provincial, gregarious but downright rude.

Few cities get under the skin like Rome. One-time *caput mundi* (capital of the world), it was here that Brutus betrayed Julius Caesar, that Christ appeared to St Peter, and that Gregory Peck tricked Audrey Hepburn at the Bocca della Verità. It's like a travertine Filofax of Western cultural anecdotes, from chapel-painting Renaissance men to ill-fated Grand Tour romantics.

Yet Rome is far from a static relic. Here, past and present fuse with intoxicating effect – temple pillars soar beside tram stops; clubbers bump and grind in 14th-century chapels; and chariot racetracks double as rock-concert arenas. Amid the jumble of imperial ruins, baroque fountains and retro espresso bars exists a kicking 21st-century cocktail of gritty street art, multiethnic neighbourhoods and Italo-fusion flavours. One minute you're walking in the footsteps of the Caesars and the next you're rocking to local indie bands in a graffiti pimped bar. It mightn't have Berlin's daring or London's edge but new millennium Rome is set on catching up to its 'with it' northern rivals. Recent years have seen the launch of two bold new contemporary art museums, a cutting-edge performing arts centre and a spate of fresh, dynamic festivals.

Of course, it's not always *perfetto* (perfect) – true love never is. Anarchic traffic, pollution and persistent beggars can give the Eternal City a whole new meaning. With an 'it's over' ready on your tongue, suddenly you stumble across a secret courtyard, a perfect zabaglione gelato or a hidden Caravaggio… and fall head over heels again.

Top Bask beneath the baroque ceiling of Chiesa del Gesù (p51) in the *centro storico* (historic city centre) **Bottom** Spend an afternoon alfresco on Vicolo del Cinque, Trastevere (p146)

IN HONOREM PRINCIPIS APOST PAVLVS V BVRGHESIVS ROMANVS PON

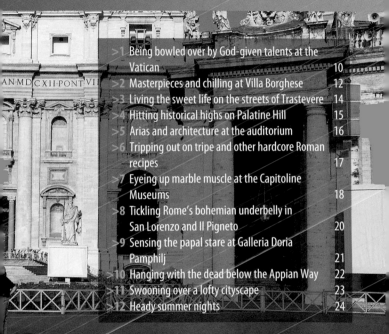

In good company outside monumental St Peter's Basilica (p163)

> 1 VATICAN CITY

BEING BOWLED OVER BY GOD-GIVEN TALENTS AT THE VATICAN

Beautiful, rich and powerful: the Vatican (Città del Vaticano; p162) is sweet Christian revenge. After all, it was in the Ager Vaticanus stadium just south of the Vatican that 1st-century emperor Nero martyred the faithful. Among them was A-list apostle Peter, whose tomb lies beneath the monumental St Peter's Basilica (Basilica di San Pietro).

Commissioned by Constantine in 315 and torn down in 1506, the basilica was ambitiously rebuilt by a league of Renaissance stars, including Bramante and Raphael. Top billing, however, goes to Michelangelo, who in 1547 (aged 72) took over where Bramante left off, designing the epic 119m high dome. Equally impressive is his heart-rending *Pietà,* which he sculpted at the age of 24; it's the only work inscribed with his name – see the ribbon on Mary's left shoulder. Other famous contributors to the basilica include Maderno, who extended the nave and revamped the façade in the early 17th century, and Gian Lorenzo Bernini, who created his bombastic baldachin with bronze from the Pantheon's portico. It soars 29m above the pope's high altar. Walk clockwise around the structure, starting at the front left, and you'll notice a woman's face carved into each pillar. Depicted in ever-increasing labour pain in the first three, the fourth pillar shows a bouncing baby. The woman was a niece of Pope Urban VIII and gave birth as Bernini worked on the structure. Bernini also whipped up St Peter's Square (Piazza San Pietro) – the Vatican's colossal welcome mat – and sculpted the pontiff's tomb, the statue of St Longinus, the Throne of St Peter and the monument to Alexander VII.

Downstairs in the Vatican grottoes are the papal tombs, among them the simple marble slab that Pope John Paul II now calls home. Far less modest are the adjacent Vatican Museums, an exhausting feast of art, and home to the world's most famous frescoes in the legendary Sistine Chapel. While 15th-century masterpieces by the likes of Botticelli, Ghirlandaio, Pinturicchio and Signorelli flatter the chapel's walls, it's Michelangelo's astounding ceiling and wall frescoes that take the cake – picture terrified sinners and ravishing prophets bursting out in 3-D brilliance. Jealous Bramante would be

turning in his grave, having convinced Pope Julius II to commission the inexperienced Michelangelo in the hope of seeing the young gun fail.

Bramante's pal Raphael frescoed the Stanze di Raffaello (the finest works are in the Stanza della Segnatura), while the Pinacoteca (art gallery) features Raphael's final effort, *La Trasfigurazione* (1517–20), as well as brushstrokes from the likes of Giotto, Leonardo da Vinci, Caravaggio, Guercino, Nicolas Poussin and Pietro da Cortona. Exquisite vintage maps fill the Galleria delle Carte Geografiche; ancient Egyptian finds line the Museo Gregoriano Egizio; Etruscan burial treasures pack Museo Gregoriano Etrusco; and early Christian antiquities call Museo Pio Cristiano home. And while Museo Gregoriano Profano stocks pagan statuary aplenty, it's no match for the Museo Pio Clementino, whose unbeatable collection of classical statues includes the gym-fit 5th-century BC *Belevedere Torso*, the 2nd-century BC masterpiece *Apollo Belvedere* and the hyperdramatic *Laocoön* (150 BC), which inspired Michelangelo.

>2 VILLA AND MUSEO E GALLERIA BORGHESE

MASTERPIECES AND CHILLING AT VILLA BORGHESE

There are good art museums. There are great art museums. And then there's the Museo e Galleria Borghese (p179). Upstaging most of the national competition (no mean feat in Italy), it's a no-excuses must-see, and one that's well worth the slight hassle of the phone call or mouse click required to book a ticket.

You have *bon vivant* Cardinal Scipione Borghese to thank for the collection. Bernini's greatest patron, Borghese was also nephew to Pope Paul V, whose nepotistic streak allowed the cashed-up cardinal to amass his enviable cultural cache. Indeed, the cardinal was the most ruthless art collector of his day, stopping at nothing to get what he wanted. He had Cavaliere d'Arpino flung into jail in order to confiscate his canvases, and had Domenichino arrested to force him to surrender *The Hunt of Diana*. Less questionable was his decision to have 17th-century wedding cake Villa Borghese built to house his ever-expanding cultural booty.

Ground-floor treasures include a Roman copy of a languid Hellenic *Hermaphroditus;* Antonio Canova's depiction of Napoleon's toy-boy-loving sister, Paolina Bonaparte Borghese, as Venus; and a young Bernini's mesmerising statues – see Pluto's hand pressing into Proserpine's thigh in the charged *Rape of Proserpine,* Apollo's ingeniously captured emotional shift in *Apollo and Daphne,* and compare Bernini's dynamic *David* to Michelangelo's languorous version.

Borghese was also a patron of the rebellious Caravaggio. There are six works by the brush-clutching rebel in the collection, including crowd-favourite *Boy with a Basket of Fruit,* the strangely beautiful *Madonna with Serpent* and the gutsy *David with the Head of Goliath,* in which the severed head is reputedly a self-portrait of the exiled bad boy.

The feast continues in the upstairs picture gallery, home to top-notch brushstrokes from the Tuscan, Venetian, Umbrian and northern European schools, among them Raphael's *Christ Being Taken Down from the Cross,* Rubens' *Lamentation over the Dead Christ* and Titian's extraordinary *Sacred and Profane Love.*

The villa, given a neoclassical makeover by architect Antonio Asprucci in 1775, stands in the verdant sprawl of Rome's best-loved park. This is the inner city's collective backyard and most locals harbour childhood memories of Sunday afternoon adventures amid the formal gardens, ornamental lakes and dreamy temples. Rome's first cricket match was played here in the 1780s, and it's home to some other cultural entities, including Museo Carlo Bilotti (p179), Silvano Toti Globe Theatre (p183) and cinephile hangout Casa del Cinema (p182). Of course, we won't think any less of you if you opt for aimless ambling instead…in which case we suggest picking up a picnic hamper from GiNa (p78) on your way.

>3 TRASTEVERE
LIVING THE SWEET LIFE ON THE STREETS OF TRASTEVERE

It may no longer boast the bohemian grit of San Lorenzo and Il Pigneto (p20), but Rome's picture-perfect 'left bank' can still sock an edgy cultural punch. Hip, contemporary galleries stud its cobbled streets, including pioneering veteran Galleria Lorcan O'Neill (p151), intelligentsia favourite Fondazione Volume! (p150) and newcomer Ex Elettro Fonica (p150), designed by two Zaha Hadad protégés. The literati still flock to bookshop Bibli (p152) for readings and launches, while a few doors down at Libreria del Cinema (p159) film types assess auteurs over coffee and Chianti.

It's no wonder sensitive souls still feel at home here. Trastevere is a visual charmer, crammed with ivy-tickled ochre façades, labyrinthine laneways, vintage trattorias and buzzing, chilled-out squares. Indeed, the area is a hit with foreigners, who flock here to live out their Roman fantasy. There's even an American university on Via della Lungara for those needing a heftier reason to linger.

Among the smitten *stranieri* (foreigners), you'll find the ever-diminishing *trasteverini*, the real-deal locals who consider themselves Rome's true classical descendants. You can help them celebrate their superiority complex in July at the Festa di Noantri (p27) street party. For the rest of the year, you won't have much trouble finding a place to indulge in a little *dolce vita;* after dark, Trastevere remains one of Rome's most happening hangouts.

>4 PALATINE

HITTING HISTORICAL HIGHS ON PALATINE HILL

In late 2007 Rome's most romantic ruins hit the headlines when archaeologist Andrea Carandini announced the discovery of a subterranean grotto believed to be the fabled Lupercale, revered by the ancient Romans as the spot where the she-wolf nursed Romulus and Remus. Camera probe images revealed a dazzling sanctuary studded with seashells and coloured mosaics buried 16m below the Palatine (Palatino; p46). Alas, it wasn't long before several other high-profile archaeologists rained on Carandini's parade, arguing that the real site lies a further 50m to 100m from what they believe is simply a nymphaeum.

In September 2009, Palatine archaeologists made another sensational claim that a 4m-wide circular pillar unearthed below the Vigna Barberini – a panoramic terrace with spectacular views of the Colosseum (p44) – belonged to Nero's fabled *coenatio rotunda*, a rotating dining hall inside the once-sprawling Domus Aurea (p95).

While bickering over the accuracy of the claim continues, a less contentious headliner is the restored Casa di Augusto. Home to Augustus in his pre-ruling days, four of its vividly frescoed rooms (including the emperor's private studio) were opened to the public in 2008.

Tranquil, commanding, and the birthplace of Rome itself, the Palatine's appeal is clear. Start your hillside exploration at Museo Palatino, then ramble through the ruins: the stucco-laced Casa dei Grifi; the 16th-century Orti Faranesi gardens; and the Casa Livia, whose frescoes wow in Museo Nazionale Romano: Palazzo Massimo alle Terme (p96).

HIGHLIGHTS

>5 AUDITORIUM PARCO DELLA MUSICA

ARIAS AND ARCHITECTURE AT THE AUDITORIUM

Rome's new-millennium performing arts centre (p182) has been hitting the high notes indeed. Since its debut in 2004, this so-called 'Music Park' has effortlessly drawn over a million spectators annually, making it Europe's most popular arts venue.

We're not surprised. Culture vultures are spoilt rotten by a programme that's as dynamic as it is democratically priced – €5 will have you tapping away to Gershwin; €15 will get you to a contemporary dance premiere. Indeed, you could spend a whole day here, hopping from a morning performance by the resident Santa Cecilia National Symphony Orchestra to an exhibition of emerging Italian artists, from a rock-music seminar to an evening performance of Brecht. With its installation by Tuscan artist Maurizio Nannucci, even the foyer is a destination. It's peppered with red neon quotes from history's creative geniuses and blue neon quotes from Nannucci's own *Antologio* project.

The list of features continues with the uncovered foundations of a 6th-century BC villa, an ancient oil press, in-house archaeological exhibits, a museum housing rare musical instruments, a well-stocked book and music shop, and slinky nosh-spot Red (p181)…not to mention the Renzo Piano–designed structure itself – a classically inspired open-air amphitheatre surrounded by three concert halls encased in huge lead-clad pods. Likened to everything from giant beetles to spacecraft (we're thinking enormous computer mice), Piano studied the interiors of lutes and violins when designing their acoustically astounding interiors. His obsession paid off.

>6 FIFTH QUARTER FEASTING

TRIPPING OUT ON TRIPE AND OTHER HARDCORE ROMAN RECIPES

Herbivores, turn the page. Carnivores, prepare for some extreme epicurean escapades – and we don't mean a little extra *panna* (cream) in your *spaghetti alla carbonara*. We're talking about that quintessential Roman ingredient, offal. We're thinking unapologetic Roman staples such as *trippa alla romana* (tripe cooked with potatoes, tomato and mint and sprinkled with *pecorino* cheese), *coda alla vaccinara* (literally, butcher-style oxtail) and the deliciously creamy pasta with *pajata* (made with veal calves' entrails, containing the mother's congealed milk).

Don't dry-retch until you've tried it. Remember, you're in a gourmand's paradise, where clued-up cooking and herbs can transform veal liver into a buttery revelation. After all, the locals have had a long time to get it right – the 4th-century Roman cookbook *Apicius* glistens with seasoned livers, hearts and brains, and up until the mid-20th century, butchers at the city's giant Mattatoio abattoir were paid in meat as well as money, taking home the innards deemed unfit for bourgeois palates. It was in these working-class kitchens that many of Rome's low-cost classics evolved.

While most Roman menus offer an organ or two, the best spot for a little nose-to-tail consumption is the earthy Testaccio district (p130). Home of the legendary Ex-Mattatoio slaughterhouse, it's where you'll find Rome's undisputed offal dining legend, Checchino dal 1887 (p135).

>7 CAPITOLINE MUSEUMS AT PIAZZA DEL CAMPIDOGLIO

EYEING UP MARBLE MUSCLE AT THE CAPITOLINE MUSEUMS

The planet's oldest public museum (p42) is a powder keg of legend, lust and melodrama, encapsulated in Rome's finest collection of classical treasures. Filling two *palazzi* (palaces or large buildings) on Michelangelo's Piazza del Campidoglio (Palazzo dei Conservatori at the southern end and Palazzo Nuovo at the northern end), the collection was established by Pope Sixtus IV in 1471, who donated a few bronze statues to the city. One of the gifts was the iconic 5th-century BC Etruscan bronze *She-Wolf* (complete with suckling Renaissance twins), now feeding happily on Palazzo dei Conservatori's 1st floor. Her famous fellow residents include 1st-century BC thorn-plucker *Spinario*, Bernini's classically inclined *Medusa* and the sumptuously frescoed Sala degli Orazi e Curiazi.

The Palazzo dei Conservatori's most recent addition is the luminous Sala di Marco Aurelio – Capitoline Museums' (modest) answer to Sir Norman Foster's Great Court at the British Museum. Designed by Italian neorealist veteran Carlo Aymonino, it skilfully shows off an epic 2nd-century equestrian statue of the hall's namesake emperor, foundations from the ancient Temple of Jupiter, and a giant bronze head of Constantine (which bears an uncanny resemblance to Sylvester Stallone). Celebrities filled the hall in June 2007 for the launch of fashion designer Valentino's 45th anniversary festivities. Finally, for fashionable yet ancient flooring, don't miss the stunning alabaster pavement in the nearby Horti Lamiani room.

On the 2nd floor, the Pinacoteca (art gallery) is a well-hung affair, with works spanning the late Middle Ages to the 18th century. Pick your favourite from masterpieces such as Guercino's *Burial of St Petronilla,* Garofalo's *Annunciation* and Pietro da Cortona's *Rape of the Sabine Women,* or opt for Caravaggio's cheeky *St John the Baptist* and his sneaky *The Fortune Teller.*

Connecting the Palazzo dei Conservatori to the Palazzo Nuovo is the basement Tabularium. Once ancient Rome's archive, its

collection of tender epigraphs and stone-carved public notices offers an intimate glimpse of daily ancient life – though the real highlight here is the balcony, with its Caesar-worthy views over the Roman Forum (p47).

Palazzo Nuovo's treasures include the timid *Capitoline Venus,* a remarkably detailed dove mosaic from Hadrian's Tivoli villa (itself a copy of a famous 2nd-century BC mosaic by Sosos of Pergamon); and the Sala dei Filosofi, which is lined with busts of classical thinkers, politicians and poets. The real show-stoppers await, however, in the Sala del Galata, where you'll find the 5th-century BC *Wounded Amazon,* and the moving *Dying Gaul,* a Roman copy of a 3rd-century BC Pergamon original depicting the anguish of a dying Frenchman.

>8 SAN LORENZO AND IL PIGNETO

TICKLING ROME'S BOHEMIAN UNDERBELLY IN SAN LORENZO AND IL PIGNETO

Political street art, grungy *centri sociali* (social centres) and hardcore leftist leanings – San Lorenzo is Rome's radical heartland. Born as a 19th-century slum and famed for its anti-Fascist history, it's now a hip hangout for real-deal bohemians, avant-garde artists and the swarms of students from the nearby La Sapienza university campus.

Creativity lines these grungy streets, from the geometric threads created by Myriam B (p109) to poetic treats at Bocca di Dama (p110). It's where you'll find iconic art incubator Pastificio Cerere (see the boxed text, p108); the late film-maker Pier Paolo Pasolini's favourite restaurant, Pommidoro (p111); and enough kicking, arty bars to work up one heavy hangover.

To the east, beyond the *Bladerunner*-style overpasses of Circonvallazione Tiburtina, raffish Il Pigneto has established itself as Rome's hippest *quartiere* (neighbourhood). The setting for neorealist films such as Rossellini's *Roma città aperta*, Visconti's *Bellissima* and Pasolini's *Accattone*, it's a beguiling mix of African migrant hangouts, counterculture cool, and slinky new bars and shops. Stencil art pimps 19th-century workers' cottages, peckish poets philosophise at Hobo ArtClub (p112), and dreadlocked radicals swill beer and politics on kerbsides.

For the best vibe, drop by in the evening, when local bohemians pour into bars such as Vini e Olii (p113) and Cargo (p112) for *aperitivo* (happy hour). Leave some room for dinner at historic Necci (p110) or in-the-know Osteria Qui Si Magna! (p110), before grungy late-night culture and clubbing at everyone's indie favourite, Fanfulla 101 (p115).

>9 GALLERIA DORIA PAMPHILJ

SENSING THE PAPAL STARE AT GALLERIA DORIA PAMPHILJ
Lavish Galleria Doria Pamphilj (p55) boasts one of the capital's richest
private art collections, with works by Raphael, Caravaggio, Titian,
Tintoretto, Brueghel, Bernini and Velázquez in the mix.

It's housed in the blingtastic Palazzo Doria Pamphilj, whose decadent
Gallery of Mirrors resembles a snack-sized Versailles. Ready to help you
tackle the booty is palace resident Jonathon Pamphilj (on the free audioguide), whose anecdotes about the art, sumptuous rooms and the odd
ancestral scandal transform the space into a living, breathing entity.

Among the many cultural stars are Titian's macabre *Salome Holding
the Head of John the Baptist* (apparently a self-portrait, with Salome
modelled on his out-of-favour ex); Quentin Massys' darkly amusing
Two Hypocrites; and two striking early works by Caravaggio, *Rest
During the Flight into Egypt* and *Penitent Magdalene,* where the artist
used the same model for both the Virgin and the prostitute.

Upstaging them all, however, is Velázquez's striking, psychological-
ly present portrait of Pope Innocent X. Upon its unveiling the pontiff
grumbled that the depiction was 'too real'. He wasn't wrong – you
can actually feel his critical gaze sizing you up. Thankfully, Bernini's
sculpted version of the 17th-century pontiff won't leave you feeling
quite as guilty.

>10 APPIAN WAY

HANGING WITH THE DEAD BELOW THE APPIAN WAY

The cypress-fringed Appian Way (Via Appia Antica; p124) is a classical Sunset Blvd; it's shrouded in legends and tales of famous faces. Only here the protagonists aren't faded divas, they're saviours and saints. Heading the cast is Christ himself, who is said to have appeared to St Peter where Chiesa del Domine Quo Vadis? (p126) now stands. In true Hollywood style, Jesus left his footprints on a slab of marble, now on show in Basilica e Catacombe di San Sebastiano (p126). The basilica's other famous relics are an arrow that was used to pierce St Sebastian, and the column to which he was tied. Depicted as a handsome, bound martyr by artists as diverse as Rubens and Pierre et Gilles, Christianity's unofficial pin-up boy was buried below the basilica after Emperor Diocletian had him beaten to death in the late 3rd century.

St Sebastian wasn't the only celestial celebrity laid to rest in these catacombs either; the bodies of St Peter and St Paul were reputedly hidden here by their persecuted fans. Close by, in Catacombe di San Callisto (p126), St Cecilia would have turned LA's botoxed beauties green with envy; her body was discovered in mint condition centuries after her death.

It's hard to dispute the otherworldly lure of Rome's ancient highway, where secret frescoes and long-forgotten epigraphs lurk below rolling hills, crumbled mausoleums and ancient chariot racetracks. If possible, hit the strip on Sundays, when traffic is banned and Rome's 'Queen of the Roads' turns into peddle-friendly bliss.

>11 ROMAN PANORAMAS

SWOONING OVER A LOFTY CITYSCAPE

Originally perched on seven hills, and now sprawling over several more, Rome seems specially made for jaw-dropping vistas. Other cities might boast taller peaks – both natural and artificial – but few can match the Eternal City's near-flawless historical sweeps.

From Gianicolo (p151), the capital's loftiest hill, Rome sprawls east in a sea of terracotta rooftops and flouncy cupolas – Il Vittoriano (itself a purveyor of perfect panoramas; see p45) sticking out like an awkward guest. For the best effect, eye it all up in Rome's sublime late-afternoon light, when the city resembles a radiant, sun-baked postcard.

Closer to the central action is St Peter's Basilica (p163), Rome's tallest building. Its dome offers a superlative overview of St Peter's Square (p167) and a sneak peek into the Vatican's well-guarded backyard. For a more intimate view of the *centro storico* (historic city centre), head to the upper terraces of Castel Sant'Angelo (p163), but not before taking in the classic Tiber views from Ponte Sant'Angelo.

If it's ruins you're craving, climb the Palatine (p46), or kick back at nearby Caffè Capitolino (p60), where cupola-sprinkled views come with a mean espresso. Gourmands can get that skyscraper feeling at Imàgo (p81), while nearby Casina Valadier (p182) is the perfect spot for Vatican-punctuated sunsets and outdoor champagne sessions.

For the ultimate in romance, however, don't miss Parco Savello (p132), where the sinking sun is viewed from a perfumed terrace.

>12 SUMMER IN THE CITY
HEADY SUMMER NIGHTS

Puccini among the ruins, Herbie Hancock under the stars: summertime in Rome is a seriously swinging affair. While temperatures continue to soar and many clubs and restaurants still shut for a little R&R, the Eternal City has shrugged off its reputation as a summertime wasteland with a bumper season of thumping festivals.

From June to September, mammoth culture fest Estate Romana (www.estateromana.comune.roma.it) transforms the city into a giant stage: conductors rouse their orchestras at the Roman Forum, celluloid classics light up the Colosseum, and parks turn into theatres. Also getting in on the act is the city's opera company, Teatro dell'Opera (www.operaroma.it), whose summer season turns the ruins of the Terme di Caracalla (p133) into an unforgettable backdrop each July and August.

Another summer-long hit is the Villa Celimontana Jazz Festival, with its season of top-notch sax in Villa Celimontana park (p123). Although gigs usually start around 10pm, head in early to grab a table and watch the sunset over a long, cool drink.

Across town at Villa Ada (Map pp176–7, F2), Roma Incontra Il Mondo (www.villaada.org in Italian) serves up world-music gigs from mid-June to early August, while from late June to September queer life gets loud and proud at the kicking Gay Village (see the boxed text, p29) – think 10 weeks of alfresco noshing, sloshing and clubbing, and flicks for bent and beautiful revellers.

>ROME DIARY

Determined to catch up with Europe's hipper hubs, Rome has revamped its social calendar with a new wave of cultural happenings. Recent additions include an international film festival, an international contemporary photography festival and a ghetto-tastic hip-hop festival. Summer is peak festival season (see opposite), when long, languid days set the scene for everything from twilight jazz to a 10-week-long queer party. Many festivals change their dates from year to year, so always check ahead. For a rundown of festival dates, hit www.romaturismo.it, as well as www.whatsonwhen.com.

Enjoy a contemplative moment in Basilica di Santa Maria Maggiore (p94) amid a busy festival schedule

FEBRUARY

Carnevale

The week leading up to Lent is a technicolour spectacle involving costumed kids throwing confetti and nostalgic adults scoffing down delectable *bignè* (profiteroles) and *fritelle* (fried pastries). It's all quite cute but comparatively tame: up until the 1880s, Romans celebrated this event with madcap riderless horse races down Via del Corso.

MARCH

Maratona di Roma

www.maratonadiroma.it

Almost 50,000 masochists huff'n'puff their way through the city's annual marathon. Get serious with the 42km course, or show yourself some mercy with the 5km fun run.

APRIL

Mostra delle Azalea

To celebrate that spring has sprung, thousands of scarlet azaleas grace the Spanish Steps, turning the famous staircase into a blazing photo opportunity.

Rome Independent Film Festival (RIFF)

www.riff.it

Based at Nuovo Cinema Aquila, RIFF offers one tasty week of fresh new flicks from Italian and foreign directors. Check the website for dates.

Procession of the Cross

On Good Friday, the pope leads a candlelit procession from the Colosseum to the Palatine. On Easter Sunday, he blesses his flock in St Peter's Square at noon.

Natale di Roma

On 21 April Rome celebrates its birthday in the Piazza del Campidoglio with live bands and loud fireworks. In 2011 the city turns a youthful 2764.

Settimana della Cultura (Week of Culture)

www.beniculturali.it in Italian

A week of free entry to public museums and otherwise closed sites. Dates change annually – check the website.

MAY

Primo Maggio

www.primomaggio.com in Italian

Rome salutes May Day with a massive open-air rock concert featuring big-name rockers.

Rome Literature Festival

www.festivaldelleletterature.it

Spilling into June, this festival offers free readings inside the Roman Forum. Past guests include Ishmael Beah.

Rome's annual marathon involves a high-intensity tour of the city's streets

La Notte dei Musei

www.museiincomuneroma.it/mostre_ed_eventi/eventi/la_notte_dei_musei
This one night sees over 50 museums and cultural sites offer free entry into the wee small hours.

JUNE

¡Fiesta!

www.fiesta.it in Italian
A sizzling, summer-long ode to Latin American tunes and food on the Capanelle racecourse on Via Appia Nuova. Past hip-shakers include Ricky Martin.

Feast of Sts Peter & Paul

On 29 June Rome honours its patron saints with mass at St Peter's Basilica and a street fair at Basilica di San Paolo Fuori-le-Mura.

JULY

Festa di Noantri

Trastevere's kicking two-week street party includes the parading of the Virgin

Mass at St Peter's Basilica celebrates the Feast of Sts Peter & Paul (p27) in June

of Carmine on the month's third Saturday. Head to Piazza Santa Maria in Trastevere, which is the hub for celebrations.

Invito alla Danza

www.invitoalladanza.it in Italian

Rome's much-loved dance festival draws top-notch international performers to the parklands of Villa Doria Pamphilj.

Rock in Roma

www.rockinroma.com

Dust down the denims for Rome's big rock fest, usually spanning the month of July. Headline acts in 2010 included Mika, The Cranberries and Skunk Anansie.

AUGUST

Ferragosto

The Feast of the Assumption on 15 August is when Rome practically shuts down and locals head to the beach or into the hills.

SEPTEMBER

FotoGrafia

www.fotografiafestival.it

Contemporary photography hits MACRO Future from late September to late October for Rome's international celebration of photographic art. Events include exhibitions, screenings and seminars.

RomaEuropa

www.romaeuropa.net

Spanning September to November, this is Rome's top arts festival, covering everything from orchestras and opera, to cutting-edge international theatre and dance.

OCTOBER

Cinema – Festa Internazionale del Film di Roma

www.romacinemafest.org

Rome's fledgling International Film Festival spans commercial premieres to emerging international talent in cinemas across town.

International Festival of Sacred Music & Art

www.festivalmusicaeartesacra.net

Some of Europe's finest classical orchestras hit Rome's four basilicas for magical evening performances from the Festival's Orchestra-in-Residence, international artists and the Vienna Philharmonic.

Via dei Coronari Mostra Mercato

In late October collectors flock to this antiques fair, held on vintage-booty heavyweight Via dei Coronari.

NOVEMBER

Roma Jazz Festival

www.romajazzfestival.it

Rome's passion for sax heats up through November, when jazz greats descend on the Auditorium Parco della Musica for a series of intoxirating jams. Guest performers at the 2009 edition included Sonny Rollins, Jamie Cullen, the So What Band and the Stefano Bollani Trio.

OFFBEAT OFFERINGS

Festa di Santa Francesca Romana Roman motorists pull up outside Monastero delle Oblate di Santa Francesca Romana (Map p41, B2; Via del Teatro di Marcello 32 & 40) on 9 March for the annual 'Blessing of the Cars'. One drive around Rome and you'll appreciate the call for divine intercession.
Gay Village Scan www.gayvillage.it for dates and locations of Rome's summer-long queer culture'n'clubbing fest.
Festa delle Catene You can kiss the chains that bound St Peter on 1 August at a sombre mass in Chiesa di San Pietro in Vincoli.
Festa della Madonna della Neve On 5 August thousands of white rose petals flutter down over the altar at Basilica di Santa Maria Maggiore to celebrate a 4th-century miracle snowfall on Esquiline hill.

DECEMBER

Piazza Navona Christmas Fair
No Nordic tea lights here, just blindingly bright stalls flogging nativity scenes, stuffed toys and jaw-breaking *torrone* (nougat). Brilliantly fun kitsch or one big eyesore? Decide for yourself.

Capodanno
Rome bids *arrivederci* (goodbye) to the year on 31 December with jubilant fireworks and free music concerts in packed-out Piazza del Popolo.

Chief among the ruins, the Colosseum (p44) makes for impressive viewing

ITINERARIES

You'll need several reincarnations to cover Rome from top to bottom, but that shouldn't be the plan. Amble lazily down side streets, linger over linguine and allow yourself to get lost in the city's mesmerising streetscapes. If you're looking for a little direction, however, tie your laces and consider the following routes.

ONE DAY

Bid Rome *buongiorno* from atop St Peter's Basilica (p163), then ogle the Sistine Chapel at Vatican Museums (p167). After lunch at Da Gino (p64), dive into the labyrinthine lanes of the *centro storico* (historic city centre); chances are you'll stumble across Piazza Navona (p58) and the mighty Pantheon (p57). If you've the energy, roam the Colosseum (p44) or Palatine (p46) before evening *aperitivo* (happy hour) at Freni e Frizioni (p159), new-school noshing at Glass Hostaria (p156) and basement blues at Big Mama (p160).

TWO DAYS

Day Two begins with masterpieces at Museo e Galleria Borghese (p179) and a soothing stroll through Villa Borghese (p180). Pop into Museo Carlo Bilotti (p179) for a quick fix of Warhol and Giorgio de Chirico, or head straight to Il Palazzetto (p79) for lunch. Once done, saunter down the Spanish Steps (p76) for catwalk couture on Via dei Condotti, or shop for edgier threads on the streets of Monti (p92). Revamped, it's time for cocktails at Salotto 42 (p69), a bubbling pizza at Da Baffetto (p63) and late-night schmoozing at Fluid (p68).

THREE DAYS

Kill the hangover with espresso at Caffè Sant'Eustachio (p68) before facing the *She-Wolf* at Capitoline Museums (p42). Don't forget to take in the views from the museum café before a well-earned soak at Acqua Madre Hammam (p70), followed by top-notch wining, dining and tunes at Auditorium Parco della Musica (p182).

Top MALRO (Museo d'Arte Contemporanea di Roma; p178) is one of the hottest hubs in Rome for contemporary art
Bottom Wend your way down the spiral staircase at the Vatican Museums (p167)

SOMETHING FOR NOTHING

Thinning wallets rejoice! Some of the best things in Rome are free, including the Vatican Museums (p167) on the last Sunday of the month. For free masterpieces, hit the city's churches, whether that's Caravaggio canvases at Chiesa di San Luigi dei Francesi (p54), Chiesa di Sant'Agostino (p54) and Chiesa di Santa Maria del Popolo (p74); Bernini sculptures inside Chiesa di Santa Maria della Vittoria (p86) and Chiesa di San Francesco d'Assisi a Ripa (p150); or Byzantine mosaics in Chiesa di Santa Prassede (p95). Must-see landmarks such as Trevi Fountain (p88), Spanish Steps (p76) and the Pantheon (p57) are also gratis, while both Auditorium Parco della Musica (p182) and culture fest Estate Romana (p24) dish out free cultural gigs. Best of all is the annual Settimana della Cultura (Week of Culture; p26), which offers free entry to all public museums. For further free options, check out www.romacheap.it (in Italian).

CONTEMPORARY CAPITAL

Dive into the new millennium at MAXXI (p178) or MACRO (p178) before passing judgment on Richard Meier's Museo dell'Ara Pacis (p75). Lunch at 'Gusto (p79), bag street-smart wares at Mondo Pop (p78), hit Pastificio

A gourmand's paradise awaits at 'Gusto (p79) in Tridente

FORWARD PLANNING

Three to four weeks before you go Check to see if your visit coincides with any festivals (see p24 & p25). If so, scan the festival websites for what's on. Music fans should hit the sites for Auditorium Parco della Musica (p182), Circolo degli Artisti (p113) and Teatro dell'Opera di Roma (p105) for upcoming gigs. Gourmands should scan the International Wine Academy of Roma (p83) website and join the Fuzzy Bar (p112) email list (in Italian) for upcoming wine and food events. Get the lowdown from the locals on their blogs and websites (p216).

Two weeks before you go A-list restaurants like Imàgo (p81), Il Palazzetto (p79) and Il Convivio Troiani (p65) should be booked around now, as well as any spa treatment at Acanto Benessere Day Spa (p69) or Acqua Madre Hammam (p70). Buy tickets online to the Vatican Museums (p167) and the Vatican Gardens (p167), and check the Alexanderplatz (p172) website if you fancy live jazz.

A few days before you go Book your tickets for Museo e Galleria Borghese (p179), scan www.060608.it for culture-scene updates, check out www.exibart.com (in Italian) for exhibitions, and book a table at Da Gino (p64).

Cerere (see the boxed text, p108) to absorb Rome's modern artistic soul, then refuel at current hot spot Ristorante Pastificio San Lorenzo (p111). Top off the night with experimental drama at Teatro India (p161) or progressive beats at Rashomon (p145).

FOODIE TRAIL

Wake the taste buds at La Tazza d'Oro (p68) before prodding the produce at Campo de' Fiori (p51). Cross the Tiber for *cannoli* (ricotta-filled pastries) at Valzani (p158), then head straight to Città del Gusto (see the boxed text, p155) to seek your culinary muse. Feast in-house or lunch adventurously at Checchino dal 1887 (p135). Stock up on organic local produce at Città dell'Altra Economia (p134), taste-test cheese at legendary Volpetti (p136), then refine your palate at International Wine Academy of Roma (p83). If you haven't booked for a wine-tasting session at the academy, instead pop in and swirl a rare local drop at Palatium (p82), then dine on the culinary cutting edge at Il Convivio Troiani (p65) or Michelin-starred Imàgo (p81).

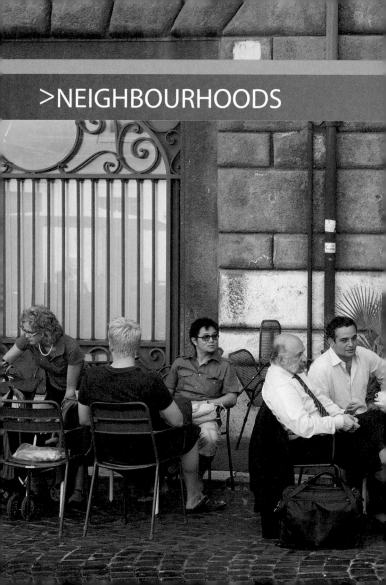

>NEIGHBOURHOODS

Catch up on the local lowdown at Caffè Sant'Eustachio (p68), in the *centro storico* (historic city centre)

NEIGHBOURHOODS

NEIGHBOURHOODS

Tickled by the Tiber, Rome is a heaving mass of superlatives – from the best of baroque to the worst of bumper-to-bumper.

Three millennia of battles and brilliance have created a city with almost too much to offer. The trick is not to sweat it – stroll the *quartieri* (neighbourhoods), lick a gelato and soak it all up like a *romano*.

The area spanning the Colosseum, Palatine and Capitoline is Rome's ancient core, home to evocative ruins and improbable legends. To the south, Caelian Hill and Lateran offer a soothing slice of medieval Rome, while to the northwest, the *centro storico* (historic city centre) is the capital's thumping heart – a heady warren of famous squares and laneways, galleries, wine bars and hip eateries and clubs.

Across the Tiber, medieval Trastevere pulls in the expats with its kicking bar scene, and neighbouring Gianicolo offers to-die-for panoramas; Vatican City needs no introduction and nearby Prati serves up respectable shopping and noshing.

Just north of the *centro storico,* elegant Tridente features designer denizens, Euro-flash retail and the look-at-me Spanish Steps; at the top of the stairs, leafy Villa Borghese harbours a smattering of cultural treasures. East of the park, and north of Tridente's Piazza del Popolo, suburban Northern Rome hosts contemporary cultural hubs, quirky architecture and off-the-radar catacombs.

Lying to the east of the *centro storico,* Trevi is home to masterpiece hot spots Galleria Colonna and Palazzo Barberini, as well as Rome's most famous fountain; Quirinal serves up a presidential palace; and Monti's snug streets harbour funky threads and intimate wine bars. Southeast of Monti, Esquiline is home to Stazione Termini, gritty multiculturalism and a clutch of must-see museums and churches. Further southeast, San Lorenzo and Il Pigneto offer real-deal Roman bohemia.

Beyond salubrious Aventine, south of the ancient centre, down-to-earth Testaccio is the city's clubbling centre. The party vibe continues into postindustrial Ostiense, before hitting the reverence of San Paolo Fuori-le-Mura and the Fascist fantasy of EUR.

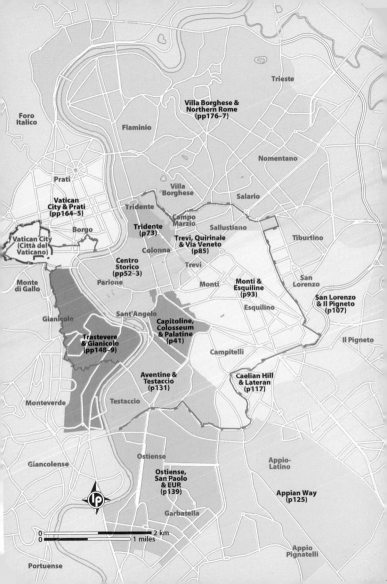

Foro
Italico

Trieste

Villa Borghese &
Northern Rome
(pp176–7)

Flaminio

Nomentano

Prati

Villa
Borghese

Vatican
City & Prati
(pp164–5)

Salario

Tridente

Campo
Marzio

Sallustiano

Vatican City
(Città del
Vaticano)

Borgo

Tridente
(p73)

Trevi, Quirinale
& Via Veneto
(p85)

Tiburtino

Colonna

Centro
Storico
(pp52–3)

Trevi

San
Lorenzo

Monte
di Gallo

Parione

Monti

Monti &
Esquiline
(p93)

San Lorenzo
& Il Pigneto
(p107)

Esquilino

Gianicolo

Sant'Angelo

Il Pigneto

Trastevere
& Gianicolo
(pp148–9)

Capitoline,
Colosseum
& Palatine
(p41)

Campitelli

Monteverde

Aventine &
Testaccio
(p131)

Caelian Hill
& Lateran
(p117)

Testaccio

Ostiense

Appio-
Latino

Giancolense

Ostiense,
San Paolo
& EUR
(p139)

Appian Way
(p125)

Garbatella

0   2 km
0   1 miles

Portuense

Appio
Pignatelli

>CAPITOLINE, COLOSSEUM & PALATINE

Rome's ancient centre reads like a gripping 3-D epic: Romulus killed Remus on the Palatine; emperors toasted to their conquests in the Roman Forum; and spectators decided the fate of gladiators in the bloody Colosseum.

Easily trekked on foot, the area's two focal points are the Colosseum to the southeast and Capitoline Hill (Campidoglio) to the northwest. In between, on either side of Via dei Fori Imperiali, sit the ruined Forums, and to the southwest lie the Palatine's relics and the hand-chomping Bocca della Verità.

Legend lingers on Capitoline Hill: Chiesa di Santa Maria in Aracoeli stands on the spot where the Tiburtine sibyl tipped off Augustus about the coming of Christ. Once the site of two ancient temples, the hill is also home to the mighty Capitoline Museums, which grace Michelangelo's handsome Piazza del Campidoglio.

Just to the north stands the less-dashing (but endearingly hideous) Il Vittoriano, and beyond it Renaissance Palazzo Venezia, home to a secret papal garden.

CAPITOLINE, COLOSSEUM & PALATINE

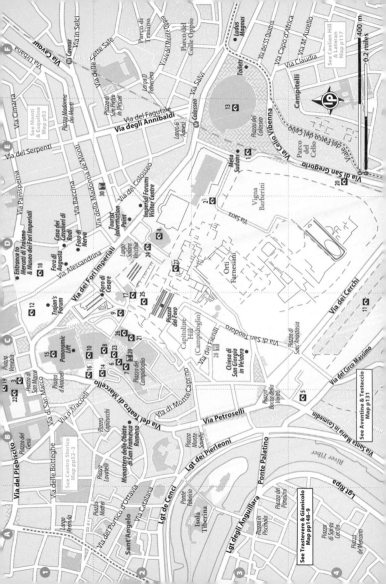

⊙ SEE

⊙ BOCCA DELLA VERITÀ & CHIESA DI SANTA MARIA IN COSMEDIN

☎ 06 678 14 19; Piazza della Bocca della Verità 18; ⏱ 9.30am-5.50pm May-late Oct, to 4.50pm late Oct-Apr; 🚊 Via dei Cerchi

The 'Mouth of Truth' is Rome's most famous lie detector: it's a mask-shaped ancient manhole cover known to bite off the hand of fibbers (priests apparently slipped scorpions in there to help it along). If you pass the test, pop into the adjoining 8th-century Chiesa di Santa Maria in Cosmedin for some stunning Cosmati interiors. The church's portico and bell tower were added in the 12th century, while the three columns embedded in the nave were part of an ancient market colonnade.

⊙ BASILICA DI SS COSMA E DAMIANO

☎ 06 699 15 40; Via dei Fori Imperiali; ⏱ 9am-1pm & 3-7pm May-late Oct, 9.30am-4.50pm late Oct-Apr; Ⓜ Colosseo

Incorporating a library from Vespasian's forum (visible through a glass wall at the end of the nave), the basilica's star turns are an explosively colourful 6th-century mosaic depicting Christ's Second Coming and a lavish 18th-century Neapolitan presepe (nativity scene; donation €1; ⏱ 10am-1pm & 3-6pm Fri-Sun

Sep-Jul) just off the 17th-century cloisters.

⊙ CAPITOLINE MUSEUMS

☎ 06 820 59 127; www.museicapitolini .org; Piazza del Campidoglio 1; adult/EU 18-25yr/EU under 18yr & over 65yr without exhibition €6.50/4.50/free, with exhibition €9/7/free, incl Centrale Montemartini with exhibition adult/student/child €11/9/free; ⏱ 9am-8pm (last tickets 7pm) Tue-Sun; 🚊 Piazza Venezia; ♿

Home to the red-marble Satiro Ridente (the inspiration for Nathaniel Hawthorne's novel The Marble Faun), the Capitoline Museums (Musei Capitolini) boast ancient sculptural marvels as well as paintings by big guns such as Titian, Tintoretto, Rubens and Van Dyck. Tackle the booty with an audioguide (one/two people €5/6.30), and make time to visit the Tate Modern–style southern outpost, Centrale Montemartini (p140).

⊙ CARCERE MAMERTINO

☎ 06 679 29 02; Clivo Argentario 1; donation requested; ⏱ closed for restoration; 🚊 Piazza Venezia

This dark, dank dungeon is the Mamertine Prison, home to anyone who got on the wrong side of the ancient Roman authorities. Holy jail bait St Peter was held here using the chains now in Basilica di San Pietro in Vincoli (p94). But even they couldn't stop him from denting the wall with his head and causing a baptismal stream to spring.

🄲 CHIESA DI SANTA MARIA IN ARACOELI

☎ 06 679 81 55; Piazza del Campidoglio 4; 🕙 9am-12.30pm & 2.30-5.30pm; 🚍 Piazza Venezia

Atop the thigh-blasting 14th-century Aracoeli staircase, this Romanesque gem is home to a 13th-century fresco by Cavallini, crisp 15th-century frescoes by Pinturicchio, and the famous *santo bambino* (holy baby) – a wooden baby Jesus believed to have the power to heal the sick.

The original was pinched in 1994 but the copy apparently does the trick. At the bottom of the Aracoeli staircase sit the ruins of a Roman apartment block or **insula**, used to house the poor.

🄲 CIRCO MASSIMO

Via del Circo Massimo; Ⓜ Circo Massimo

This sorry stretch of grass was once Rome's largest chariot-racing stadium. Seating 250,000 spectators, and sometimes flooded for mock sea battles, its 600m racetrack boasted ornate lap indicators and Egyptian obelisks, one of which now punctuates Piazza del Popolo (p75).

Become the object of the ancient gaze in the Capitoline Museums' Hall of Philosophers

MAD EMPERORS

President not withdrawing troops? Prime Minister not slashing taxes? Spare a thought for the ancient Romans, who suffered their fair share of megalomaniac leaders. One of the worst was Caligula ('Little Shoes'; r AD 37–41), who specialised in extravagance, extortion and murder, and was in love with his sister. Even nastier was Nero (r AD 54–68). Augustus' last descendant, he had his pushy stage mum murdered, his first wife's veins slashed, his second wife kicked to death, and his third wife's ex-husband topped off. (And that was just his private life.) One thing Nero may not have been responsible for is the great fire of AD 64, traditionally attributed to him but now increasingly doubted by historians.

◉ COLONNA DI TRAIANO

☎ 06 820 59 127; www.mercatidi traiano.it; Via dei Fori Imperiali; 🚇 Via dei Fori Imperiali

Set among the ruins of Trajan's Forum, Trajan's column (AD 113) is adorned with painfully intricate reliefs depicting the victories over the Dacians (from modern-day Romania). It became Trajan's tomb, with his ashes buried underneath and a golden statue resting on top (later replaced by one of St Peter by Pope Sixtus V). Casts of the column at Museo della Civiltà Romana (p141) will spare you the sore neck.

◉ COLOSSEUM

☎ 06 399 67 700; www.pierreci.it; Piazza del Colosseo; adult/EU 18-24yr/ EU under 18yr & over 65yr incl Palatine & Roman Forum €12/7.50/free; ⏰ 8.30am-7.15pm Apr-Aug, to 7pm Sep, to 6.30pm Oct, to 4.30pm Nov-Dec & Jan–mid-Feb, to 5pm mid-Feb–mid-Mar, to 5.30pm mid-end Mar (last tickets 1hr before closing); Ⓜ Colosseo; ♿

Had the World Society for the Protection of Animals existed in ancient times, Emperor Vespasian's 50,000-seater would have been in strife: at its 100-day-long inauguration party in AD 80, 5000 animals were slaughtered in gladiatorial battles. Karma caught up with the stadium in the 6th century, when the empire's fall kick-started its devolution into a forlorn quarry – travertine from its exterior clads Chiesa di Sant'Agostino (p54). It's now home to fascinating temporary exhibitions (a recent show examined Vespian's political and social image). Beware the 'gladiators' lingering outside who will charge to have your photo taken with them, as well as the 'official' guides touting discounted entry and shorter queues. If you do want to save time, prepurchase your ticket at the Palatine (p46). Standing beside the Colosseum, the 4th-century **Arco di Costantino** honours Constantine's victory at Ponte Milvio (p180).

◉ IL VITTORIANO

☎ 06 699 17 18; Piazza Venezia; admission free; ⏱ 9.30am-6.30pm Mon-Sun; 🚇 Piazza Venezia

It's a case of architecture on steroids at this overscale, overly white marble monument to Italy's first king, Vittorio Emanuele II. Home to the tomb of the Unknown Soldier, its one true redeeming feature is the 360-degree panorama from the rooftop, reached via the **panoramic lift** (adult/10-18yr & over 65yr/under 10yr €7/3.50/free; ⏱ 9.30am-6.30pm Mon-Thu, to 7.30pm Fri-Sun, last admission 45min before closing) at the back of the building.

◉ MERCATI DI TRAIANO & MUSEO DEI FORI IMPERIALI

☎ 06 820 59 127; www.mercatidi traiano.it; Via IV Novembre 94; adult/ EU 18-25yr/EU under 18yr & over 65yr €6.50/4.50/free; ⏱ 9am-7pm Tue-Sun (last tickets 1hr before closing); 🚇 Via IV Novembre

Incorporating the Great Hall of the 2nd-century Trajan markets (an ancient three-level shopping mall), the striking new Museum of the Imperial Fora showcases ancient artefacts found in Trajan's Forum and the surrounding fora of Cesare (Caesar), Nerva and Augusto

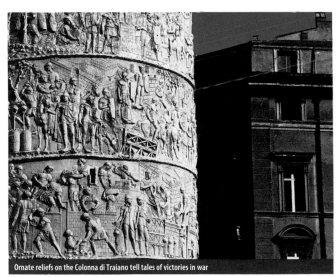

Ornate reliefs on the Colonna di Traiano tell tales of victories in war

(Augustus). In its heyday, Trajan's Forum boasted libraries, a temple, a triumphal arch, Rome's largest basilica, the Colonna di Traiano (p44) and the impressive market complex. You can still peek into the ancient shops and bars, now a dramatic backdrop for temporary art exhibitions, as well as download the free audioguide podcast from the museum website.

◎ PALATINE
🕿 06 399 67 700; www.pierreci.it; Via di San Gregorio 30; adult/EU 18-24yr/EU under 18yr & over 65yr incl Colosseum & Roman Forum €12/7.50/free; 🕒 8.30am-7.15pm Apr-Aug, to 7pm Sep, to 6.30pm Oct, to 4.30pm Nov-Dec & Jan–mid-Feb, to 5pm mid-Feb–mid-Mar, to 5.30pm mid-end Mar (last tickets 1hr before closing); Ⓜ Colosseo

Ancient Rome's Beverly Hills, lofty Palatine (Palatino) was home to the capital's 'somebodies' – from egotistical emperors to cerebral celebrity Cicero. Studded with ruined villas, remnants of the Orti Faranesi (Europe's first private botanical gardens) and lavish views, its Museo Palatino is home to valuable hillside artefacts, including Palaeolithic 'kitchenware' and a beautiful sculptured head of Giovane Principessa (daughter of emperor Marcus Aurelius). Tickets (which include admission to the Colosseum and Roman

Forum) are valid until 6.30pm the following day, allowing you to visit each site once over two days. The Palatine is also directly accessible from the Roman Forum (opposite).

◎ PALAZZO VENEZIA
🚃 Piazza Venezia

Designed by Francesco del Borgo in the 15th century, Rome's first great Renaissance palace is home to **Museo del Palazzo di Venezia** (🕿 06 699 94 318; Via del Plebiscito 118; admission €4, extra for exhibitions; 🕒 8.30am-7.30pm Tue-Sun; ♿). The museum holds an eclectic collection of Byzantine and early Renaissance paintings, camp ceramics, tapestries, arms and armour. Major exhibitions are often held in Sala del Mappamondo (Mussolini's ex-office), while around the back, facing Piazza San Marco, **Basilica di San Marco** (Piazza San Marco; 🕒 8.30am-noon & 4-6.30pm Tue-Sat, 9am-1pm & 4-8pm Sun) is worth a glance for its scrumptious 9th-century mosaic.

◎ PIAZZA DEL CAMPIDOGLIO
🚃 Piazza Venezia

Michelangelo's urban masterpiece is best approached via the **Cordonata**, his equally graceful ramp leading up from Piazza d'Aracoeli. Built for the 16th-century visit of Emperor Charles V, the piazza is guarded by a row of ancient sculptures, among them the giant Castor and Pollux, uncovered in the Jewish ghetto. At the top of the ramp, beyond the gate to the right, lies a lesser-known romantic terrace.

○ ROMAN FORUM

☎ 06 399 67 700; www.pierreci.it; entrance at Largo Salara Vecchia; admission incl Colosseum & Palatine adult/EU 18-24yr/EU under 18yr & over 65yr €12/7.50/free; ☼ 8.30am-7.15pm Apr-Aug, to 7pm Sep, to 6.30pm Oct, to 4.30pm Nov-Dec & Jan–mid-Feb, to 5pm mid-Feb–mid-Mar, to 5.30pm mid-end Mar (last tickets 1hr before closing); Ⓜ Colosseo

These badly labelled ruins were once the centre of the ancient world, lined with gleaming marble temples, law courts and offices. Rev your imagination with the sweeping overview from behind **Palazzo Senatorio** on Piazza del Campidoglio (opposite) before grabbing an audioguide (€4) or, if you understand Italian, joining the Sunday 10am tour (€4; departure from the ticket office at the Largo Salara Vecchia entrance). Anecdotes pepper the toppled columns: Mark Antony asked Romans to lend them his ears at the **Rostrum**; the **Lapis Niger** supposedly sits on Romulus' tomb; the Vestal

Exercise your imagination as well as your legs among the ruins of the Roman Forum

Virgins tended the sacred flame at **Tempio di Vesta**; and Roman Jews avoided passing under the **Arco di Tito** – built to celebrate Vespasian and Titus' victories against Jerusalem, and the historical symbol of the Diaspora's beginning. The Roman Forum is now also directly accessible from the Palatine (p46).

EAT

While you'll find few culinary options among the ruins, the neighbourhoods of Monti, Caelian Hill and Lateran are easily reached on foot.

SAN TEODORO

Ristorante €€€

☎ 06 678 09 33; Via dei Fienili 49-50;
🕐 1-3.15pm & 8-11.30pm Mon-Sat;
🚌 Teatro di Marcello

San Teodoro's formula for success is no secret: a romantic setting on a medieval piazza, local contemporary art, a quaffable wine list and sophisticated takes on traditional dishes. Seafood is the star attraction (think baby squid sautéed with artichokes), and chocolate, ricotta and ice cream make an appearance in various dessert guises.

Caffè Capitolino serves its coffee spiked with grand vistas

▼ DRINK

▼ CAFFÈ CAPITOLINO *Café*
☎ 06 691 90 564; Capitoline Museums, Piazza del Campidoglio 19; ⏱ 9am-7pm Tue-Sun; 🚍 Piazza Venezia

If you insist on a view with your *caffè* (coffee), head up to the Capitoline Museums' sleek rooftop café (you don't even need a museum ticket: there's a street entrance to the right of Palazzo dei Conservatori). The light snacks (panini, salads and pizza) won't leave you breathless, but the vistas most certainly will.

▼ CAVOUR 313 *Wine Bar*
☎ 06 678 54 96; Via Cavour 313; ⏱ 12.30-2.45pm & 7.30pm-12.30am, closed Sun Jul–mid-Sep; Ⓜ Cavour

A popped cork away from the Colosseum and Roman Forum, snug Cavour 313 charms everyone from ministers to fledgling Romeos. Wines span low-cost locals to New World vintages, and are matched by yummy cheese platters; an inspired *culatello* (prosciutto) involtini dish with goats cheese, hazelnut cream and *dragoncello* (tarragon); and sweet, low-key service.

>CENTRO STORICO

Show-off piazzas, frescoed *palazzi* (palaces) and a mouth-watering market: the tightly packed *centro storico* (historic city centre) delivers the Rome you're most likely pining for, whether its church crawling for Caravaggios, sun-soaking on Piazza Navona or late-night lounging on Campo de' Fiori.

There's no better, or easier, place to get lost in. Dusty artisan studios line skinny side streets, contemporary galleries stud medieval buildings,

CENTRO STORICO

Please see over for map

and vintage kosher bakeries perfume Via del Portico d'Ottavia: heart of the Jewish Ghetto. Slip into a laneway and trust where the city takes you.

Carved in two by Corso Vittorio Emanuele II, the *centro storico* was once the ancient Campo Marzio (Field of Mars), a flood-prone spread of barracks, bawdy theatres and temples, including the 'I'm-still-standing' Pantheon. Incorporated into the city proper in the Middle Ages, it found its groove in the Renaissance and baroque, when masters such as Bramante, Bernini and Borromini turned its medieval mash into an unforgettable showcase.

◉ SEE

◉ AREA ARCHEOLOGICA DEL TEATRO DI MARCELLO E DEL PORTICO D'OTTAVIA

Via del Teatro di Marcello 44; admission free; 🕙 **9am-7pm summer, 9am-6pm winter;** 🚊 **Via del Teatro di Marcello**
Eras fuse dramatically at this archaeological site, where a Renaissance palace by Baldassare Peruzzi is ingeniously grafted onto Augustus' Teatro di Marcello (a model for the Colosseum). The recycling continues at the 1st-century BC Portico d'Ottavia, where columns from an ancient temple complex form part of Chiesa di Sant'Angelo in Pescheria (named for the area's former fish market).

◉ BIBLIOTECA E RACCOLTA TEATRALE DEL BURCARDO

☎ **06 681 94 71; www.burcardo.org; Via del Sudario 44; admission €1.50;** 🕙 **9am-1.30pm Mon-Fri;** 🚊 🚋 **Largo di Torre Argentina;** ♿
Rome's little-known theatre museum includes dazzling costumes worn by acting greats such as Eleonora Duse, *fin de siècle* playbills, set-design artwork and exquisite 18th-century Chinese marionettes. The lack of English info doesn't detract from the appeal and there's a well-stocked theatre library (mostly Italian) on the 2nd floor.

◉ CAMPO DE' FIORI

🚊 **Corso Vittorio Emanuele II**
By day, Rome's only churchless square is a colourful spectacle of heaving market stalls. By night, 'Il Campo' becomes an open-air party, its vaguely trashy pubs and bars overflowing with revellers. No doubt many a sleepless local wishes them the fate of heretical monk Giordano Bruno, burnt here in 1600 and honoured by Ettore Ferrari's sinister statue.

◉ CHIESA DEL GESÙ

☎ **06 69 70 01; Piazza del Gesù;** 🕙 **6.45am-12.30pm & 4-7.30pm Mon-Sat, 7.30am-1.15pm Sun;** 🚊 🚋 **Largo di Torre Argentina**
Built in the 16th century, Rome's first Jesuit church is a bombastic

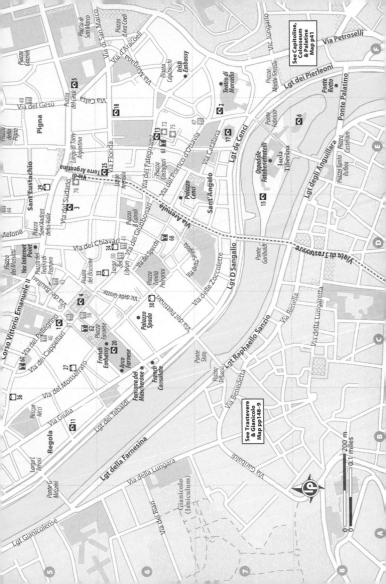

CENTRO STORICO

VIA GIULIA

While there's no shortage of picture-perfect streets in the *centro storico*, Via Giulia (Map pp52-3, B5) is a strip you simply must stroll. Lined with Renaissance *palazzi* (palaces) and potted orange trees, it was designed by Bramante in 1508 as an approach to the Vatican.

At its southern end, the **Fontana del Mascherone** depicts a gob-smacked 17th-century hippy spewing water from his mouth. Close by, the ivy-dripping Arco Farnese (built to a design by Michelangelo) was part of an ambitious, unfinished project meant to link Palazzo Farnese (p57) with Villa Farnesina (p152) across the Tiber. Continuing north, on the left, in Via di Sant'Eligio, is **Chiesa di Sant'Eligio degli Orefici** (buzz at Via di Sant'Eligio 7 for admission; 🕙 10-11am Mon-Fri), the 16th-century goldsmiths' church designed by Raphael.

Counter-Reformation extravaganza, starring Giovanni Battista Gaulli's electric, 3-D vault fresco *Triumph of the Name of Jesus* (1676–79). If you can pull your eyes away, look out for Andrea del Pozzo's tomb for Jesuit founder Ignatius Loyola and Bernini's bust of St Roberto to the left of Antonio Sarti's high altar.

🖸 CHIESA DI SAN LUIGI DEI FRANCESI

☎ 06 68 82 71; Piazza di San Luigi dei Francesi; 🕙 10am-12.30pm & 4-7pm Fri-Wed, 10am-12.30pm Thu; 🚌 Corso del Rinascimento

Caravaggio connoisseurs are spoilt rotten at Rome's French national church, with three of the master's canvases hanging in the fifth chapel on the left. Known as the St Matthew cycle (1600–02), they showcase Caravaggio's astounding chiaroscuro technique. A lesser-known highlight is Domenichino's 17th-century frescoes of St Cecilia in the second chapel on the right.

🖸 CHIESA DI SANTA MARIA SOPRA MINERVA

☎ 06 679 39 26; Piazza della Minerva; 🕙 8am-7pm Mon-Sun; 🚌 🚋 Largo di Torre Argentina

Built over the ancient temple of Minerva in the 13th century, Rome's only Gothic church sports electric-blue vaulting and Renaissance gems such as Filippino Lippi frescoes, Fra Angelico's tomb and Michelangelo's daring sculpture of a naked *Christ Bearing the Cross* (the prudish bronze loincloth is a baroque aberration). Don't miss the eerie flood markers on the façade and Bernini's too-cute *Elefantino* sculpture on the square.

🖸 CHIESA DI SANT'AGOSTINO

☎ 06 688 01 962; Piazza di Sant'Agostino; 🕙 7.45am-noon & 4-7.30pm; 🚌 Corso del Rinascimento

Boasting one of the earliest Renaissance façades in Rome, top billing at this 15th-century number goes to Jacopo Sansovino's clucky sculpture *Madonna del Parto* (1521), Raphael's striking fresco of Isaiah (1512) on the nave's third column, and Caravaggio's *Madonna dei Pellegrini,* whose unflattering brutal realism caused outrage upon its being revealed in 1604.

◉ FONTANA DELLE TARTARUGHE
Piazza Mattei; 🚌 🚋 **Largo di Torre Argentina**
Depicting four boys hoisting turtles up into a bowl of water, Taddeo Landini's playful little fountain was apparently created overnight in 1585, on behalf of the Duke of Mattei who had gambled away his fortune and was about to lose his fiancée (it worked, the Duke got the girl). Bernini added the turtles in 1658.

◉ GALLERIA DORIA PAMPHILJ
☎ **06 679 73 23; www.doriapamphilj.it; Via del Corso 305; adult/over 65yr & student €9/7;** ⏰ **10am-5pm Mon-Sun, last entry 4.15pm;** 🚌 **Piazza Venezia;** ♿
One of Rome's richest private art collections is housed in the mid-15th-century Palazzo Doria Pamphilj, which is still home to Rome's aristocratic Pamphilj family. Masterpieces aside, look out for St Theodora's mummified corpse in the 17th-century family chapel, designed by architect Carlo Fontana.

◉ ISOLA TIBERINA
🚌 **Lungotevere dei Pierleoni**
The world's smallest inhabited island was home to a 3rd-century temple dedicated to Aesculapius, the Greek god of healing. The temple's columns now line the nave of

The breathtaking light and shade of Caravaggio's *Life of St Matthew* in Chiesa di San Luigi dei Francesi

The Pantheon's 2nd-century architecture allows it to be lit by natural light

Romanesque **Chiesa di San Bartolomeo** (🕒 9.30am-1pm & 3.30-7pm Mon-Fri, to 7.30pm Sat, 9am-1pm & 7-8pm Sun), while the remains of Rome's first stone bridge, Ponte Rotto (Broken Bridge), are visible from the island's south side.

📷 MUSEO CRIMINOLOGICO
☎ 06 683 00 234; www.museocrimino logico.it; Via del Gonfalone 29; adult/ under 18yr & over 60yr €2/free; 🕒 9am-1pm Tue-Sat plus 2.30-6.30pm Tue & Thu; 🚌 Corso Vittorio Emanuele II
Boost your revenge fantasies at Rome's Criminology Museum, with its motley assortment of vintage torture devices, weapons and executioners' knives. Eye-up fake Picassos and confiscated smut, read about the gun-toting *contessa* and peek into the infamous

trunk used in the 1964 kidnapping of Israeli spy Mordechai Louk.

📷 MUSEO EBRAICO DI ROMA
☎ 06 684 00 661; www.museoebraico .roma.it; Lungotevere de Cenci; adult/student/under 10yr €7.50/4/free; 🕒 10am-7pm Sun-Thu, 9am-4pm Fri Jun-Sep, 10am-5pm Sun-Thu, 9am-2pm Fri Oct-May; 🚌 Lungotevere de Cenci; ♿
Twenty-two centuries strong, Rome's Jewish community is Europe's oldest, and this small but savvy museum chronicles its historical, cultural and artistic heritage – from exquisitely embroidered textiles to moving Holocaust artefacts. Best of all, the hourly tours take you into the city's splendid Great Synagogue, Europe's second-largest synagogue, completed in 1904.

⊙ MUSEO NAZIONALE ROMANO: CRYPTA BALBI

☎ 06 399 67 700; Via delle Botteghe Oscure 31; adult/EU 18-24yr/EU under 18yr & over 65yr incl Palazzo Altemps, Palazzo Massimo & Terme di Diocleziano €7/3.50/free, plus €3 supplement if there's an exhibition; 🕑 9am-7.45pm Tue-Sun; 🚌 🚋 Largo di Torre Argentina
Built around medieval and Renaissance ruins, themselves plonked on top of the 1st-century BC Theatre of Balbus, this oft-overlooked museum vividly illustrates Rome's multilayered history. Duck into the underground excavations, and view well-labelled exhibitions, complete with 6th-century bling and Byzantine toys.

⊙ MUSEO NAZIONALE ROMANO: PALAZZO ALTEMPS

☎ 06 683 35 66; Piazza Sant'Apollinare 46; admission incl Crypta Balbi, Palazzo Massimo & Terme di Diocleziano adult/ EU 18-24yr/EU under 18yr & over 65yr €7/3.50/free, plus €3 supplement if there's an exhibition; 🕑 9am-7.45pm Tue-Sun; 🚌 Corso del Rinascimento; ♿
Heavenly bodies fill the frescoed rooms of this exquisite Renaissance palace, home to Cardinal Ludovico Ludovisi's prized collection of sculpture. Highlights include the mesmerising 6th-century *Galata Suicida* (Gaul's Suicide) and *Ludovisi Ares,* as well as the legendary 5th-century BC *Trono Ludovisi* (Ludovisi

Throne). Five recently restored rooms house the museum's Egyptian Collection (tours 11am, noon, 4pm and 5pm Tuesday to Sunday, unrestricted access Sunday only), its pieces reflecting the influence of Egyptian culture and spirituality on ancient Roman art.

⊙ PALAZZO FARNESE

☎ 06 688 92 818; visitefarnese@france -italia.it; Piazza Farnese; admission free, children under 15yr not admitted, 15-18yr admitted with adult; 🕑 1hr tours depart 3pm, 4pm & 5pm Mon-Thu early Sep–mid-Jul; 🚌 Corso Vittorio Emanuele II
Home to the French Embassy, this show-stopping 16th-century palace is the work of Antonio da Sangallo, Michelangelo and Giacomo della Porta. Inside, Annibale Carracci's astounding frescoes are worth the slight hassle of booking a spot on one of the guided tours (in Italian or French). Photo ID is required for entry. Bookings should be made one to four months in advance. The twin fountains in Piazza Farnese were giant baths taken from Terme di Caracalla (p133).

⊙ PANTHEON

☎ 06 683 00 230; Piazza della Rotonda; admission free; 🕑 8.30am-7.30pm Mon-Sat, 9am-6pm Sun; 🚌 🚋 Largo di Torre Argentina; ♿
Built by Hadrian where Marcus Agrippa's original temple (27 BC)

stood (you can still see Agrippa's name in the inscription on the pediment), this stoic temple-turned-church has been hanging around since circa AD 120. Sporting original bronze doors, it's the dome that takes the breath away: a perfect semisphere and the ancient Romans' finest architectural feat. Lit by a 9m oculus, it's a surreal sight when rain falls through in a mesmerising column.

📷 PIAZZA NAVONA
🚍 **Corso del Rinascimento**

Sun-roasted *palazzi*, extravagant fountains and spritz-sipping poseurs in shades: Rome's most iconic piazza sits on the ruins of an ancient arena, built by Domitian in AD 86 and still partially visible from nearby Piazza di Tor Sanguigna. Paved over in the 15th century, it was often flooded for communal summertime splashing. Its centre-

piece is Bernini's ostentatious Fontana dei Quattro Fiumi (Fountain of the Four Rivers), depicting the Nile, Ganges, Danube and Plata. The veiled Nile was reputedly shielding his eyes from **Chiesa di Sant'Agnese in Agone** (🕐 9.30am-12.30pm & 4-7pm Tue-Sat, 10am-1pm & 4-8pm Sun) – designed by Bernini's antithesis, Borromini. In truth, it simply denotes that the river's source was unknown at the time. The church occupies the spot where St Agnes literally lost her head. You'll find the martyred teen's skull inside.

📷 PIAZZA SANT'IGNAZIO
🚍 **Via del Corso**

When we say that Filippo Raguzzini's 18th-century square steals the stage, we're serious. Resembling a theatrical set, complete with exits into 'the wings' at either end of its northern side, it's also home to 17th-century **Chiesa di**

TALKING HEADS

At the eastern end of Piazza Pasquino (C4) you'll find a grubby statue covered with tatty bits of paper: meet Pasquino, Rome's most famous 'talking statue'.

During the 16th century, with no safe outlets for dissent, a Vatican tailor named Pasquino began sticking *pasquinade* (notes) to the statue with satirical verses lampooning the church and aristocracy. Others soon joined in, many of whom worked closely with the Pope and his posse and were privy to hushed-up scandals. Before long, chattering statues sprang up across the city.

Understandably, Pasquino's 'big mouth' wasn't a big hit with the pontiffs: Pope Adrianus VI (r 1522–3) considered throwing him into the Tiber, but wisely decided against punishing stone. Centuries on, Pasquino refuses to shut up, with a new generation's *pasquinade* stuck to his weathered base.

CENTRO STORICO

The holy art of perfumery is revealed at Ai Monasteri

Sant'Ignazio di Loyola (⊗ 7.30am-12.15pm & 3-7.15pm) and its deceptive trompe l'oeil ceiling perspective by Andrea Pozzo in the 'dome'.

📖 SHOP

Head to Via del Governo Vecchio for vintage and independent threads, with favourites including Maga Morgana at No 27, Vestiti Usuati Cinzia at No 45 and Omero & Cecilia at No 110. Scour Via del Pellegrino and Via del Monserrato for cute boutiques, antiques and jewellery, as well as Via de' Cestari and surrounds for cardinal caps and colourful Catholic statues.

📷 AI MONASTERI *Toiletries*
☎ 06 688 02 783; Corso del Rinascimento 72; ⊗ 10am-1pm & 3.30-7.30pm Fri-Wed, 10am-1pm Thu; 🚊 Corso del Rinascimento
This heavenly scented shop peddles beautifully packaged products made by monks, from liqueurs and spirits to soaps, balms and anti-wrinkle creams. Boost your love life with the Elixir d'Amore (Elixir of Love), though why monks are expert at this is anyone's guess.

📷 ANTICHI KIMONO
Fashion, Accessories
☎ 06 681 35 876; www.antichikimono .com in Italian; Via del Monserrato 43b-44; ⊗ 4-8pm Mon, 10.30am-1.30pm & 4-8pm Tue-Fri, 10am-8pm Sat; 🚊 Corso Vittorio Emanuele II
Not only does local designer Gloria Gobbi turn vintage Japanese *obis* into corsets and bags, she's known to transform vintage Oriental carpets into coats, selling them alongside her eclectic handmade jewellery and other fetching accessories by Euro artisans. There's even a **small selection of silk and cashmere scarves an**d quirky accessories for male individualists.

🏠 ARSENALE *Fashion*

☎ 06 686 13 80; www.patriziapieroni.it; Via del Governo Vecchio 64; 🕑 3.30-7.30pm Mon, 10am-7.30pm Tue-Sat; 🚌 Corso Vittorio Emanuele II

Female fashionistas revere the understated cool of Arsenale, where you'll find heavenly fabrics worked into svelte, structuralist creations by Roman designer Patrizia Pieroni.

🏠 BORINI *Shoes*

☎ 06 687 56 70; Via dei Pettinari 86-87; 🕑 3.30-7.30pm Mon, 9.30am-1pm & 3.30-7.30pm Tue-Sat; 🚌 🚊 Via Arenula

Don't be fooled by the dowdy interior: fashionistas pile into this unglitzy shop for some of Rome's sassiest shoes. Whatever is 'in' this season, Borini will have it, at reasonable prices and in every delicious candy hue.

🏠 CITTÀ DEL SOLE *Toys*

☎ 06 688 03 805; Via della Scrofa 65; 🕑 10am-7.30pm Tue-Sat, 11am-7.30pm Sun, 3.30-7.30pm Mon; 🚌 Corso del Rinascimento

At Città del Sole, brain-numbing gimmicks are ditched for educational, well-made toys stocked under categories such as 'Imagination and Creativity' and 'Making Theatre'. Wrap your little darling's mind around Escher nano-puzzles or awaken the Bramante within with a build-your-own-basilica model kit.

Guaranteed to put a smile on your face: Confetteria Moriondo & Gariglio makes chocolate to vintage recipes

◩ CONFETTERIA MORIONDO & GARIGLIO Confectionery
☎ 06 699 08 56; Via del Piè di Marmo 21-22; ⏱ 9am-7.30pm Mon-Sat Sep-Jun, 9am-7.30pm Mon-Fri, 9am-3pm Sat Jul; 🚌 Via del Corso

Roman poet Trilussa was so smitten with this vintage confectionery shop – established by confectioners to the royal house of Savoy – that he dedicated several sonnets in its honour. Many of the handmade chocolates and bonbons are still made to 19th-century recipes.

◩ I LOVE TOKYO! Shoes
☎ 06 686 91 04; www.ilovetokyo.it; Via dei Giubbonari 72; ⏱ 10am-1.30pm & 3-8pm Mon-Sun; 🚌 🚊 Via Arenula

Pimp up your feet with one of Rome's coolest collections of sneakers, including limited-edition Saucony, Dutch brand Patta and New York label Alife. Street-smart threads include reversible DC Double Label jumpers and French-designed Qhuit tees. Flash your student card for a discount.

◩ IBIZ – ARTIGIANATO IN CUOIO Accessories
☎ 06 683 07 297; Via dei Chiavari 39; ⏱ 9.30am-7.30pm Mon-Sat; 🚌 Corso Vittorio Emanuele II

In their diminutive workshop, Elisa Nepi and her father craft exquisite, well-priced leather goods spanning classic chic to contemporary funk. Pick up a quirky pistachio-hued handbag, suave laptop satchel or style-up your shave with a handmade leather toiletry bag.

◩ MERCATO DELLE STAMPE Antiques
Piazza Borghese; ⏱ 9am-5pm Mon-Sat; 🚌 Piazza Augusto Imperatore

Best midweek when crowds are lighter and vendors more helpful, this cluster of street stalls is worth a snoop if you're a fan of vintage books and old prints.

◩ MONDELLO OTTICA Accessories
☎ 06 686 19 55; www.mondelloottica .it; Via del Pellegrino 97-98; ⏱ 10am-1.30pm & 4-7.30pm Tue-Sat; 🚌 Corso Vittorio Emanuele II

Piazza posing requires a pair of shades, so head here for A-list frames from Anne et Valentin, IC-Berlin, Oliver Peoples, Cutler and Gross, and Belgian designer Theo. Prescription glasses can be ready the same day.

◩ NARDECCHIA Antiques
☎ 06 686 93 18; Piazza Navona 25; ⏱ 4.30-7.30pm Mon, 10am-1pm & 4.30-7.30pm Tue-Sat; 🚌 Corso del Rinascimento

Nardecchia is famed for its antique prints, ranging from exclusive

BASSETTI TESSUTI

Hidden away in a run-of-the-mill *palazzo* (palace), **Bassetti Tessuti** (☎ 06 689 23 26; Corso Vittorio Emanuele II 73; 3.30-7.30pm Mon, 9am-1pm & 3.30-7.30pm Tue-Sat) is a sprawling, technicolour temple to textiles. From fine Italian wools and silks, to cheetah-print faux fur, a jaw-dropping 200,000 fabrics line its endless sea of soaring, cracked rooms. Brothers Emidio and Lorenzo Bassetti set up shop in 1954, serving everyone from couture royalty to needle-savvy homemakers. It's a fabulously atmospheric place, caught in a retro time warp of linoleum floors and wizened old men pushing cart after cart of rare and luscious threads.

18th-century etchings of Rome by Giovanni Battista Piranesi to more affordable 19th-century panoramas to inspire the John Keats within.

RETRO Design

☎ 06 681 92 746; www.retrodesign.it; Piazza del Fico 20; 4-8pm Mon, 11am-1pm & 4-8pm Tue-Sat; Corso del Rinascimento

Design buffs squeeze into Retro for colourful rows of mid-century glassware, cult designer furniture, bakelite jewellery and retro architectural drawings.

TEMPI MODERNI Jewellery

☎ 06 687 70 07; Via del Governo Vecchio 108; 10am-1pm & 4-7.30pm Mon-Sat; Corso Vittorio Emanuele II

Thank Streisand for Tempi Moderni, run by a team of camp *signori* and packed with must-have vintage costume bling, from art nouveau and deco trinkets, to poptastic 1960s bangles and chichi options from the likes of

Balenciaga and Dior. Mix and match with vintage catwalk couture, including '70s Armani coats.

EAT

From adventurous Michelin-star dens to rough'n'ready pizzerias, the *centro storico* has all budgets and predilections covered. For a taste of Jewish Roman grub, follow your nose to Via del Portico d'Ottavia.

AL BRIC Ristorante €€€

☎ 06 687 95 33; www.albric.it; Via del Pellegrino 51-52; 7.30pm-midnight Tue-Sat, 12.30-3pm & 7.30pm-midnight Sun, closed 2 weeks Aug; Corso Vittorio Emanuele II

Is it the display of Italian and French cheeses, the intimate bistro-chic air, or the Michelin-lauded menu with its focus on meat in winter and fish in summer? Ponder Al Bric's appeal over simple, innovative dishes like smoked Sardinian goats-milk ricotta with marmalade, or lamb with Predappio *pecorino*. Book ahead.

🍴 ANTICO FORNO ROSCIOLI
Bakery €

☎ 06 686 40 45; www.anticofornoroscioli.it; Via dei Chiavari 34; ☽ 7.30am-8pm Mon-Fri, 7.30am-2.30pm Sat, closed Sat Aug; 🚍 🚊 Via Arenula

For a delicious bite-to-go, dive into this ever-buzzing bakery. Its drool-inducing counter bursts with luscious *pizza al taglio* (by the slice) and fresh-from-the-oven treats like juicy *crostate* (fruit tarts) and *tortine di ricotta e cioccolato* (ricotta-and-chocolate minicakes).

🍴 ARMANDO AL PANTHEON
Trattoria €€

☎ 06 688 03 034; Salita dei Crescenzi 31; ☽ 12.30-3pm & 7-11pm Mon-Fri, 12.30-3pm Sat Sep-Jul; 🚍 🚊 Largo di Torre Argentina

Neither its touristy locale or past clientele (Jean-Paul Sartre and Pelé have noshed here) mess with this family-run bolthole's genuine service and soulful staples such as luscious roast duck with prunes and the legendary *torta antica romana* (Roman-style cake).

🍴 CASA BLEVE *Enoteca* €€€

☎ 06 686 59 70; Via del Teatro Valle 48-49; ☽ 12.30-3pm & 7.30-10.30pm Tue-Sat, closed 3 weeks Aug; 🚍 🚊 Largo di Torre Argentina

Ideal for a romantic or Epicurean assignation, chichi Casa Bleve dazzles with its column-lined courtyard, complete with stained-glass roof. The fetching wine list accompanies hard-to-find *salumi* (cold cuts), sublime cheese and innovative flavour combos like lentil soup with peperoncino, shrimps and lime peel.

🍴 CUL DE SAC *Enoteca* €€

☎ 06 688 01 094; Piazza Pasquino 73; ☽ noon-4pm & 6pm-12.30am Mon-Sat; 🚍 Corso Vittorio Emanuele Ii

The French love narrow, unaffected Cul de Sac, where 1500 international labels and Gallic-inspired grub such as homemade pâté and hearty onion soup fuel lingering conversation. If you're heading in after 8pm, call ahead to get on the waiting list and minimise the wait.

🍴 DA BAFFETTO *Pizzeria* €

☎ 06 686 16 17; Via del Governo Vecchio 114; ☽ 6.30pm-1am; 🚍 Corso Vittorio Emanuele Ii

Loud locals, lovingly worn furniture and thin-crust pizza perfection. Spin-off **Baffetto 2** (☎ 06 682 10 807; Piazza del Teatro di Pompeo 18; ☽ 6.30pm-12.30am Mon & Wed-Fri, 12.30-3.30pm & 6.30pm-12.30am Sat & Sun) opens for lunch on weekends.

🍴 DA GIGGETTO *Trattoria* €€

☎ 06 686 11 05; Via del Portico d'Ottavia 21-22; ☽ 12.30-3pm & 7.30-11pm Tue-Sun; 🚍 🚊 Piazza Benedetto Cairoli

For a crash course in Roman-Jewish flavours, dive into this

SECRET SQUARE

At Via del Pellegrino 19, you'll stumble across a dimly lit archway called the **Arco degli Acetari** (Vinegar-makers' Arch). Wander through it and into a magical medieval courtyard, flanked by sorbet-hued façades, flower-filled balconies and ivy-clad staircases spilling onto the cobbled square. It's like watching a play as residents pop in and out of doors and call to each other, window to window. Chances are you'll feel a little déjà vu – while few visitors make it here, many take home souvenirs plastered with this surreptitious charmer.

fabulous Ghetto landmark, famed for its glorious deep-fried *carciofi* (artichokes) and *fiori di zucca* (courgette flowers fried and flavoured with anchovies). If the weather's on your side, bag an outside table next to the 1st-century ruins of Portico d'Ottavia.

🍴 DA GINO *Trattoria* €€
☎ 06 687 34 34; Vicolo Rosini 4; ⏰ 1-2.45pm & 8-10.30pm Mon-Sat, closed Aug; 🚍 Via del Corso
Though Gino is tucked in a laneway, its culinary brilliance is no secret. Book ahead or miss out on Rome's finest home cooking, where old-school know-how turns classics like *pollo con peperoni* (chicken with peppers) into richly flavoured revelations. No credit cards.

🍴 ENOTECA CORSI
Enoteca €€
☎ 06 679 08 21; Via del Gesù 87; ⏰ 12.15-3pm Mon-Sat; 🚍 🚊 Largo di Torre Argentina
Merrily worse-for-wear, Enoteca Corsi is old-school Rome down

to its rustic *cacio e pepe* (pasta with cheese and pepper) on bare wooden tables. Expect filthy fresh ingredients and a freshly photocopied menu true to the culinary calendar, with gnocchi on Thursdays and *baccalà* (salted cod) on Fridays. Go early or queue.

🍴 FILETTI DI BACCALÀ
Trattoria €
☎ 06 686 40 18; Largo dei Librari 88; ⏰ 5-10.40pm Mon-Sat; 🚍 🚊 Via Arenula
This tiny veteran sells fish and chips, Italian-style (fried 'fillet of cod' without the chips). Never mind. Make mamma proud and have the crispy battered veggies instead.

🍴 FORNO DI CAMPO DE' FIORI
Pizza al Taglio €
☎ 06 688 06 662; Campo de' Fiori 22; ⏰ 7.30am-2.30pm & 4.40-8pm Mon-Sat, closed Sat afternoon Jul & Aug; 🚍 Corso Vittorio Emanuele II
Slap bang on market square Campo de' Fiori, this ever-buzzing bakery makes obscenely good *pizza al taglio*. Grab a slice or three

(the olive-oil-drizzled *pizza rossa* – pizza with tomato sauce – is divine), pair it with an *occhio di bue* (apricot jam tartlet) and munch to your heart's content on the perfect piazza outside.

🍴 GIOLITTI *Pasticceria*   €
☎ 06 699 12 43; Via degli Uffici del Vicario 40; 🕑 7am-1.30am;
🚌 Via del Corso

When Gregory Peck and Audrey Hepburn stopped by gelato-tastic Giolitti in *Roman Holiday,* they were onto a good thing. Elbow your way through the photo-snapping hordes for succulent, natural-tasting sorbets (the pear is unmissable) and richer must-licks such as marrons glacés and hazelnut.

🍴 IL CONVIVIO TROIANI
Ristorante   €€€
☎ 06 686 94 32; www.ilconviviotroiani .com; Vicolo dei Soldati 31; 🕑 8-11pm Mon-Sat; 🚌 Corso del Rinascimento

Tucked away in a 16th-century *palazzo,* this intimate, elegant, Michelin-star heavyweight is a progressive gourmand's nirvana – think lemongrass-scented calamari sauté with candied toma-toes and licorice polenta, or bay leaf–scented roasted pigeon in a green pepper casserole with spicy peach salad. Predictably, bookings are a must.

🍴 IL GELATO DI SAN CRISPINO *Gelateria*   €
☎ 06 976 01 190; www.ilgelatodisan crispino.com; Piazza della Maddalena 3; 🕑 noon-midnight Sun-Thu, noon-12.30am Fri & Sat; 🚌 🚋 Largo di Torre Argentina

Rome's finest gelateria (p91) now has a second branch, close to the Pantheon. Like the original, flavours are made from scratch, meaning no nasty industrial bases.

🍴 LA ROSETTA *Seafood*   €€€
☎ 06 686 10 02; www.larosetta.com; Via della Rosetta 8-9; 🕑 12.45-2.45pm & 7.30-11pm Mon-Sat, 12.30-3pm Sun, closed 3 weeks Aug; 🚌 🚋 Largo di Torre Argentina

Supreme seafood, superlative service and a refreshing lack of pretension keep this legend in the 'bookings only' league. Secure a spot and swoon over simple, bril-liantly prepared revelations such as raw sea bass with orange and Cata-lan lobster salad with fried onion.

🍴 LO ZOZZONE
Pizza al Taglio   €
☎ 06 688 08 575; Via del Teatro Pace 32; 🕑 9am-9pm Mon-Fri, 10am-11pm Sat, 11.30am-5.30pm Sun; 🚌 Corso del Rinascimento

No men in trench coats at 'The Dirty One', just gut-filling *pizza rustica* served in no-frills surrounds.

NEIGHBOURHOODS

CENTRO STORICO

Take your coffee upright in true Italian style at Caffè Sant'Eustachio (p68)

Pay at the till for a regular or large *pizza bianca* (pizza with olive oil and sea salt), get it stuffed with your belly's desire at the bar and wash it down with a mighty beer (preferably at a tiny outdoor table).

OBIKÀ
Mozzarella Bar €€
☎ 06 683 26 30; www.obika.it; Piazza di Firenze; noon-11.30pm; Corso del Rinascimento

Rome's still-hip 'mozzarella bar' serves up mouth-watering variations of the white stuff, brought in fresh daily from the neighbouring Campania region. Don't miss the *affumicato* (smoked) version and make room for the gluttonous Sunday brunch (€24). A second branch (minus brunch) sits on the Campo de' Fiori (☎ 06 688 02 366).

TRATTORIA *Ristorante* €€
☎ 06 683 01 427; www.ristorantetrattoria.it; Via del Pozzo delle Cornacchie 25; 12.30-3pm & 7.30-11.30pm Mon-Sat, closed 3 weeks Aug; Corso del Rinascimento

A glass wall separates diners from the young-gun chefs at this Massimiliano Fuksas–designed restaurant-bar. Guided by celebrity chef Fabio Campoli, Trattoria whips up mod-Sicilian creations like pineapple-marinated calamari with pistachio *puntarelle* (chicory). Sweet tooths should not miss the manna.

Y DRINK

Although tourist-types love sloshing the night away on Campo de' Fiori, the *centro storico* harbours an eclectic mix of drinking gems across the district, ranging from quiet and intimately candlelit wine bars to chic contemporary lounges.

☿ BAR DELLA PACE *Café, Bar*
☎ 06 686 12 16; Via della Pace 5; ⏱ 4pm-2am Mon, 9am-2am Tue-Sun; 🚍 Corso Vittorio Emanuele II

Live the Euro cliché at this perennially fashionable art nouveau café, complete with ivy-clad façade, alfresco tables for Proust-reading poseurs, and a cosy gilt-and-wood interior once frequented by Danish sculptor Bertel Thorvaldsen.

☿ BARNUM CAFÉ *Café*
☎ 06 647 60 483; Via del Pellegrino 87; ⏱ 9am-2am Mon-Sat, 11am-2am Sun, closed Aug; 🚍 Corso Vittorio Emanuele II

If your idea of a café involves eclectic furniture, contemporary art, and the odd design magazine to flick through, Barnum has your name all over its cool white brickwork. Killer coffee aside, the well-priced drinks include teas, fresh juices and alcoholic tipples, while nibbles include croissants and tasty *panini*.

☿ BARTARUGA *Bar*
☎ 06 689 22 99; Piazza Mattei 9; ⏱ 6pm-1am Tue-Thu & Sun, to 2am Fri & Sat; 🚍 🚊 Via Arenula

VIPs, theatre darlings and those with bohemian tendencies adore this snug, Ghetto classic, with its mock-baroque ensemble of antique divans, velvet fabrics and Liberty wall lamps. Order an Alexander (brandy, cocoa and cream) and dream away to Sinatra. No credit cards.

☿ CAFFÈ FARNESE *Café*
☎ 06 688 02 125; Via dei Baullari 106; ⏱ 7am-2am; 🚍 Corso Vittorio Emanuele II

We're with Goethe, who thought Piazza Farnese one of the world's most beautiful squares. Judge for yourself from the vantage point of this unassuming café, famed for its secret recipe *caffè alla casa* (house coffee).

KING KONG, ROMAN-STYLE

In his novel *The Marble Faun*, American scribe Nathaniel Hawthorne recounts a Roman anecdote in which a pet monkey snatches an infant from its cot, carries it to the top of a medieval tower and swings it around like a handbag. Aghast, the newborn's parents pray to the Virgin Mary for help, promising to build her a shrine if she saves their cradle-snatched tot. The Virgin agrees to the deal, the monkey brings the baby down and the parents deliver the shrine. The tower belongs to **Palazzo Scapucci** (Via dei Portoghesi 18), the statue to Mary perched at its top.

▼ CAFFÈ SANT'EUSTACHIO
Bar

☎ 06 686 13 09; Piazza Sant'Eustachio 82; ⏱ 8.30am-1am Sun-Thu, 8.30am-1.30am Fri, 8.30am-2am Sat; 🚌 Corso del Rinascimento

The coffee at this retro standing-room-only bar enjoys cult status, created through a special process – note how the *baristi* (coffee makers) turn away to complete the secret recipe. Served sugared (specify if you want it *amaro* – bitter, or *poco zucchero* – with little sugar) with a layer of froth, it's dangerously addictive.

▼ ETABLÌ *Wine Bar, Restaurant*

☎ 06 976 16 694; Vicolo delle Vacche; ⏱ 6pm-2am Mon, noon-2am Tue-Sat, noon-midnight Sun; 🚌 Corso del Rinascimento

Another ubercool lounge-bar-restaurant combo, laid-back Etablì pairs French antiques with chandeliers, a crackling fireplace and a low-key urbane crowd. Slip into an armchair with a glass of red, nibble on fabulous *aperitivi,* or tuck into the Italo-Chilean owners' wonderful Roman/Mediterranean dishes.

▼ FLUID *Bar*

☎ 06 683 23 61; Via del Governo Vecchio 46; ⏱ 6pm-2am; 🚌 Corso del Rinascimento

Glowing ice-cube stools, glass floor panels and ink-infused tabletops set a sleek scene at this popular evening hangout, where a tasty, abundant *aperitivo* spread (6pm to 10pm) meets well-mixed drinks (try the Grasshopper house speciality), slinky DJ tunes and a chatty, chilled, eye-candy crowd.

▼ IL GOCCETTO *Wine Bar*

☎ 06 686 42 68; Via dei Banchi Vecchi 14; ⏱ 11am-2pm & 6.30pm-midnight Mon-Sat, closed Aug; 🚌 Corso Vittorio Emanuele II

Had anyone decided to make an Italian version of *Cheers,* it would have been recorded at this wood-panelled number, where a colourful cast of regulars finish each other's sentences, banter with the owners and work their way through a learned list of wines at the bar. Eavesdrop over an *assaggio* (tasting platter) of boutique, northern Italian cheeses.

▼ LA TAZZA D'ORO *Bar*

☎ 06 679 27 68; Via degli Orfani 84-86; ⏱ 7am-8pm Mon-Sat; 🚌 Via del Corso

'The Golden Cup' boasts some of the best coffee in the capital, which means it's criminally good. A speciality is the *granita di caffè,* a crushed-ice, sugared coffee served with a generous dollop of cream added both top and bottom. If you're not looking for a double hit and only want cream on the top/bottom, ask for *solo sopra/sotto.*

OPEN BALADIN
Beer Bar, Restaurant
☎ 06 683 89 89; Via degli Specchi 5-6;
🕐 noon-2am; 🚌 🚊 Via Arenula
This friendly temple to liquid amber boasts 38 Italian brews *alla spina* (on tap) alone. Indeed, national brews are the speciality, from classic blondes and golden ales to champagne-yeast and lavender-infused concoctions. Soak them up with fresh, Slow Food grub like local *trippa* (tripe) and lusty Piedmontese steaks.

SALOTTO 42 *Bar*
☎ 06 678 58 04; www.salotto42.it in Italian; Piazza di Pietra 42; 🕐 10am-2am Tue-Sat, 10am-midnight Sun; 🚌 Via del Corso
It might face 11 giant Corinthian columns belonging to a long-gone Tempio di Adriano, but this slinky lounge-bar has modernity on the mind – think suede lounges, newspaper-themed wallpaper and designer tomes lining the walls.

Clever cocktails include the spicy Basil (vodka, strawberry, chilli and basil).

SOCIÉTÉ LUTÈCE *Bar*
☎ 06 683 01 472; Piazza di Monte Vecchio 17; 🕐 6pm-2am Tue-Sun, closed 2 weeks Aug; 🚌 Corso del Rinascimento
Like its Trastevere sibling, Freni e Frizioni (p159), Société Lutèce remains one of the city's most kicking *aperitivo* bars, its effortlessly sexy crowd more art-school cool rather than D&G diva. Nibble inside or go alfresco on the tiny piazza.

⭐ PLAY

ACANTO BENESSERE DAY SPA *Spa*
☎ 06 681 36 602; www.acantospa.it; Piazza Rondanini 30; 1hr massage €90; 🕐 10am-9pm Mon-Sat, closed Aug; 🚌 Corso del Rinascimento
Sporting a space-pod entrance by local architects Marco and Luigi Giammetta, this is *the* place for a

---

TICKETS & RESERVATIONS
Prices for concert and theatre tickets range enormously depending on the venue and artist. Hotels can often reserve tickets for guests, or you can contact the venue or organisation directly. Otherwise try the following agencies:
> **Hellò Ticket** (☎ 800 90 70 80, 06 480 78 400; www.helloticket.it in Italian)
> **Orbis** (Map p93, B2; ☎ 06 474 47 76; Piazza dell'Esquilino 37; 🕐 9.30am-1pm & 4-7.30pm Mon-Fri, closed Aug)

You can also get tickets to concerts at major record outlets, including **Messaggerie Musicali** (Map p73, B4; ☎ 06 679 81 97; Via del Corso 123).

CAPITAL CAT-ASTROPHE

In the summer of 2007 alone, 400 kittens were abandoned at Rome's volunteer-run **Torre Argentina Cat Sanctuary** (☎ 06 687 21 33; www.romancats.com; Via di Torre Argentina; ⌚ noon-6pm), a sadly common occurrence in a country where neutering pets is not yet as common as it is in many other developed nations. Yet, a recent decrease in abandoned cats (around 50 in 2009) has the sanctuary – itself focused on sterilising, nursing and finding good homes for its four-legged guests – hopeful that local attitudes are finally changing.

The centre itself inhabits part of a mostly unexcavated Roman temple in the Area Sacra di Largo di Torre Argentina, close to the spot where Julius Caesar was slain in 44 BC. For the historical lowdown (ask to see the ancient latrine), join the sanctuary's **tour** (⌚ 4.30pm Wed, Fri & Sat Jun-Oct, 4pm Wed, Fri & Sat Nov-May). It's free... although a little donation is good for your karma and furry Roman friends.

designer detox. There's a blissful selection of facials and massages, a vaulted-ceiling hammam for atmospheric sweating and uberluxe options such as flower-infused milk baths for two. It's best to book treatments 48 hours ahead, especially on weekends.

⭐ ACQUA MADRE HAMMAM
Hammam

☎ 06 686 42 72; www.acquamadre.it; Via di Sant'Ambrogio 17; hammam €50, 50min massage from €60; ⌚ 2-7pm Tue, 11am-7pm Thu, Sat & Sun, women only 11am-7pm Wed & Fri, last exit 9pm; 🚌 🚋 Via Arenula

At Rome's chic new hammam, frazzled urbanites soak their way from *tepidarium* (warm room) to *caldarium* (hot room) to *frigidarium* (cold room), or give into seriously sublime massage and beauty treatments. First-timers need to buy a bathing glove and slippers (€10), and you can also buy a bathing costume (€10/15). Book ahead.

⭐ ANIMA *Nightclub*
☎ 06 688 92 806; Via di Santa Maria dell'Anima 57; ⌚ noon-4am; 🚌 Corso Vittorio Emanuele II

Mock-baroque Anima pulls a fashionable crowd who are hot and loving it. Head in before 8pm for the daily brunch or slip in for crafty evening cocktails and booty-shaking house, electronica, R&B and soul.

⭐ LA MAISON *Nightclub*
☎ 06 683 33 12; www.lamaisonroma .it; Vicolo dei Granari 4; ⌚ 11pm-4am Wed-Sun Oct-May; 🚌 Corso Vittorio Emanuele II

Crystal chandeliers, velvet banquettes and a *palazzo* vibe set a decadent scene at this playpen for 30-something fashion slaves. Count on smooth commercial tunes and a kicking vibe (assuming you get past the door bitch). Don't expect a crowd before 2am.

⭐ RIALTOSANTAMBROGIO
Centro Sociale

☎ 06 681 33 640; www.rialto.roma.it; Via di Sant'Ambrogio 4; admission free-€5; ⏰ varies; 🚌 🚋 Via Arenula
Expected to relocate (check the website for updates), Rome's most central *centro sociale* (social centre) oozes radical art-school cred with its edgy melting pot of art shows, film, theatre, live music and killer DJ sets.

⭐ TEATRO ARGENTINA *Theatre*
☎ 06 684 00 11; www.teatrodiroma.net in Italian, bookings www.helloticket .it in Italian; Largo di Torre Argentina 52; tickets €16-27, discounted Thu; ⏰ box office 10am-2pm, 3-7pm & 8-10pm Tue-Sun on performance days; 🚌 🚋 Largo di Torre Argentina

Opened in 1792, Rome's theatrical diva is a lavish affair, decked out with red-curtained boxes and a garlanded frescoed ceiling. Rossini's *Barber of Seville* debuted here and its theatre programme spans Shakespeare to Ray Bradbury (mostly in Italian). It also occasionally hosts major dance productions, best booked early.

⭐ WONDERFOOL *Spa*
☎ 06 688 92 315; www.wonderfool.it; Via dei Banchi Nuovi 39; ⏰ 10am-8pm Tue-Sat, noon-8pm Sun; 🚌 Corso Vittorio Emanuele II
Still male-focused but now offering treatments for women, this urban retreat boasts a day spa, vintage-style barber, Neapolitan tailor and a savvy grooming store. Counter Rome's smog and cobblestones with a revitalising facial (€160) and a heavenly reflexology massage (€80 for 50 minutes). Book ahead.

>TRIDENTE

Tridente is unapologetically glam: home to Victoria Beckham clones, double-parked limos and the show-off Spanish Steps. Fashion pilgrims flock to Via dei Condotti; celebrities sip at Stravinsky Bar; and fastidious foodies take in sweeping city views at dining hot spot Imàgo. It's all about names, darling: Goethe scribed on Via del Corso; Keats slipped away on Piazza di Spagna; and Fellini lived *la dolce vita* on dreamy Via Margutta.

Topping the district is neoclassical showpiece Piazza del Popolo, where Chiesa di Santa Maria del Popolo flaunts the works of its own famous posse – think Caravaggio, Raphael, Bramante and Bernini. From the piazza, Via di Ripetta runs south to Richard Meier's Museo dell'Ara Pacis; fashion-fabulous Via del Babuino hits ever-popular Piazza di Spagna; and main drag Via del Corso shoots down to Piazza Venezia in a chic-challenged combo of high-street chains and flash-trash teens.

TRIDENTE

👁 SEE
Chiesa della Trinità
  dei Monti **1** D4
Chiesa di Santa Maria
  del Popolo **2** B1
Keats-Shelley House **3** C4
Louis Vuitton **4** C4
Mausoleo di Augusto **5** B4
Museo dell'Ara Pacis **6** A4
Piazza del Popolo **7** B2
Porta del Popolo **8** A1
Spanish Steps **9** D4

🛍 SHOP
Alinari **10** C3
Anglo-American
  Bookshop **11** C5

Bomba **12** A2
Buccone **13** B2
Fabriano **14** B2
Fausto Santini **15** C5
Furla **16** C4
Gente **17** B2
Mondo Pop **18** B3
My Cup of Tea **19** C3

🍴 EAT
Babette **20** B2
GiNa **21** C3
'Gusto **22** A3
Il Palazzetto **23** D4
Imàgo **24** D4
La Buca di Ripetta **25** A3
Margutta RistorArte **26** B2

Osteria della Frezza **27** B3
Osteria Margutta **28** C3

🍸 DRINK
Antica Enoteca **29** C4
Caffè Greco **30** C4
Hi-Res at Hotel
  Valadier **31** B2
Palatium **32** C5
Stravinsky Bar at Hotel de
  Russie **33** B2

⭐ PLAY
International Wine Academy
  of Roma **34** C4

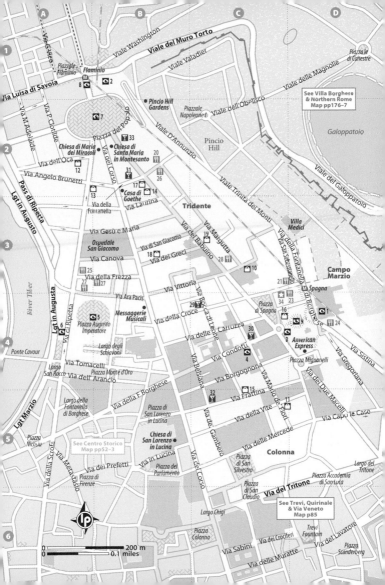

NEIGHBOURHOODS

TRIDENTE

 SEE

CHIESA DI SANTA MARIA DEL POPOLO

☎ 06 361 08 36; Piazza del Popolo;
🕑 7am-noon & 4-7pm Mon-Sat,
8am-1.30pm & 4.30-7.30pm Sun;
Ⓜ Flaminio

This cultured 15th-century Catholic church boasts 16th-century vault frescoes by Pinturicchio, two canvases by Caravaggio, Rome's first stained-glass windows (1509) in the Bramante-designed apse, and the elegant Chigi chapel – designed by Raphael and mostly completed by Bernini some 100 years later in the mid-17th century. Back in 1099 Pope Paschal II had a chapel built here to exorcise the spirit of Nero, believed to inhabit a walnut tree on the site. The tree was felled and its ashes dumped into the Tiber.

KEATS-SHELLEY HOUSE

☎ 06 678 42 35; www.keats-shelley -house.org; Piazza di Spagna 26; admission €4; 🕑 10am-1pm & 2-6pm Mon-Fri, 11am-2pm & 3-6pm Sat; Ⓜ Spagna

The Keats-Shelley House is where a 25-year-old John Keats coughed his last in February 1821. The fol-

Stepping up to Meier's modernist Museo dell'Ara Pacis

MEIER'S MAYHEM

Love it or loathe it, there's no denying that Richard Meier's Museo dell'Ara Pacis (below) knows how to whip up a storm. The controversy began in 1999, when then-mayor Francesco Rupelli announced the US architect would design the historic centre's first major civic building in more than half a century. That a *straniero* (foreigner) was given the honour was enough to make many locals indignant, but it was nowhere near as vexing as the fact that the commission, rather than having been won, was personally offered to Meier. In 2005, two years after the building's completion, 35 Italian architects wrote an open letter condemning the 'invasion' of foreign designers on the local scene.

As for the building itself, it's been compared to everything from a coffin to a petrol station. One journalist denounced it as 'absurdly overscale', while in 2008 Rome's new right-wing mayor Gianni Alemanno declared plans to have the enclosure dismantled and banished to the suburbs. One man who most likely toasted Alemanno's bombshell is popular art critic Vittorio Sgarbi, who infamously damned Meier's creation as an 'indecent cesspit by a useless architect', burning a model of the building for added effect.

lowing year, his partner-in-verse Percy Bysshe Shelley drowned off the Tuscan coast. Snoop through the atmospheric, stuck-in-time rooms that are crammed with memorabilia from the poets' short lives, including letters from Mary Shelley and Keats' death mask.

📷 MUSEO DELL'ARA PACIS

☎ 06 820 59 127; www.arapacis.it; Lungotevere in Augusta; adult/EU 18-25yr/EU under 18yr & over 65yr €6.50/4.50/free; ⏱ 9am-7pm Tue-Sun; 🚇 Lungotevere in Augusta

Set inside Richard Meier's muck-making modernist pavilion (also see the boxed text, above), the 1st-century BC Ara Pacis Augustae (Altar of Peace) is a marble masterpiece, laden with exqui-sitely carved reliefs in honour of peacemaker emperor Augustus. The downstairs exhibition space hosts oft-fabulous temporary exhibitions, from contemporary photography to industrial design retrospectives. Across the street, the once-glorious 28 BC **Mausoleo di Augusto** is the burial site of the emperor and his favourite nephew, Marcellus.

📷 PIAZZA DEL POPOLO

Ⓜ Flaminio

Once a hot spot for public executions, the 16th-century 'People's Square' was given a dashing 19th-century make-over by Giuseppe Valadier. Spot the differences between Carlo Rainaldi's not-so-twin baroque churches, and walk through the Bernini-

DESIGNER DETAIL
Forget handbags. The star turn at Rome's latest **Louis Vuitton** (☎ 06 699 40 000; www.louisvuitton.com; Via dei Condotti 13; ☼ 10am-7.30pm Mon-Sat, 11am-7.30pm Sun) store is a show-stopping, plasma-screen staircase. Based on a concept by New York–based architect Peter Marino (and looking like it's straight off a Madonna concert set), this visual tour de force transforms itself from psychedelic snake to technicolour torrent in seconds. For the full effect, head in after hours when the stairs are free of clutter and at their hi-tech best.

decorated **Porta del Popolo**, located on the piazza's northern flank, a one-time entry point for Grand Tour arrivals.

🅖 SPANISH STEPS
Ⓜ **Spagna**
Designed by Italian Francesco De Sanctis, financed by a French diplomat, and named after the nearby Spanish Embassy, Rome's most famous staircase (completed in 1725) keeps it global with daily hordes of camera-clicking tourists, migrant hawkers and crush-struck local teens. Head to the top for **Chiesa della Trinità dei Monti** (☼ 10am-noon & 4-6pm Mon-Sun) or to the bottom for the boat-shaped Barcaccia (1627) fountain on Piazza di Spagna, attributed to

Pietro Bernini (father of the famous Gian Lorenzo).

🛍 SHOP
To shop for Armani to Zegna, strut to Via dei Condotti, Via Borgognona and Piazza di Spagna. Via del Babuino is home to ab-fab concept store TAD at No 155A, while Via Margutta is best for fine art and antiques. Mosey down Via di Ripetta for wine, perfume and a Geppetto-like dolls' hospital at No 29.

🛍 ALINARI *Prints, Books*
☎ 06 679 29 23; Via Alibert 16; ☼ 3.30-7pm Mon, 10am-1pm & 3.30-7pm Tue-Fri, 10.30am-1pm & 3.30-7pm Sat; Ⓜ **Spagna**
Head here for evocative sepia prints and postcards of Rome and Italy by 19th-century Florentine photographers the Alinari brothers. A smattering of chunky photography tomes will keep your coffee table humming.

🛍 ANGLO-AMERICAN BOOKSHOP *Books*
☎ 06 679 52 22; Via della Vite 102; ☼ 3.30-7.30pm Mon, 10am-7.30pm Tue-Sat; Ⓜ **Spagna**
Titles span contemporary architecture to the Jewish history of Greece at this well-stocked English-language bookshop. There's a sound selection of travel

guides and maps, and enough classics, novels and kids' books to keep roaming bookworms busy.

☐ BOMBA *Fashion*
☎ 06 361 28 81; www.cristinabomba
.com; Via dell'Oca 39-41; ⏲ 3.30-
7.30pm Mon, 11am-7.30pm Tue-Sat;
Ⓜ Flaminio

Discerning Romans worship Cristina Bomba's sartorial creations. Here they're mixed with Metradamo and Liviana Conti gowns, Nafi De Luca millinery, Donatella Pellini jewellery and idiosyncratic footwear from Fiorentini & Baker. There's a small selection of modish ties and shoes for men, while bespoke fans can book a Monday appointment with the in-house tailor (a basic dress or suit takes about a week to complete).

☐ BUCCONE *Wine, Food*
☎ 06 361 21 54; www.enotecabuccone
.com; Via di Ripetta 19-20; ⏲ 9am-
8.30pm Mon-Thu, to 11.30pm Fri & Sat;
Ⓜ Flaminio

Salivate over soaring vintage shelves crammed with foodie-fabulous oils, vinegars, sauces, pasta, regional Italian *biscotti* (biscuits) and wines from Sicily to South Australia. If you can't wait till you get home, sit and scoff well-priced old-school grub at the little in-house **enoteca** (⏲ 12.30-3pm Mon-Thu, 12.30-3pm & 7.30-10.30pm Fri & Sat).

☐ FABRIANO *Stationery*
☎ 06 326 00 361; www.fabriano
boutique.com; Via del Babuino 173;
⏲ 10am-7.30pm Mon-Sat; Ⓜ Flaminio
or Spagna

Fabriano makes stationery sexy with a collection of deeply desirable diaries, funky notebooks and products embossed with street maps of Rome. Enlightened extras include quirky paper jewellery made by local designers and stylish paper-thin wallets.

☐ FAUSTO SANTINI *Shoes*
☎ 06 678 41 14; www.faustosantini
.com; Via Frattina 120; ⏲ 11am-7.30pm
Mon, 10am-7.30pm Tue-Sat, noon-7pm
Sun; Ⓜ Spagna

The kind of shoe store *Sex and the City's* Carrie Bradshaw would happily die in (yes, you'll find bags here, too). Fausto Santini is God to fashionable feet, designing show-stopping mules and boots in obscenely soft leather.

☐ FURLA *Accessories*
☎ 06 692 00 363; www.furla.com;
Piazza di Spagna 22; ⏲ 10am-8pm Mon-
Sat, 10.30am-8pm Sun; Ⓜ Spagna
Drop in for hot handbags and fashion-savvy accessories at the Tridente branch of this well-priced designer favourite (see p168).

NEIGHBOURHOODS

TRIDENTE

☐ GENTE
Fashion, Accessories

☎ 06 322 59 54; Via del Babuino 185;
🕑 10.30am-7.30pm; Ⓜ Spagna
Savvy Gente stocks superlative
Italian and foreign labels including
Prada, Cesare Attolini and Tom
Ford. Female fashion junkies can
get their fix across the street at
No 81. Those with more style than
savings should pop into Outlet
Gente (p169) for remainders and
last-season reductions.

☐ MONDO POP
Street Art

☎ 06 364 92 313; www.mondopop.it;
Via dei Greci 30; 🕑 10.30am-7.30pm
Tue-Sat; Ⓜ Spagna
Mondo Pop is for those Gen-X
and Gen-Y pop freaks who have it
all. This gallery-cum-shop stocks
a rotating selection of products
designed by cultish street artists
such as Gary Baseman, Cesko and
MTV's Jeremyville – from pop-print
T-shirts and poufs, to art toys and
'where-did-you-get-that?' bags.

☐ MY CUP OF TEA
Concept Store

☎ 06 326 51 061; www.mycupoftea.it in
Italian; Via del Babuino 65; 🕑 10am-
6pm Mon-Fri; Ⓜ Spagna
In a hard-to-find converted artist's
studio (walk through the main
entrance and ring the bell at the
courtyard door), this self-dubbed

'creative incubator' showcases the
work of emerging, mostly Italian,
artists and designers (with an
emphasis on women's fashion).
Expect anything from hand-sewn
cocktail dresses and felt jewellery to
sculptural candelabra and designer
dog bowls.

🍴 EAT

🍴 BABETTE
Ristorante   € €

☎ 06 321 15 59; Via Margutta 1; 🕑 8-
11pm Mon, 1-3pm & 8-11pm Tue-Sun,
closed Aug; Ⓜ Flaminio or Spagna
Come here for an atmospheric
mix of soaring warehouse ceilings,
1930s alley-style lamps, eclectic art
and a tranquil courtyard. Babette
loves sexing-up Italian classics,
whether that might be brioche
stuffed with *baccalà* (salted cod)
or pasta with zucchini, saffron and
pistachio pesto. Simpler options
dominate the lunch buffet (€12
Tuesday to Friday, €25 Saturday to
Sunday), and dinner is best booked
in advance.

🍴 GINA *Café*   € €

☎ 06 678 02 51; Via San Sebastianello
7A; 🕑 11am-8pm; Ⓜ Spagna
Just around the corner from the
Spanish Steps, trendy white-on-
white GiNa does luscious light
meals, including soups, bruschetta
and fresh, inspired salads. The

Mealtimes are approached with a typically Roman enthusiasm at 'Gusto

latter are a hit with Gucci-garbed princesses, who come to check out the Prada-preened pin-ups on their lunch break. Should romance spark, Villa Borghese picnic hampers (€40) are available for two.

🍴 'GUSTO
Pizzeria, Ristorante   €

☎ 06 322 62 73; Piazza Augusto Imperatore 9; 🕙 lunch buffet noon-3.30pm Mon-Fri, brunch noon-4pm Sat & Sun, restaurant 7pm-midnight, pizzeria 7pm-1am, wine bar noon-2am; 🚌 Via del Corso

Terence Conran would approve of this sprawling loft-style restaurant,

pizzeria and wine bar combo, complete with a warehouse-worthy kitchenware emporium. While the restaurant's efforts can be a bit hit-and-miss, Gusto's star attractions remain the jumbo-sized pizzas and bountiful, bargain-priced weekday lunch buffet (€9).

🍴 IL PALAZZETTO
Ristorante   € € €

☎ 06 699 34 1000; www.ilpalazzettoroma .com; Vicolo del Bottino 8; 🕙 12.30-2.30pm & 7.30-10.30pm Tue-Fri & Sun, noon-4pm Sat, closed Aug; Ⓜ Spagna

Take a light lunch on the terrace (with views of the Spanish Steps)

Francesco Apreda
Executive Chef, Imàgo (opposite)

Your culinary inspiration? My travels. The markets, restaurants and ingredients I encounter inspire me. Essentially my cooking is Italian, but I enjoy adding foreign twists like *inogi* mushrooms to a plate of anchovy linguine. It comes spontaneously. **The dining scene in Rome...** has definitely changed in the past five years. Young chefs are exposing themselves to foreign techniques and flavours and getting creative, while still respecting Italian culinary traditions. Chef Enzo di Tuoro at Il Palazzetto (p79) is a good example. **A good place for authentic Roman classics?** I'm always on the lookout for places in Trastevere, where I might be offered something really genuine, like robust homemade salami. **Where do you buy your vegetables?** At the market on Campo de' Fiori (p51). I'm a regular at Claudio's stall, which is right in the middle. I love the fact that I can get exotic products I won't find anywhere else, like huge Indian papayas.

or dine on new-school wonders in the old-school library room (think chestnut *tagliolini* pasta with whelks and black truffle). Wine buffs take note: the International Wine Academy of Roma (p83) awaits downstairs.

🍴 IMÀGO *Ristorante* €€€
☎ 06 699 34 726; www.imagorestau rant.com; Piazza della Trinità dei Monti 6; 🕐 12.30-2.30pm & 7.30-10.30pm Mon-Sat, 12.30-3pm & 7.30-10.30pm Sun; Ⓜ Spagna

The Hassler Hotel's rooftop showcase is *hot* – we're talking Michelin-star credentials, seamless city views (request the corner table), sexy mirrored tables, and bold mod-Italian creations from culinary star Francesco Apreda (see opposite). Book ahead.

🍴 LA BUCA DI RIPETTA
Ristorante €€
☎ 06 321 93 91; www.labucadiripetta .com; Via di Ripetta 36; 🕐 12.30-3pm & 7-11pm; Ⓜ Flaminio

Understatedly refined, and a hit with local actors and directors, this is one of Rome's best value-for-money foodie destinations. Classics are given inspired make-overs – think fried artichokes with melted *tellagio* cheese, or pear ravioli served with a subtle orange sauce spiked with green pepper-corns. Head in before 2pm to avoid the lunch crowds, and book for dinner.

🍴 MARGUTTA RISTORARTE
Vegetarian €€
☎ 06 678 60 33; www.ilmargutta.it; Via Margutta 118; 🕐 12.30-3.30pm & 7.30-11.30pm; Ⓜ Flaminio or Spagna

Vegetarians and vegans can breathe easy at restaurant-gallery Margutta. Svelte design and bilingual staff pair perfectly with an impressive wine list and gems like artichoke hearts with potato cubes and smoked Provolone cheese. The *parmigiana di melan-zane* (aubergine parmigiana) is the house speciality and around 70% of ingredients are organic. Best value is the Saturday/Sunday buffet brunch (€15/25).

🍴 OSTERIA DELLA FREZZA
Osteria €€
☎ 06 322 62 73; Via della Frezza 19; 🕐 12.30-4pm & 6.30pm-midnight; 🚌 Via del Corso

Part of the 'Gusto complex (p79), this Scandi-style *osteria/enoteca/tapas* bar is a perfect spot to chill out with a glass of Frascati, a platter of cheese and a good book. Between 6.30pm and 9pm, €4 will get you a small grazing plate from the buffet. The bar itself remains open until 2am.

🍴 OSTERIA MARGUTTA
Trattoria €€€

☎ 06 323 10 25; Via Margutta 82; ⏰ 12.30-3pm & 7.30-11pm Mon-Sat; Ⓜ Spagna

Looking straight out of *Moulin Rouge* with its red velvet curtains and fancy fringed lampshades, Osteria Margutta has plaques on its chairs testifying to the famous thespian bums they've supported. The menu includes a devilishly good *tortelloni al tartufo* (pasta dumplings stuffed with truffle) and market-fresh fish specials on Tuesdays, Fridays and Saturdays.

🍸 DRINK

🍸 ANTICA ENOTECA *Enoteca*

☎ 06 679 08 96; Via della Croce 76B; ⏰ noon-1am; Ⓜ Spagna

Local shoppers and shopkeepers pack this much-loved wine bar, which is full of frescoes and 19th-century trimmings. Plonk yourself at the long wood-and-brass counter and take your pick from 60 Italian drops by the glass; or plunge into the back room for soul-food staples such as pasta and polenta.

🍸 CAFFÈ GRECO *Café*

☎ 06 679 17 00; Via Condotti 86; ⏰ 10am-7pm Mon & Sun, 9am-7.30pm Tue-Sat; Ⓜ Spagna

Keats, Wagner and Casanova were regulars at the legendary Greco, which has been clattering cups since 1760. Still going strong, it's

of more interest for its history than anything it serves, so soak up its past with a coffee at the bar.

🍸 HI-RES AT HOTEL VALADIER
Rooftop Bar, Ristorante

☎ 06 361 19 98; Via della Fontanella 15; ⏰ 10.30am-1am; Ⓜ Flaminio

Demand a view with your *prosecco*? Take it in at Hotel Valadier's gorgeous rooftop bar-restaurant. Champagne-hued lounges and mosaic-trimmed floors ensure an appropriate setting as you gaze over Roman rooftops and sip on regional wines, cocktails or con-science-clearing juices and shakes. Drop in for a pre-dinner drink and complimentary nibbles.

🍸 PALATIUM *Enoteca*

☎ 06 692 02 132; Via Frattina 94; ⏰ 11am-11pm Mon-Sat, closed Aug; Ⓜ Spagna

Drop those Valentino shopping bags and refuel at this sleek, kosher showcase for Lazio's bumper produce. Explore lesser-known local drops such as Aleatico, and snack on local artisan cheese, olives and salami. Lunch is served from 1pm to 3pm and dinner from 8pm to 10.30pm.

🍸 STRAVINSKY BAR AT HOTEL DE RUSSIE *Hotel Bar*

☎ 06 328 88 874; Via del Babuino 9; ⏰ 9am-1am; Ⓜ Flaminio

With its lushly planted terraces, potted orange trees and just-love-to-please-you waiters, Hotel de Russie's chichi courtyard bar is hard to beat for that garden-party vibe. Go ahead – order the smoky Lapsang martini, slip on some shades and scan the bar for checked-in stars.

⭐ PLAY

⭐ INTERNATIONAL WINE ACADEMY OF ROMA
Wine Tasting
☎ 06 699 08 78; www.wineacademy roma.com; Vicolo del Bottino 8; 🕑 varies; Ⓜ Spagna

Get the lowdown on Italy's wine regions and tone up your tasting skills with a €180 half-day (90-minute) course, which includes lunch or dinner, or head out of town on one of the academy's sublime winery and restaurant tours (€330 to €360; minimum four people). There are regular themed tastings (free to €50), spanning Italian shiraz to Bourgogne beauties. Bookings essential.

>TREVI, QUIRINAL & VIA VENETO

Home to *that* fountain, Trevi's lively medieval streets can feel a bit like a circus with their camcorder crowds, tacky touts and endless souvenir shops. Beyond the hype, however, is a line-up of distinguished Roman residents, including mighty art repositories Palazzo Barberini and Palazzo Colonna, Bernini's ecstatic St Teresa, and the frozen revelations of Gelato di San Crispino.

The proliferation of policy-talking bureaucrats at linen-covered restaurant tables reminds you that you're in the shadow of the Quirinal (Quirinale), home to lofty presidential pad Palazzo del Quirinale, its stable-turned-gallery Scuderie Papali al Quirinale, and baroque high-achievers Chiesa di Sant'Andrea al Quirinale and Chiesa di San Carlo alle Quattro Fontane, designed by rival architects.

North of Quirinal, the once glamorous Via Vittorio Veneto curves gracefully towards Villa Borghese with its own cast of grandiose 19th-century façades, bored porters, overpriced cafés and faded celebrity memories. It's where you'll also find a creepy crypt decked out with creative Capuchin bones.

TREVI, QUIRINAL & VIA VENETO

👁 SEE
Chiesa di San Carlo alle
  Quattro Fontane **1** C3
Chiesa di Santa Maria della
  Concezione **2** C2
Chiesa di Santa Maria della
  Vittoria **3** D2
Chiesa di Sant'Andrea al
  Quirinale **4** C3
Gagosian Gallery **5** B2
Palazzo Barberini –
  Galleria Nazionale d'Arte
  Antica **6** C3
Palazzo del Quirinale **7** B4
Palazzo e Galleria
  Colonna **8** B4
Scuderie Papali al
  Quirinale **9** B4
Trevi Fountain **10** A3

🛍 SHOP
Galleria Alberto Sordi ..**11** A3
Victory **12** B3

🍴 EAT
Al Moro **13** A3
Al Presidente **14** B3

Cantina Cantarini **15** D1
Colline Emiliane **16** B3
Da Michele **17** A4
Dagnino **18** D2
Il Gelato di San
  Crispino **19** B3
Moma **20** C2

⭐ PLAY
Gregory's 21 B2

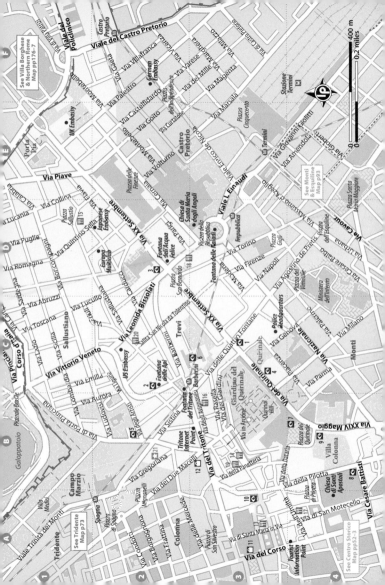

SEE

CHIESA DI SAN CARLO ALLE QUATTRO FONTANE

☎ 06 488 32 61; Via del Quirinale 23; ⏱ 10am-1pm & 3-6pm Mon-Fri, 10am-1pm Sat & Sun; 🚌 Via Nazionale

This tiny church is a sterling baroque work – not bad considering it was Borromini's first solo effort. Completed in 1641, it bears all the hallmarks of his tortured genius, from the play of convex and concave surfaces to its incredible honeycomb dome, which seems to float above your head (the secret's in the cunningly hidden windows).

CHIESA DI SANTA MARIA DELLA CONCEZIONE

☎ 06 487 11 85; Via Vittorio Veneto 27; admission by donation; ⏱ 9am-noon & 3-6pm; 🚇 Barberini

Beneath this boring 17th-century church, the fantastically ghoulish Capuchin cemetery takes recycling to extremes, with the bones of 4000 departed monks revamped into everything from lanterns to flouncy fleurs-de-lys. There's even a child-sized skeleton (scales of justice in one hand, scythe of death in the other) for the ultimate pick-me-up.

CHIESA DI SANTA MARIA DELLA VITTORIA

☎ 06 482 61 90; Via XX Settembre 17; ⏱ 8.30am-noon & 3.30-6pm Mon-Sat, 3.30-6pm Sun; 🚇 Repubblica

Religion gets racy with Bernini's *Ecstasy of St Teresa,* in the last chapel on the left of this modest baroque church. Arguably his finest sculpture, it depicts the Spanish saint floating in questionable pleasure while an angel pierces her with a golden arrow. Whatever Teresa's up to, it's a mesmerising work, best viewed in sensual afternoon light.

BATTLE OF THE BAROQUE

Before Paris and Nicole, there were Bernini and Borromini – the Italian baroque's most famous bitter rivals. While Bernini was an ebullient, urbane player (he seduced the pope's niece to nab the commission for the Fontana dei Quattro Fiumi (Fountain of the Four Rivers; in Piazza Navona, p58), Borromini was neurotic, reclusive and tortured. Despite getting his break in Rome working in Bernini's studio, Borromini looked down on his contemporary's lack of architectural training and formal stone-carving technique. No love was lost: Bernini believed Borromini 'had been sent to destroy architecture'.

Centuries on, the rivalry lives on in the works they left behind, from Borromini's Chiesa di San Carlo alle Quattro Fontane (above) and Bernini's neighbouring Chiesa di Sant'Andrea al Quirinale (opposite), to their back-to-back creations in Piazza Navona.

☉ CHIESA DI SANT'ANDREA AL QUIRINALE

☎ 06 489 03 187; Via del Quirinale 29; ⏱ 8.30am-noon & 3.30-7pm Mon-Sat, 9am-noon & 4-7pm Sun; 🚊 Via Nazionale

Long before IKEA did clever things with small spaces, Bernini created this ingeniously deceptive number, deploying an elliptical floor plan and eight deep chapels to create a grand effect in a rather tight squeeze. The magic continues with the statue of Sant'Andrea, which looks ready to float out of the church and into the heavens.

☉ GAGOSIAN GALLERY

☎ 06 420 86 498; www.gagosian.com; Via Francesco Crispi 16; admission free; ⏱ 10.30am-7pm Tue-Sat; Ⓜ Barberini

In December 2007, contemporary art heavyweight Gagosian added Rome to its portfolio, converting a 1920s bank into a gallery designed by Firouz Galdo and Caruso St John. Its debut exhibition featured the work of Rome-based American artist Cy Twombly.

☉ PALAZZO BARBERINI – GALLERIA NAZIONALE D'ARTE ANTICA

☎ 06 482 41 84; www.galleriaborghese .it; Via delle Quattro Fontane 13; adult/ EU 18-25yr/EU under 18yr & over 65yr €5/2.50/free; ⏱ 9am-7.30pm Tue-Sun; Ⓜ Barberini

A who's who of baroque architects created this magnificent 17th-century palace, now home to fine artistic booty. Compare Bernini's stately staircase with Borromini's spiral number, then take in works by Caravaggio, Raphael, El Greco, Tintoretto, Bronzino and Hans Holbein. For the ultimate rush, soak up Pietro da Cortona's almighty ceiling fresco, *Triumph of Divine Providence* (1632–39) in the main salon; it celebrates the power (and ego) of the *palazzo's* founder, Pope Urban VIII. Note that the entrance will be from Via Barberini 18 from late 2009.

☉ PALAZZO DEL QUIRINALE

☎ 06 4 69 91; www.quirinale.it; Piazza del Quirinale; admission €5; ⏱ 8.30am-noon Sun Sep-Jun; 🚊 Via Nazionale

Hilltop Palazzo del Quirinale was the pope's summer pad for almost three centuries until, prompted by a gun, the keys were handed over to Italy's new king (in 1870), who then handed them to the president of the Republic (in 1948). Domenico Fontana designed the main façade, Carlo Maderno the chapel, and Bernini the wing running the length of the street.

Across the Piazza del Quirinale, Italian architect Gae Aulenti (of Musée d'Orsay fame) reworked the palace's former stables. The resulting **Scuderie Papali al Quirinale** (☎ 06 69 62 70; bookings 06 399 67 500; www.scuderiequirinale.it; Via XXIV Maggio 16;

Rome's most famous film star – the Trevi Fountain

admission varies; 🕒 9.30am-8pm Mon-Thu, 9.30am-10.30pm Fri, 9am-10.30pm Sat, 9am-8pm Sun during exhibitions only) is one of Rome's slickest exhibition venues, host to shows spanning pop art to Renaissance retrospectives.

🄲 PALAZZO E GALLERIA COLONNA
☎ 06 678 43 50; www.galleriacolonna.it; Via della Pilotta 17; adult/under 10yr & over 60yr €10/8; 🕒 9am-1pm Sat, closed late Jul-Aug; 🚊 Via IV Novembre
On Saturday mornings, the aristocratic Colonna clan allows curious commoners into its opulent 17th-century gallery. The space is

crowned by loud, glorious ceiling frescoes recording the family's virtuous deeds. Below them hang the works of artistic greats, including Bronzino, Veronese, Salvatore Rosa and Annibale Caracci, whose humble *Bean Eater* is the crowd favourite. Don't trip on the cannonball lodged in the marble steps, an uncanny memento from the 1849 siege of Rome.

🄲 TREVI FOUNTAIN
Piazza di Trevi; 🚊 Via del Tritone
Rococo extravaganza Trevi Fountain (Fontana di Trevi) was immortalised by Anita Ekberg's

midnight dip in *La Dolce Vita*. Designed by Nicola Salvi in 1732, it depicts Neptune's chariot being led by Tritons with sea horses – one wild, one docile – representing the various moods of the sea. For some of that Fellini magic, ditch the hordes and come at dawn.

SHOP

GALLERIA ALBERTO SORDI
Shopping Centre
Piazza Colonna; 🕐 **10am-10pm;** 🚊 **Via del Corso**
Film buffs may recall this elegant stained-glass arcade from Alberto Sordi's 1973 film classic, *Polvere di Stelle* (Stardust). The film starred Rome's favourite actor, for whom the gallery was renamed in 2003. Retail protagonists include Trussardi, Zara, AVC and Feltrinelli, and there are two chic little cafés for cinematic posing.

VICTORY *Fashion*
☎ **06 699 24 280; Via dei Due Macelli 32;** 🕐 **10am-8pm Mon-Sat, noon-7.30pm Sun;** Ⓜ **Barberini**
Rome's penchant for mainstream catwalk crud bypassed Victory, which flies the flag for harder-to-find male wardrobe winners. Must-buys include Dondup jeans, Gaetano Navarra shirts and Barcelona footwear label Munich. Clued-up female fashionistas can get their fix across the street at No 103–4.

EAT

AL MORO *Ristorante*   €€€
☎ **06 678 34 96; Vicolo delle Bollette 13;** 🕐 **1-3.30pm & 8-11.30pm Mon-Sat;** 🚊 **Via del Corso**
This one-time Fellini haunt feels like a step back in time with picture-gallery dining rooms, Liberty wall lamps, cantankerous buttoned-up waiters and old-money regulars with nicknames like *la Principessa* (the Princess). Join faux royals for classic *cicoria al brodo* (chicory in broth) or melt-in-your-mouth veal liver with crusty sage and butter.

AL PRESIDENTE
Seafood   €€€
☎ **06 679 73 42; Via in Arcione 95;** 🕐 **1-3pm & 8-11pm Tue-Sun;** 🚊 **Via del Tritone**
In the shadow of the presidential palace, Al Presidente spikes its stately white interiors with twisted copper chandeliers, Bordeaux-red chairs and black-clad waiters. Seafood is the forte, with classic-meets-contemporary highlights including fettucine with calamari and mullet roe. Don't forget to book.

CANTINA CANTARINI
Osteria   €€
☎ **06 485 52 81; Piazza Sallustio 12;** 🕐 **12.30-3pm & 7.30-10.30pm Mon-Sat, closed Aug;** 🚊 **Via XX Settembre**
Expect meat in the first half of the week and fish thereafter at this

crowded, salt-of-the-earth cente-narian. The menu focuses on the simple, robust flavours of Italy's Lazio and Le Marche regions, delivered by veteran staffer Mario Fattori (on the floor since 1946). Get in early or queue.

🍴 COLLINE EMILIANE
Trattoria € €
☎ 06 481 75 38; Via degli Avignonesi 22; ⏱ 12.45-2.45pm & 7.30-10.45pm Tue-Sat, 12.45-2.45pm Sun, closed Aug; Ⓜ **Barberini**
Flying the flag for Emilia-Romagna, the Italian region that gave the world Parmesan, balsamic vinegar, Bolognese sauce and Parma ham, this warm, elegant foodie staple is all about cream, veal and scrumptious homemade pasta fillings such as mashed pumpkin. Don't miss the pork cutlet stuffed

with prosciutto and cheese, and remember to *always* book.

🍴 DA MICHELE
Pizza al Taglio €
☎ 349 252 53 47; Via dell'Umiltà 31; ⏱ 9am-8pm Sun-Thu, 9am-3pm Fri; 🚌 **Via del Corso**
Only a schmuck would pass on a slice of pizza at this little kosher legend, which includes a can't-stop-at-one, pan-tossed spinach and tomato number. Crusts are light and crispy, and the owners really do love each other despite the seasoned insults.

🍴 DAGNINO
Pasticceria €
☎ 06 481 86 60; Galleria Esedra, Via Vittorio Emanuele Orlando; ⏱ 7am-11pm Mon-Sat, 7.30am-11pm Sun; Ⓜ **Repubblica**

Choosing your favourite flavour of gelato ought to be child's play...but is it?

Sweet tooths cram this chintzy *pasticceria* (pastry shop) for sublime Sicilian treats, from moreish ricotta-filled *cannoli* (pastries) and ice-cream brioche to velvety marzipan fruits. While the savoury offerings are hit and miss, the *arancini* (rice balls) would make Palermo proud.

IL GELATO DI SAN CRISPINO *Gelateria*   €

☎ 06 679 39 24; Via della Panetteria 42; ⏰ noon-12.30am Mon, Wed, Thu & Sun, noon-1.30am Fri & Sat; Ⓜ Barberini

We forgive the stingy servings simply because this is possibly the world's best gelato. Religiously stored under stainless steel lids, the flavours are seasonal, strictly natural and unforgettable – the liquorice root and *mandarancia* (orange/mandarin) flavours are a heavenly match.

MOMA
Ristorante, Café   €€€

☎ 06 420 11 798; Via San Basilio 42; ⏰ 7am-11pm Mon-Sat; Ⓜ Barberini

Paging London with its concrete floors and sexed-up boardroom style, metropolitan Moma splits itself in two: downstairs bar for stand-up espresso and ab-fab nibbles, and upstairs dining room for mod-Med creations such as

THE LICKERS' LOWDOWN

Roman gelato is addictive, assuming you get the real, freshly made deal. A good tip is to check the banana: bright yellow equals bad; grey equals good. Gelato stored in plastic containers is often a sign of mass production, while top-notch gelaterie use seasonal ingredients. Best-in-Rome contenders include heavenly Il Gelato di San Crispino (left), historic Giolitti (p65), as well as off-the-radar Al Settimo Gelo (p169) and Palazzo del Freddo di Giovanni Fassi (p102).

grilled *capesante* (scallops) served with quenelle red lentils, *velo di Colonnata* (thin slices of Colonnata lard) and rosemary gelato. Book for dinner.

⭐ PLAY

⭐ GREGORY'S *Live Music*

☎ 06 679 63 86; www.gregorysjazz .com; Via Gregoriana 54D; admission €5; ⏰ 8pm-3am Tue-Sun, closed Aug; Ⓜ Spagna

This husky, soulful jazz den is a popular hangout for local musicians and a good bet for top local sax. Unwind in the downstairs bar, then find a squashy sofa upstairs and muse about Manhattan over Teddy Wilson tunes.

>MONTI & ESQUILINE

Tucked in between three ancient hills, Monti is a hit with discerning urbanites, who are drawn to its village vibe and fashion-forward boutiques. Shopkeepers showcase local artists and kick back together at buzzing summer street parties. In imperial times this was the notorious Suburra – Rome's sleazy red-light district and the childhood home of Julius Caesar. These days, you're more likely to stumble across a pair of April 77 drill pants or a bar selling books and Caprioskas on atmospheric streets such as Via del Boschetto, Via Leonina, Via Urbana, Via degli Zingari and sinister-sounding Via dei Serpenti (Street of Snakes).

East of Monti, misunderstood Esquiline (Esquilino) flies the flag for shab with its budget hotels, dodgy after-dark crowds and cookie-cutter 'Made in China' shops. But beyond the lunching pimps is a heady mix of Pakistani spice shops, bargain-hunting Polish maids and wizened pavement tarot readers. Add cultural heavyweights such as Museo Nazionale Romano: Palazzo Massimo alle Terme and Basilica di Santa Maria Maggiore, throw in a secret magic door, and you have yourself one exotic urban escapade.

MONTI & ESQUILINE

🟢 SEE

Basilica di San Pietro in Vincoli	1	B3
Basilica di Santa Maria Maggiore	2	C2
Chiesa di Santa Croce in Gerusalemme	3	E4
Chiesa di Santa Prassede	4	C2
Domus Aurea	5	B4
Magic Doorway	6	D3
Museo Nazionale d'Arte Orientale	7	C3
Museo Nazionale Romano: Palazzo Massimo alle Terme	8	C1
Museo Nazionale Romano: Terme di Diocleziano	9	C1
Palazzo delle Esposizioni	10	A2

🅰 SHOP

Abito	11	B2
Bookàbar	(see 10)	
C.A.M	12	B2
Contesta Rock Hair	13	B3
Fabio Piccioni	14	B2
Furla	15	B2
I Vetri di Passagrilli	16	B3
La Bottega del Cioccolato	17	B3
MAS	18	C3
RAP	19	B2
Stazione Termini	20	C2
Super	21	B3
Tina Sondergaard	22	A2

🍽 EAT

Africa	23	C1
Agata e Romeo	24	C3
Castroni	25	B2
Da Ricci	26	B2
Doozo	27	B2
Indian Fast Food	28	D3
Palazzo del Freddo di Giovanni Fassi	29	D3
Panella l'Arte del Pane	30	C3
Trattoria Monti	31	C3

🍷 DRINK

Ai Tre Scalini	32	A3
Al Vino al Vino	33	A3
Bar Zest at Radisson SAS es. Hotel	34	D2
Bohemien	35	B3
La Barrique	36	B2
La Bottega del Caffè	37	B3

⭐ PLAY

Hangar	38	B3
Micca Club	39	E3
Teatro dell'Opera di Roma	40	B2

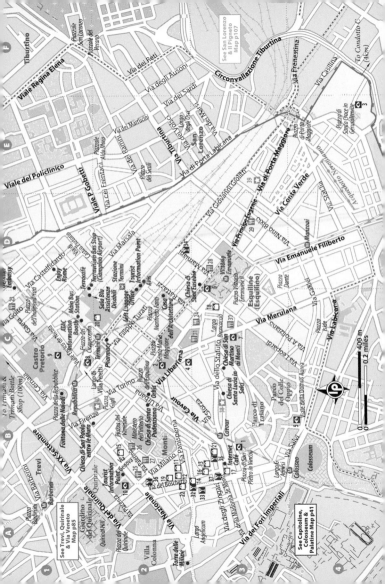

👁 SEE

👁 BASILICA DI SAN PIETRO IN VINCOLI

☎ 06 488 28 65; Piazza di San Pietro in Vincoli 4A; ⏱ 8am-12.30pm & 3-6pm; Ⓜ Cavour

Beneath the altar of this 5th-century number sit the chains used to bind St Peter. According to legend, the chains miraculously rejoined after returning to Rome from Constantinople in two pieces. Miracles give way to misunderstandings with Michelangelo's monumental unfinished tomb of Pope Julius II – its horned Moses resulted when the Hebrew word for 'radiant' was mistranslated as 'horned'.

👁 BASILICA DI SANTA MARIA MAGGIORE

☎ 06 48 31 95; Piazza Santa Maria Maggiore; ⏱ 7am-7pm Mon-Sun; 🚌 Piazza Santa Maria Maggiore

This hilltop diva boasts a classical 5th-century triple nave, a Romanesque bell tower (Rome's tallest), an 18th-century façade, a kaleidoscopic Cosmati marble floor, a 15th-century gilded coffered ceiling, and riotously coloured 5th-century mosaics.

Step inside the marble marvel of Basilica di Santa Maria Maggiore

Such grandiosity befits the tomb of baroque maestro Gian Lorenzo Bernini, which lies to the right of the altar.

CHIESA DI SANTA CROCE IN GERUSALEMME

☎ 06 706 13 053; Piazza di Santa Croce in Gerusalemme 12; ⏰ 7am-12.30pm & 3.30-7.30pm; 🚌 Piazza di Porta Maggiore

Back from a trip to Jerusalem, St Helena (mother of Emperor Constantine) founded this pilgrim pit stop in 320 to house her holy souvenirs: bits from Christ's cross, a nail, two spines from his crown and a slice of St Thomas' doubting finger.

CHIESA DI SANTA PRASSEDE

☎ 06 488 24 56; Via Santa Prassede 9A; ⏰ 7am-noon & 4-6.30pm; 🚌 Piazza Santa Maria Maggiore

Humble Santa Prassede will blow you away with its dazzling 9th-century mosaics, whipped up by Byzantium artists brought in especially by Pope Paschal I. Swoon over those on the triumphal arch and apse, before hitting the jackpot with the razzle-dazzle extravaganza in the Chapel of San Zenone (where you'll also find a piece of the column Christ was tied to when flagellated).

DOMUS AUREA

☎ 06 399 67 700; www.pierreci.it; Viale della Domus Aurea; admission €4.50; ⏰ closed for restoration; Ⓜ Colosseo

Hollywood homes would have had nothing on Nero's 'Golden House' estate, built after the fire of AD 64 and covering a third of the city. Clad in gold and mother-of-pearl, the palace itself boasted frescoed banqueting halls, nymphaeums, baths, and an artificial lake where the Colosseum (p44) now stands. Among the few survivors is a series of frescoes, which inspired the likes of Ghirlandaio and Raphael. The ruins were scheduled to reopen in 2011.

MUSEO NAZIONALE D'ARTE ORIENTALE

☎ 06 469 74 801; www.museorientale.it; Via Merulana 248; adult/EU 18-24yr/EU under 18yr & over 65yr €6/3/free; ⏰ 9am-2pm Tue, Wed & Fri, to 7.30pm Thu, Sat & Sun, closed Mon; Ⓜ Vittorio Emanuele; ♿

Swap continents at Rome's little-known but impressive National Museum of Oriental Art. Set in a fabulously camp *palazzo* (palace), its collection of Near and Far Eastern treasures includes carved ancient Afghani marble, richly hued 15th-century Kubachi ceramics, painted Tibetan fans from the 11th to 18th centuries

THE MAGIC DOORWAY

Hidden away in the northeast corner of Piazza Vittorio Emanuele II is a mysterious limestone doorway covered in cabbalistic symbols and mysterious Latin inscriptions. It's guarded by two ancient Egyptian demigods and topped by a limestone disc engraved with the Star of David. The door once led to the private gardens of Villa Palombara, which stood here until the late 19th century.

According to legend, the villa's occult-loving owner, the Marquis Palombara, had sponsored the experiments of a young necromancer named Giuseppe Francesco Borri, who was set on discovering the legendary philosopher's stone (which turns matter into gold). But Borri vanished one day, leaving behind a pile of papers inscribed with secret formulae that the marquis hoped would unlock the magic formula. When even the best alchemists were left scratching their heads, Palombara engraved the symbols into the doorway, hoping that an expert would one day see them and finally crack the code.

and intricate Nepalese textiles. English-language information is wanting, but the pieces speak for themselves.

◉ MUSEO NAZIONALE ROMANO: PALAZZO MASSIMO ALLE TERME

☎ 06 399 67 700; Largo di Villa Peretti 1; adult/EU 18-24yr/EU under 18yr & over 65yr €7/3.50/free, special exhibitions extra €2; ⏰ 9am-7.45pm Tue-Sun; Ⓜ Termini; ♿

A must for classical connoisseurs. Start with ancient cash, souvenirs and a mummified Roman child in the basement, then hit the ground floor for egotastic sculptures – don't miss *Pugile* (The Resting Boxer) and the moving 5th-century BC *Niobide dagli Horti Sallustiani* (Niobide from the Gardens of Sallust). Admire ancient hairstyles on the next floor

before heading up another flight of stairs for exquisite mosaics and frescoes, among them erotic wall paintings from an Augustan-period villa found in the grounds of Villa Farnesina (p152), and the sublimely delicate *Garden Painting* from Villa di Livia near Rome. The audioguide (€4) is a worthwhile investment.

◉ MUSEO NAZIONALE ROMANO: TERME DI DIOCLEZIANO

☎ 06 399 67 700; Viale Enrico De Nicola 78; adult/EU 18-24yr/EU under 18yr & over 65yr €7/3.50/free, special exhibitions extra €3; ⏰ 9am-7.45pm Tue-Sun; Ⓜ Termini; ♿

The 3rd-century Diocletian Baths were ancient Rome's largest, accommodating 3000 pleasure seekers in a sprawl of pools, libraries, concert halls and gardens. Part of the surviving structure, recently reopened to the public, houses two 2nd-century burial chambers discovered beneath the city's modern suburbs – one featuring beautiful stucco decoration, the other smothered in frescoes. The museum itself, housed in a 16th-century convent designed by Michelangelo, is famed for its collection of revealing ancient epigraphs.

PALAZZO DELLE ESPOSIZIONI
☎ 06 399 67 500; www.palazzo esposizioni.it; Via Nazionale 194; adult/under 26yr & over 65yr €12.50/10; 🕐 10am-8pm Thu & Sun, to 10.30pm Fri & Sat; 🚇 Via Nazionale; ⚫

This former Communist Party hangout packs a punch with its revamped 19th-century grandeur and ubercool art exhibitions; recent shows include a Stanley Kubrick retrospective and 21st-century Chinese photography. Watch exhibition-themed flicks in the cinema or shop'n'sip in the seriously sleek Bookàbar (right).

🛍 SHOP
ABITO *Fashion*
☎ 06 488 10 17; www.abito61.blogspot .com in Italian; Via Panisperna 61; 🕐 10.30am-8pm; Ⓜ Cavour

Wilma Silvestri and her daughters Giorgia and Carlotta whimsically rework retro threads into chic, fashion-forward statements. Their fabulously affordable *Confezione Express* range allows you to pick a garment from 20 prototypes, choose a fabric, and have it sewn to your exact measurements within 24 hours. Genius!

BOOKÀBAR *Books, Music*
☎ 06 489 13 361; Via Milano 15-17; 🕐 10am-8pm Tue-Thu & Sun, to 10.30pm Fri & Sat; 🚇 Via Nazionale

A cool place simply to hang out in, this stunning Firouz Galdo-designed bookshop/bar stocks drool-worthy tomes (art, architecture, design and film), DVDS, CDs and design-savvy gifts. Part of the Palazzo delle Esposizioni (left), it has its own street entrance on Via Milano.

C.A.M *Fashion & Accessories*
☎ 06 489 07 175; www.myspace.com/ classeartigianamonti; Via del Boschetto 76; 🕐 3-8pm Mon, 11am-8pm Tue-Sat; Ⓜ Cavour

This former poultry shop, complete with original marble counter, is home to up-and-coming fashion duo Valentina Bacci and Giorgio Maroni. Inspired by vintage fabrics, their creations meld Scandi simplicity with rave culture undercurrents and irreverent twists – think slinky frocks splattered with silicone.

ART & SCANDAL IN SUBURBIA

In less than three years, alleyway-turned-art space **Condotto C** (☎ 377 151 98 71; www .condottoc.com; Via Re Filippo 8A; ⏰ varies; Ⓜ Quadraro-Porta Furba) has established itself as a dynamic platform for the work of emerging Italian and foreign artists in genres spanning performance art to site-specific installations. As sculptor and Condotto C co-founder Marco Bernardi explains: 'We own the space, which allows us to exhibit artists that bigger galleries with bigger overheads wouldn't take a risk on.' Indeed, the tiny creative room has come a long way from the days when locals believed it was a setting for Satanic rituals. Bernardi recalls: 'We once featured a half-naked dancer simulating electric shocks on a hospital bed. Some of the neighbours freaked out but after a debate at the local bar they concluded it was art.' Condotto C sits 500m northwest of Quadraro-Porta Furba metro station. Check the website for upcoming events and call ahead as opening hours are erratic.

🏠 CONTESTA ROCK HAIR
Fashion

☎ 06 489 06 975; Via degli Zingari 10; ⏰ 10am-8pm Mon-Sat; Ⓜ Cavour
Minimalist style, neon rods and a disco ball set the scene for clued-up guys and girls looking for edgy threads. Snap up in-the-know indie labels such as Italy's Jucca, NDLPRK & PHCY, Spain's Mariona Gen & Skunkfunk, America's Joe's Jeans & Australia's Insight.

🏠 FABIO PICCIONI *Jewellery*

☎ 06 474 16 97; Via del Boschetto 148; ⏰ 2-8pm Mon, 10.30am-1pm & 2-8pm Tue-Sat, closed Sat Jun-Aug; Ⓜ Cavour
Under a sea of chandeliers, artisan Fabio Piccioni turns old trinkets into must-have deco-inspired jewellery. A hit with film and theatre divas, what Fabio doesn't sell he wears himself. Also opens 10.30am to 1pm and 2pm to 8pm Saturdays from November to April.

🏠 FURLA *Accessories*

☎ 06 487 01 27; www.furla.com; Via Nazionale 54-55; ⏰ 9.30am-8pm Mon-Sat; Ⓜ Via Nazionale
Another option for affordable accessorising from this savvy fashion staple (p168).

🏠 LA BOTTEGA DEL CIOCCOLATO *Food*

☎ 06 482 14 73; Via Leonina 82; ⏰ 9.30am-7.30pm Mon-Sat Sep-May; Ⓜ Cavour
Scarlet hues and a boudoir vibe set the mood for dietary sins at this seductive chocolate peddler. Give in to wickedly smooth, freshly made pralines and truffles; pick up a cute chocolate car; or succumb to the thick hot chocolate.

MAS *Department Store*
☎ 06 446 80 78; Via dello Statuto 11;
⊙ 9am-12.45pm & 4-7.45pm Mon-Sat,
10am-12.45pm & 4-7.30pm Sun;
Ⓜ **Vittorio Emanuele**

Intensely atmospheric, fun and
trashy MAS (Magazzino allo
Statuto) is a sprawling retro emporium of J-Lo wannabe assistants,
multicultural crowds and floor
after floor of bargain finds. Pick up
€15 jeans, dirt-cheap suits, knickers, hats, shoes, fabrics, crockery
and almost anything in between.

STAZIONE TERMINI
Shopping Centre
Piazza dei Cinquecento; Ⓜ **Termini**
It mightn't make retail hot lists,
but Rome's central station is un-
disputedly handy, with more than
100 outlets spanning ubiquitous

chains such as Sisley and Benet-
ton, to a multilevel bookshop,
late-night **pharmacy** (platform 1;
⊙ 7.30am-10pm) and three supermarkets – the best of the lot being
basement **Conad** (⊙ 6am-midnight).

SUPER *Fashion, Accessories*
☎ 06 454 48 500; www.super-space
.com; Via Leonina 42; ⊙ 3.30-8pm
Mon, 10.30am-2pm & 3.30-8pm Tue-Sat;
Ⓜ **Cavour**

Lauded by French *Vogue* and
Japanese *Elle*, minimalist, unisex
Super ditches big-name bones for
hard-to-find threads from Italian
innovators February, Crossley
and Mario's, and progressive
foreigners such as London's Ash,
Belgium's Raf Simons and French
label Sessùn. There's also a quirky
collection of designer novelties.

More than just a transport hub, Stazione Termini caters for all your retail needs

Carla Zaia
Tour guide and passionate Roman

Describe Rome as a person Looking out from Gianicolo (p151), she evokes a curvaceous aristocrat, her undulating sprawl a tattered, elegant gown. As for her temperament, it's feline. She loves attention but can turn on you like a mad cat. **Your heart belongs to…**The area between Trastevere (p146), the Ghetto and the Campo de' Fiori (p51). On a summer's night, sitting beside the Fontana delle Tartarughe (p55) is bliss. **Architecturally and artistically…** I adore the simplicity and exoticness of Rome's early-Christian monuments, like the Case Romane below the Chiesa di SS Giovanni e Paolo (p119) and the layered Basilica di San Clemente (p118). That said, Bernini's baroque *Ecstasy of St Teresa* in the Chiesa di Santa Maria della Vittoria (p86) makes me cry. The spirituality is so entrenched in the flesh.**What would you change about Rome?** Romans are famous moaners! I'd say we need fewer protagonists and more consideration for others.

TINA SONDERGAARD
Fashion

☎ 06 979 90 565; Via del Boschetto 1D; ⏱ 3-7.30pm Mon, 10.30am-1pm & 1.30-7.30pm Tue-Sat, closed Aug; Ⓜ Cavour

Sublimely cut and whimsically retro-esque, these handmade threads are a hit with female fashion cognoscenti, including Italian rock star Carmen Consoli and the city's theatre and TV crowd. Each piece is a limited edition and new creations hit the racks every week.

🍴 EAT

🍴 AFRICA *Ethiopian, Eritrean* €

☎ 06 494 10 77; Via Gaeta 26-28; ⏱ 8am-midnight Tue-Sun; Ⓜ Castro Pretorio

Forget what your mother said and eat with your hands at this boldly hued ethnic veteran, serving up authentic Ethiopian and Eritrean grub in technicolour *mesobs* (traditional Ethiopian woven baskets). Dig into spicy stews and delicious *sambusas* (fried savoury pastries); lick your fingers to upbeat Afro tunes; and soak up a refreshingly different scene of worldly Roman cool.

🍴 AGATA E ROMEO
Ristorante €€€

☎ 06 446 61 15; Via Carlo Alberto 45; ⏱ 12.30-3pm & 7.30-10.30pm Mon-Fri, closed 2 weeks in Jan & Aug; Ⓜ Vittorio Emanuele

A luxe epicurean classic, Agata e Romeo is headed by legendary chef Agata Parisella, whose deceptively simple-sounding Roman dishes are often complex and always perfectly balanced – think *baccalà* (salted cod) spiked with fragrant orange. Husband Romeo curates the cellar; daughter Maria Antonietta chooses the cheeses; and service is smooth and unobtrusive. Book ahead.

🍴 CASTRONI *Deli* €

☎ 06 489 87 474; Via Nazionale 71; ⏱ 7.30am-8pm Mon-Sun; 🚌 Via Nazionale

Another outlet of this glutton's paradise (p169).

🍴 DA RICCI *Pizzeria* €

☎ 06 488 11 07; Via Genova 32; ⏱ 7pm-midnight Tue-Sun, closed Aug; 🚌 Via Nazionale

Tucked away on a cosy cul-de-sac, Est! Est! Est! (as it's also known) is possibly Rome's oldest pizzeria. Beginning life as a wine shop in 1905, it's famed for its deep-crust *pizza alla napoletana* (Neapolitan-style pizza), served up in old-school surrounds packed with boisterous, satisfied regulars.

🍴 DOOZO *Japanese* €€

☎ 06 481 56 55; www.doozo.it; Via Palermo 51; ⏱ 12.30-3pm & 8-11.30pm Tue-Sat, 8-11.30pm Sun; 🚌 Via Nazionale

Japanese nosh meets art and coffee-table tomes at this cool yet relaxed hybrid. Eye-up contemporary photography exhibitions over a cup of roasted rice tea; bag a Japanese tea set; or relax in the Zen garden with perfect sushi and sashimi, soothing soba soup and heavenly *mochi* sweets prepared by a real-deal Tokyo chef.

🍴 INDIAN FAST FOOD
Indian   €

☎ 06 446 07 92; Via Mamiani 11;
🕑 11am-4pm & 5-10pm; Ⓜ Vittorio Emanuele

Blaring Hindi pop, curious stares and kick-ass curries define this no-frills takeaway joint, complete with Ganesh statue above the drinks fridge. Pig out on cheap, authentic Indian grub such as spicy samosas, flavoursome pakoras and day-glo Indian sweets.

🍴 PALAZZO DEL FREDDO DI GIOVANNI FASSI
Gelateria   €

☎ 06 446 47 40; Via Principe Eugenio 65-67; 🕑 noon-midnight Tue-Fri, to 12.30am Sat, 10am-midnight Sun; Ⓜ Vittorio Emanuele

Sprinkled with old-fashioned marble table tops and vintage gelato-making machinery, Rome's oldest ice-cream peddler is one of its best. Undecided palates should opt for a heavenly *riso* (rice), pistachio and *nocciola* (hazelnut) combo.

🍴 PANELLA L'ARTE DEL PANE
Bakery   €

☎ 06 487 24 35; Via Merulana 54; 🕑 8am-2pm & 5-8pm Mon-Wed & Fri, 8am-2pm & 4.30-8pm Sat, 8am-2pm Thu & Sun; Ⓜ Vittorio Emanuele

Just steps away from the Museo Nazionale d'Arte Orientale (p95), this devilishly tempting bakery-cum-providore defies moderation with its gluttonous array of *pizza al taglio* (pizza by the slice), focaccia, Sicilian rice balls, fried croquettes and pastries, as well as breads made to ancient Roman recipes. Upgrade the glee-factor with a glass of chilled *prosecco* (sparkling wine), then scan the shelves for pantry treats to take home.

🍴 TRATTORIA MONTI
Trattoria   € €

☎ 06 446 65 73; Via di San Vito 13A; 🕑 12.45-2.45pm & 7.45-10.45pm Tue-Sat, 12.45-2.45pm Sun, closed Aug; Ⓜ Vittorio Emanuele

Savvy journalists and fine-looking families flock to this well-bred favourite, which is run by the charming Cameruccis. Like the owners, the top-notch seasonal fare hails from the Le Marche region – think gamey stews, truffles and *pecorino di fossa* (sheeps cheese aged in caves), all of which is skilfully deployed in dishes like *mezze maniche* pasta with *pecorino,* sausage and black pepper. Be sure to make reservations for dinner.

DRINK

AI TRE SCALINI *Enoteca*
☎ 06 489 07 495; Via Panisperna 251;
🕑 12.30pm-1am Mon-Fri, 6pm-1am Sat & Sun; Ⓜ Cavour

Sporting the quintessential ivy-clad exterior, this vintage slosh spot opts for eclectic interior decorating, with theatre masks, grandfather clock and rustic frescoes in the mix. Nosh options include fresh salads and a gut-filling strudel; tunes span blues to jazz; and the popular *aperitivo* (happy hour) is a hit with Monti's younger crowd.

AL VINO AL VINO *Wine Bar*
☎ 06 48 58 03; Via dei Serpenti 19;
🕑 9.30am-2.30pm & 5.30pm-12.30am Sun-Thu, to 1.30am Fri & Sat, closed 2 weeks Aug; Ⓜ Cavour

The perfect epilogue to a Monti shopping escapade, affable Al Vino melds rustic chic with contemporary art. Expect 500 drops lining the cellar (including 25 wines by the glass), a savvy selection of whiskies and grappas, and spiced-up Sicilian nosh if you care to line your stomach.

BAR ZEST AT RADISSON SAS ES. HOTEL
Rooftop Bar & Ristorante
☎ 06 44 48 41; www.rome.radissonsas .com; Via Filippo Turati 171; 🕑 10.30am-1am Apr-Sep, 10am-midnight Oct-Mar; Ⓜ Termini

Atop the Radisson SAS es. Hotel and opposite Stazione Termini, Bar Zest swaps Esquiline grit for cool, clean chic: we're talking Jasper Morrison chairs, floor-to-ceiling windows and a sexy rooftop pool (usually open to the public May

Rooftop splashing and lounging at Bar Zest, Radisson SAS es. Hotel

NEIGHBOURHOODS

MONTI & ESQUILINE

to September – call ahead). Sip a perfume-inspired cocktail, nibble on Med-twist nosh and forget the mayhem below.

�Y BOHEMIEN *Bar*

☎ 06 890 10 626; Via degli Zingari 36; ☽ 6pm-2am Wed-Mon; Ⓜ Cavour

Suitably shabby with its worn velvet armchairs, crooked painted lampshades and Amy Winehouse tunes, this boho-inclined bolthole is a hit for its potent €5 cocktails and small-but-scrumptious *aperitivo* spread (€8) from 7pm. The art on the wall is local, the books are for sale, and arty-types pack the place after 10.30pm.

☓Y LA BARRIQUE *Wine Bar*

☎ 06 478 25 953; Via del Boschetto 41B; ☽ 1-3pm & 7pm-1.30am Mon-Fri, 7pm-1.30am Sat; 🚃 Via Nazionale

Intimate and softly lit, laid-back La Barrique boasts an erudite selection of Italian and French wines, 120 types of champagne, rare whiskies and a friendly vino-versed owner, Fabrizio. Delectable snacks include an unmissable pancetta and anchovy *crostone* (bruschetta), which happens to be Fabrizio's *favorito*.

☓Y LA BOTTEGA DEL CAFFÈ *Café*

☎ 06 474 15 78; Piazza della Madonna dei Monti; ☽ 8am-2am; Ⓜ Cavour

Contemporary, buzzing and situated right on a picture-perfect square complete with trickling fountain, this café is a sound spot to don that black polo-neck sweater, scan the papers and watch the locals sip, flirt and gossip. Vino aside, you'll find fine coffee, freshly squeezed juices and grazing options ranging from simple pizzas to cheeses and salamis.

☓Y TRIMANI *Wine Bar*

☎ 06 446 96 30; Via Cernaia 37B; ☽ 11.30am-3pm & 6pm-12.30am Mon-Sat, closed Aug; Ⓜ Termini

Head here for an ample selection of vineyard gems, complemented by changing daily dishes such as delicately flavoured ravioli stuffed with nuts and dressed with fabulously sharp *pecorino romano*. It's part of the Trimani family's wine empire, whose celebrated **bottle shop** (☎ 06 446 96 61; Via Goito 20; ☽ 9am-1.30pm & 3.30-8.30pm Mon-Sat) just around the corner is Rome's biggest.

⭐ PLAY

⭐ HANGAR *Gay Club*

☎ 06 488 13 971; www.hangaronline .it; Via in Selci 69; ☽ 10.30pm-2.30am Wed-Mon, closed 3 weeks Aug; Ⓜ Cavour

Rome's veteran gay bar is still a hit with local Lotharios and cruising out-of-towners, all of who come

VIA DEL BOSCHETTO

While Monti has no shortage of cool streets, Via del Boschetto (Map p93, A2) is the neighbourhood's stand-out strip. Home to whimsical Tina Sondergaard (p101) and newcomer C.A.M (p97), it's a fusion of eclectic boutiques, bric-a-brac boltholes and the odd wine bar.

It's also home to some idiosyncratic artist studios. One long-standing favourite is **I Vetri di Passagrilli** (☎ 06 474 70 22; www.ivetridipassagrilli.it; Via del Boschetto 94; ✆ 10.30am-2pm & 3-7.30pm Mon-Sat), the workshop/showroom of Domenico Passagrilli and his organic glassware. Equally inspired is **RAP** (☎ 06 474 08 76; www.chiararapaccini .com in Italian; Via del Boschetto 61; ✆ varies), where children's-book author and artist Chiara Rapaccini lets her imagination run riot in objects like chicken-legged tables.

for the down-to-earth yet raunchy vibe. For a kicking crowd, turn up on weekends, Mondays (porn night) or Thursdays (striptease). There's even a dark room for turned-on punters.

⭐ MICCA CLUB
Live Music, Nightclub
☎ 06 874 40 079; www.miccaclub .com; Via Pietra Micca 7A; admission free Tue, Thu & Sun, €10 via the website or €15 at the door Fri & Sat; ✆ 9pm-2am Mon, 10pm-2am Tue & Thu, 10pm-4am Fri & Sat Sep-May, also 6pm-1am Sun Oct-Apr; Ⓜ Vittorio Emanuele
Channelling the '60s with its shagadelic pop art vibe, this swinging basement venue spins out live bossa nova to French jazz, burlesque workshops, retro Italian rock and DJ-spun dance. Fill up on *aperitivo* from 7pm to 10pm

Thursday to Tuesday, or graze and shop at the Sunday *aperitivo*-cumflea market (from 6pm October to April).

⭐ TEATRO DELL'OPERA DI ROMA *Opera House*
☎ 06 481 60 255; www.operaroma.it; Piazza Beniamino Gigli 1; opera tickets €30-€140, ballet tickets €13-€65; ✆ box office 9am-5pm Tue-Sat, to 1.30pm Sun, indoor opera season Dec-Jun, ballet season Dec-Jun; Ⓜ Repubblica
Puccini premiered Tosca at Rome's opera house, whose stern Fascist exterior belies its classic gilt and velvet interior, much loved by mink-pimped signore and their programme-clutching husbands. Its hit-and-miss acoustics mean it's best to book a box. In July and August, the season goes alfresco at Terme di Caracalla (p133).

>SAN LORENZO & IL PIGNETO

Murphy's Law hit San Lorenzo hard on 19 July 1943, when the famously anti-Fascist district was the only one damaged by an Allied air raid. Thousands were killed and Basilica di San Lorenzo Fuori-le-Mura reduced to rubble. That San Lorenzo boasts the city's largest cemetery only amplifies the irony.

Squeezed between the dead and Rome's ancient Aurelian wall, today's district oozes old-school Berlin soul – think hammer-and-sickle graffiti, the smell of pot in the air, and a live-and-let-live attitude where *nonni* (grandpas) chat with tongue-pierced punks and rough'n'ready dives share the curb with fine-dining gems.

A quick tram ride southeast, Il Pigneto is the 'new' San Lorenzo. Built to house railway workers in the 19th century, it was until a few decades ago better known for petty theft and slums. These days it's a hub for artists and trend-seeking urbanites, who cram its *enoteche* (wine bars), indie bars and funky offbeat shops.

East of the railway, suburban side streets such as Via Fazio degli Uberti and Via Alipio serve up an eclectic mix of Arabesque flats, mock-Moorish pads and sun-bleached vegetable gardens.

SAN LORENZO & IL PIGNETO

◉ SEE
Basilica di San Lorenzo
  Fuori-le-Mura **1** C1
Cimitero di Campo
  Verano **2** C2
Galleria Pino
  Casagrande .... (see 3)
Pastificio Cerere **3** B2

⬚ SHOP
Claudio Sanò **4** A3
La Grande Officina **5** B2
Le Terre di AT **6** B2

Myriam B **7** A3
Radiation Records **8** D4

🍴 EAT
Bocca di Dama **9** A3
Formula Uno **10** A3
Necci **11** D5
Pommidoro **12** B2
Ristorante Pastificio San
  Lorenzo .... (see 3)
Rouge **13** B2
Said **14** B2

🍸 DRINK
Baràbook **15** B3
Cargo .... (see 18)
Fuzzy Bar **16** A3
Hobo ArtClub **17** C5
Vini e Olii **18** C5

★ PLAY
Circolo degli Artisti 19 C5
Fanfulla 101 ....20 D5
Locanda Atlantide 21 B3
Nuovo Cinema Aquila ..22 C4

SEE

CIMITERO DI CAMPO VERANO

Piazzale del Verano; ☙ **7.30am-7pm Mon-Sun Apr-Sep, to 6pm Oct-Mar;** 🚌 **Piazzale del Verano**

It may seem a little morbid, but in fact San Lorenzo's cemetery is an interesting and strangely moving place, peppered with brooding mausoleums, yearning epigraphs and mournful marble angels. Located to the left of the cemetery, **Basilica di San Lorenzo Fuori-le-Mura** (☎ 06 49 15 11; ☙ 8am-noon & 4-6.30pm Mon-Sun) sits on St Lawrence's burial place. The basilica features a 13th-century frescoed portico and sumptuous mosaics in the Chapel of Pio IX behind the high altar.

GALLERIA PINO CASAGRANDE

☎ **06 446 34 80; Via degli Ausoni 7A; admission free;** ☙ **5-8pm Mon-Fri;** 🚌 **Via Tiburtina**

Take the goods lift to the 5th floor of the legendary **Pastificio Cerere** (see the boxed text, below) for intelligent, progressive art at this small, top-notch gallery. Past exhibitors include German photographer Jan Bauer and local sound artist Piero Mottola.

SHOP

CLAUDIO SANÒ
Accessories

☎ **06 446 92 84; www.claudiosano.it; Largo degli Osci 67A;** ☙ **10am-1pm & 4.30-8pm Mon-Sat;** 🚌 **Via Tiburtina**

Fancy a fish-shaped handbag or a moustached briefcase? San

ART AL DENTE

It might be an icon of modern Italian art, but **Pastificio Cerere** (☎ 06 454 22 960; www.pastificiocerere.com; Via degli Ausoni 7; ☙ 3-7pm Mon-Fri; 🚌 Via Tiburtina) started life as a giant pasta factory in 1905. Abandoned in 1960, its empty loft spaces would eventually draw six emerging artists – Nunzio, Giuseppe Gallo, Piero Pizzi Cannella, Gianni Dessì, Marco Tirelli and Bruno Ceccobbelli. Dubbed the Nuova Scuola Romana (New Roman School), they took the nation's art scene by storm in the early 1980s, rebelling against mainstream minimalism with a revival of old-school techniques mixed with new-school edge. Now, a new generation of artists is pushing boundaries inside this industrial monolith, including Maurizio Savini, famed for his mind-blowing bubble-gum sculptures. To explore the studios, email a request (from the website) to Fondazione del Pastificio Cerere, specifying which artists' studios you'd like to visit. The website has links that let you explore the residents' work and also lists upcoming exhibitions.

Lorenzo artisan Claudio Sanò is the Salvador Dalí of leather, transforming mundane everyday accessories into quirky lifelike creations. They're not cheap, but masterpieces seldom are.

🔲 LA GRANDE OFFICINA
Jewellery
☎ 06 445 03 48; Via dei Sabelli 165B; ⏲ 10.30am-7.30pm Mon-Fri; 🚋 🚋 Via dei Reti

Under dusty workshop lamps, husband-and-wife team Giancarlo Genco and Daniela Ronchetti turn everything from old clock parts and Japanese fans into edgy geometric jewellery.

🔲 LE TERRE DI AT *Ceramics*
☎ 06 49 17 48; www.leterrediangela.it; Via degli Ausoni 13; ⏲ 4-8pm Mon-Sat; 🚋 Via Tiburtina

Local ceramicist Angela Torcivia has a knack with the wheel, spinning out stunning pieces such as richly hued bijoux and bottle-stoppers, and smoky Raku (Japanese pottery) lamps and bowls.

🔲 MYRIAM B
Fashion & Accessories
☎ 06 443 61 305; www.myriamb.it; Via dei Volsci 75; ⏲ 11am-1pm & 5-8pm Tue-Sat, 5-8pm Mon; 🚋 Via Tiburtina

Mass-produced mediocrity is a foreign concept at this local designer's bolthole boutique. Here,

chic deconstructionist threads mix it with hand-painted gloves, scarves made from recycled ties, industrial rings and sculptural necklaces that are nothing less than artworks.

🔲 RADIATION RECORDS *Music*
☎ 06 454 49 836; www.radiation records.net; Circonvallazione Casilina 44; ⏲ 4.30-8pm Mon, 10.30am-2pm & 4-8pm Tue-Fri, 10.30am-8pm Sat; 🚌 105 to Circonvallazione Casilina 🚋 Via Prenestina

Off-the-radar Radiation stocks vinyl, CDs and DVDs spanning ska and funk, to rock steady, garage and local indie acts such as the Intellectuals. Occasional in-store gigs have seen the likes of punk chick Penelope Houston rock the shop.

🍴 EAT

🍴 ARANCIA BLU
Vegetarian, Enoteca   € €
☎ 06 445 41 05; www.aranciabluroma .com; Via Prenestina 396; ⏲ 4pm-midnight Mon-Fri, noon-midnight Sat, Sun & public holidays; 🚋 19 to Via Prenestina

Now in larger bistro-chic premises 3km east of Il Pigneto, the 'Blue Orange' continues to sex-up herbivorous fare (potato tartlet with Brie de Meaux and black truffle, anyone?). Though service has slipped a bit, the degustation menus (€35 and €37) continue to impress. Check online for upcoming cultural events.

🍴 SAID *Café*   €
☎ 06 446 92 04; Via Tiburtina 135; ⏰ noon-12.30am Mon-Sat; 🚊 Via Tiburtina
Set in a 1920s chocolate factory, this industrial-cool café/chocolate shop/restaurant peddles thick hot chocolate, luscious cakes and pralines, and savoury gems like *tagliatoni* pasta with pistachio pesto and speck (book ahead for dinner). Adventurous chocoholics should request *un'assaggio di cioccolatini particolari* (a tasting platter of 'interesting' chocolates) to avoid a run-of-the-mill selection.

🍴 BOCCA DI DAMA *Pasticceria, Café*
☎ 06 443 41 154; www.boccadidama .it in Italian; Via dei Marsi 2-6; ⏰ 11am-8pm Tue-Sat, 11am-1pm & 1.30-4.20pm Sun; 🚊 Via Tiburtina
Run by fresh, creative types, this new-school pastry shop/café injects traditional sweet recipes with a dash of contemporary quirkiness – think handmade chocolates sold with euphemisms and architect-concocted bonbons with names such as *bacio dell'architetto* (the architect's kiss). Stock up on all-natural sea-

sonal cakes, biscuits and heavenly handmade marmalades.

🍴 FORMULA UNO *Pizzeria*   €
☎ 06 445 38 66; Via degli Equi 13; ⏰ 6.30pm-12.30am Mon-Sat; 🚊 Via Tiburtina
Beneath whirling rooftop fans and Ferrari posters, swarms of local students and slumming up-towners tuck into crunchy bruschetta, golden *supplì al telefono* (rice croquettes with a mozzarella centre) and cheap-as-chips thin-crust pizzas served by potbellied waiters.

🍴 NECCI *Café, Trattoria*   €
☎ 06 976 01 552; www.necci1924 .com in Italian; Via Fanfulla da Lodi 68; ⏰ 8am-2.30am, kitchen closes 1.15am; 🚊 105 to Circonvallazione Casilina
Cinema great Pier Paolo Pasolini loved the place, and bohemians still flock to retro-tastic Necci to down beers on the terrace or tuck into hearty grub to Little Tony jukebox tunes. The Sunday evening buffet (€10, from 7pm) is great value, and Micca's (p105) ever-popular Sunday flea market migrates here from May to September (from 7pm).

🍴 OSTERIA QUI SE MAGNA! *Osteria*   €
☎ 06 27 48 03; Via del Pigneto 307A; ⏰ 12.30-3pm & 8-11pm Mon-Sat, dinner only Aug; 🚊 Via Casilina

Dining alfresco at popular Necci

A real neighbourhood secret, this buzzing, gay-friendly *osteria* (wine bar serving food) serves cheap, lip-smacking dishes such as *pasta all'amatriciana* (pasta with tomato, pancetta and chilli-pepper sauce), grilled meats and *puntarella* (Lazio chicory with anchovies, garlic and a splash of vinegar) to loud'n'merry locals. Book for weekends.

☷ POMMIDORO *Trattoria* €€
☎ 06 445 26 92; Piazza dei Sanniti 44;
⏱ 1-3pm & 8-10.30pm Mon-Sat, closed Aug; 🚌 Via Tiburtina
Despite the famous fans (among them Nicole Kidman), centenarian Pommidoro remains true to its San Lorenzo roots, cooking up perfected heirlooms such as *spaghetti alla carbonara* (spaghetti

with an egg, cheese and pancetta sauce) and oxtail stew. Grilled meats are a speciality, and the huge fireplace is a winter night's dream.

☷ RISTORANTE PASTIFICIO SAN LORENZO
Ristorante, Bar €€
☎ 06 972 73 519; www.pastificio cerere.com/ristorante; Via Tiburtina 196;
⏱ 7pm-2am Tue-Sun, kitchen closes 11.30pm; 🚌 Via Tiburtina
Located in the Pastificio Cerere (see the boxed text, p108), this cool-yet-convivial restaurant/bar/lounge fuses industrial architecture with white-tiled walls, low-slung lamps and suede banquettes. Nibble on cheese and *affetatati* (cold cuts) at the bar, or score a table for progressive delights like duck with caramelised cabbage and clementine compote. Book ahead.

☷ ROUGE *Osteria* €
☎ 06 494 08 63; Via dei Sabelli 193;
⏱ 1-3pm & 8-11.30pm Mon-Fri, 1-3pm Sat; 🚌 🚋 Via dei Reti
Local artists, academics and labourers can't get enough of this place, with its kooky caged parrot, op-shop glassware and soul-glow specials like spicy lentil soup and *fettucine Rouge* (pasta with spicy 'Nduja salami and spinach pesto). It's like a communal retro dining

room, complete with Portishead tunes.

DRINK

☿ BARÀBOOK
Wine Bar

☎ 06 960 43 014; www.barabook.it in Italian; Via dei Piceni 23; ☽ 4pm-midnight Tue-Thu, to 2am Fri & Sat, 11am-midnight Sun, closed Aug; ⊕ ▣ Via dei Reti

Yes, it's a bar… with books, which line the walls alongside oddball retro finds and art. In the middle, at a long communal table lit by low-strung lamps, locals read, chat and sip the house speciality spritzer. *Aperitivo* (happy hour; €8) comes with DJ tunes on Fridays and Saturdays from 7.30pm, and the Sunday brunch (12.30pm to 3pm) is tasty fuel for cultured brains.

☿ CARGO *Bar*

☎ 06 976 17 820; Via del Pigneto 20; ☽ 5.30pm-2am daily, from 9am 4th Sun of the month; ⊕ 105 to Circonvallazione Casilina

Hipster hangout Cargo has all the right moves: communal tables, retro lamps, local artwork and quirky extras like old theatre seats. Celebrate Pigneto's effortless cool with well-priced libations and nibbles ranging

from bruschetta and cheeses to Malaga speck and *salame d'oca* (duck salami).

☿ FUZZY BAR
Wine Bar

☎ 06 445 11 62; Via degli Aurunci 6; ☽ 6pm-2am, closed Sun summer & Mon winter; ⊕ Via Tiburtina

Fuzzy is seriously clued-up about wine and food. New World drops are snubbed for Old World gems; the gourmet *aperitivo* focuses on small-scale Italian producers; and regular tasting events span oils and wines to regional cuisines. The kitchen closes at 12.30am from Sundays to Thursdays and at 1am Fridays and Saturdays. If you write/read Italian, join the email list (fuzzybar@libero.it) for the lowdown on upcoming events.

☿ HOBO ARTCLUB *Bar, Café*

☎ 06 64 80 19; www.hoboartclub.word press.com in Italian; Via Ascoli Piceno 3; ☽ 6pm-2am; ⊕ 105 to Circonvallazione Casilina

Cultured Hobo's book-lined walls, stacked wine boxes and odd parked bike sit somewhere between secondhand bookshop and mate's garage. Cheap, well-chosen wines mix it with fresh juices and smoothies (including a 'Keith Richard's Wish' liver detox) and cheap, salubrious grub like chickpea and bulgar soup.

▼ VINI E OLII *Enoteca*

Via del Pigneto 18; ⏱ **6.30pm-2am;**
🚍 **Circonvallazione Casilina**
Looking like a dimly lit cellar-
garage, Vini e Olii is a favourite
aperitivo haunt for local bohemians. Perched on tiny wooden
stools that spill out onto the
pedestrianised street, they drink
decent house vino from plastic
cups, eat old-school *porchetta*
(sliced pork) on disposable plates,
and talk life and Lacan to soulful
funk and blues.

⭐ PLAY

⭐ CIRCOLO DEGLI ARTISTI
Live Music, Nightclub
☎ **06 703 05 684; www.circoloartisti.it**
in Italian; **Via Casilina Vecchia 42; admis-**
sion varies; ⏱ **7pm-2am Tue-Thu for**
concerts only, 7pm-4.30am Fri & Sat,
7pm-1am Sun, closed 1 week Aug;
🚍 **Via Casilina**
East of Il Pigneto, laid-back Circolo
is the spot for alternative music
gigs (think Glasvegas and Corner-
shop), innovative cultural events

SUBURBAN BUZZ

More than just home to blingy teens, suburban Rome harbours some seriously kicking clubs:
Brancaleone (off Map pp176–7; ☎ 06 820 04 382; www.brancaleone.eu; Via Levanna 11;
admission usually €10; ⏱ 10.30pm-4am Thu-Sat Oct-Jun; 🚍 Via Nomentana) This *centro*
sociale (social centre) is one of the hottest underground clubs in Rome, pulling in a young,
alternative crowd and electronica meisters such as Stockholm's Tomas Andersson, Berlin's Paul
Kalkbrenner and Detroit's Jeff Mills.
Forte Prenestino (off Map p107; ☎ 06 218 07 855; www.forteprenestino.net in Italian; Via
Federico Delpino Centrocelle; admission free–€20; ⏱ varies; 🚍 Via Prenestina) Housed in a
fort east of the city centre, this active *centro sociale* hosts everything from counterculture gigs,
vintage markets and shiatsu massage (€15) to a brilliant May Day festival.
Piper Club (Map pp176–7, F4; ☎ 06 855 53 98; www.piperclub.it in Italian; Via Tagliamento
9; ⏱ 11pm-5am Fri, 4-8pm & 11pm-5am Sat, hours vary other days, closed Mon; 🚍 Via
Salaria) Born in 1965, Piper has worked through its midlife crisis and is rediscovering its mojo
as the life and soul of the party. Unfashibly funky nights aside, this clubbing classic attracts
big-name gigs (think Peaches and Babyshambles).
Qube (off Map p107; ☎ 06 438 54 45; www.qubedisco.com in Italian; Via di Portonaccio 212;
admission free before midnight, then €5 Thu, €16 incl 1 drink Fri, free with phone booking or €10
incl 1 drink at door Sat; ⏱ 10.30pm-4am Thu, 11.30pm-5am Fri & Sat mid-Sep–May; 🚍 Via
di Portonaccio) Rome's clubbing giant offers Radio Rock on Thursday, gay night Muccassassina
(www.muccassassina.com in Italian) on Friday, and regular international DJs at Saturday staple
Babylon. In July and August, the party moves outdoors – check the website for details.

Beatrice Bertini
Founder and curator, Ex Elettro Fonica (p150)

Ex Elettro Fonica's design was inspired by… The human body. The architects envisioned a 'skin' wrapped around the building's interior. The end result is an anthropomorphic space that reflects the vitality of young, contemporary artists. **The gallery's most outrageous exhibition to date?** Davide D'Elia's collection of abstract mould compositions. Preparation involved exposing the gallery to 100% humidity for three weeks. When the mould began to form we were pretty excited. **Zaha Hadid's MAXXI (p178) will…** Give Rome more of an international edge and hopefully become a dynamic meeting place for people. Museums in Rome are too often stuffy and institutional. Hopefully MAXXI will prove otherwise. **Other good bets for contemporary art?** The Pastificio Cerere (see the boxed text, p108), home to the studios of internationally renowned artists like Giuseppe Gallo; Fondazione Volume! (p150), which allows artists to reinvent the space itself; and Condotto C (see the boxed text, p98).

and thumping club nights. Friday is gay Omogenic, Saturday serves up punk-funk, ska and new-wave, and Sunday melds *aperitivo* with indie art and fashion 'happenings'. There's an open-air bar to boot.

⭐ FANFULLA 101
Arts, Nightclub
www.fanfulla.org in Italian; Via Fanfulla da Lodi 101; admission €5, free with Arci-card; 🕒 **varies, usually 9pm-2am;** 🚌 **105 to Circonvallazione Casilina**
This raw'n'retro cultural centre (hidden behind an unmarked workshop door) keeps left-leaning loafers oiled with dirt-cheap drinks and anything from live indie, jazz and rock, to art-house films, and DJ-spun reggae, house and Jap-pop kitsch. The shack on the corner across the street starred in Pasolini's *Accattone*.

⭐ LOCANDA ATLANTIDE
Arts, Nightclub
☎ **06 447 04 540; www.locandatlantide .it in Italian; Via dei Lucani 22B; admission free-€10;** 🕒 **varies, usually 9pm-2am mid-Sep-mid-Jun;** 🚌 🚊 **Viale dello Scalo San Lorenzo**
Culture and clubbing collide at ever-jamming Locanda Atlantide, tucked down a graffiti-covered backstreet, decked out in retro junk, and home to attitude-free counterculture crowds. Expect anything from experimental theatre, fashion, dance and video art, often followed by DJ-spun electro. Check the website for gigs.

⭐ NUOVO CINEMA AQUILA
Cinema
Via L'Aquila 68; 🚌 🚊 **Via Prenestina**
A venue for RIFF (p26), Il Pigneto's restored 'deco' picture palace houses three intimate screening rooms (one with 3-D screen), a modest exhibition space and a petite bar for thirsty cinephiles.

>CAELIAN HILL & LATERAN

One of Rome's original seven hills, Caelian Hill (Celio) rises to the south of the Colosseum with refreshing serenity – picture medieval churches, weathered stone walls and rambling orchards. In imperial times the area was prime real estate, home to cashed-up nobility and politicians. Less fortunate were the sharp-clawed inmates of the local zoo, fodder for the nearby Colosseum.

These days, Caelian Hill is a repository of early Christian struggle. Frescoes ooze with tales of martyrdom and conversion – from torture tableaux in Chiesa di Santo Stefano Rotondo and Basilica di San Clemente, to a depiction of Emperor Constantine's religious Christian conversion in Chiesa di SS Quattro Coronati. Beneath Chiesa di SS Giovanni e Paolo – dedicated to beheaded martyrs St John and St Paul – ancient rooms recall the days of secret Christian worship.

Trouble gives way to triumph in neighbouring Lateran; Christian relics, kneeling pilgrims and the mighty Basilica di San Giovanni in Laterano provide a glorious epilogue to Caelian's wince-inducing carnage.

CAELIAN HILL & LATERAN

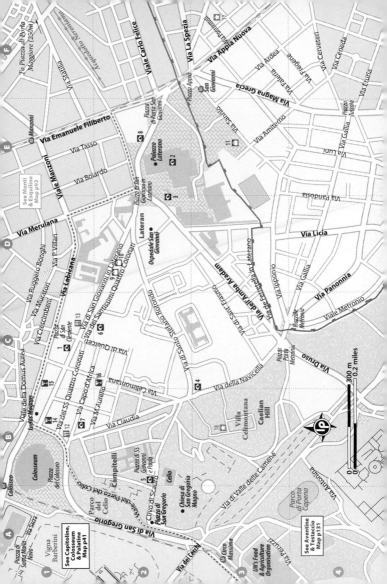

👁 SEE

◉ BASILICA DI SAN CLEMENTE

☎ 06 774 00 21; www.basilicasan clemente.com; Via di San Giovanni in Laterano; excavations adult/student under 26yr €5/3.50; ⏰ 9am-12.30pm & 3-6pm Mon-Sat, noon-6pm Sun; Ⓜ Colosseo

This is a case of architectural time travel: a 12th-century basilica plonked on a 4th-century church, which was built over a 1st-century house containing a 2nd-century pagan temple dedicated to Persian god Mithras. Come for Renaissance frescoes by Masolino and Masaccio, subterranean 11th-century frescoes of St Clemente and the eerie sound of an underground river.

◉ BASILICA DI SAN GIOVANNI IN LATERANO

☎ 06 698 86 433; Piazza di San Giovanni in Laterano 4; ⏰ 7am-6.30pm; Ⓜ San Giovanni; ♿

Rome's gleaming cathedral is also its oldest basilica, founded by Constantine in the 4th century. Papal headquarters until the 14th century, its imposing 18th-

A 15th-century Cosmati floor underpins the 'wow' factor inside Basilica di San Giovanni

century Alessandro Galilei façade is a magnificent example of late Roman baroque. Much older are the bronze doors, moved here from the Roman Forum (p47). Borromini revamped the interior, which flaunts 15th-century Cosmati floors and a snippet of a Giotto fresco behind the nave's first right-hand pillar. The next pillar, the Sylvester II monument, is said to sweat and creak when the death of a pope is imminent. Below the baldachin, the *confessio* houses pieces of what's thought to be St Peter's wooden altar table, while the dome in the **baptistry** (🕙 7.30am-12.30pm & 4-6.30pm) features modern copies of frescoes by Andrea Sacchi.

🄶 CHIESA DI SANTO STEFANO ROTONDO

🕿 06 42 11 91; Via di Santo Stefano Rotondo 7; 🕙 9.30am-12.30pm & 3-6pm Tue-Sat, 9.30am-12.30pm Sun Apr-late Oct, 9.30am-12.30pm & 2-5pm Tue-Sat, 9.30am-12.30pm Sun late Oct-Mar, closed 3 weeks Aug; 🚊 Via della Navicella

Built in the 5th century, Rome's first round church features graphic 16th-century frescoes by Pomarancio and Antonio Tempesta à la *How to Kill a Christian Martyr*. All the boiling and hacking was too much for Charles Dickens, who remarked: 'Such a panorama of horror and butchery no man could imagine in his sleep, though he were to eat a whole pig, raw, for supper.'

🄶 CHIESA DI SS GIOVANNI E PAOLO

🕿 06 700 57 45; Piazza di SS Giovanni e Paolo; 🕙 8.30am-noon & 3.30-6pm; 🄼 Colosseo or Circo Massimo

Below this much-tweaked 4th-century church of little note lies the engrossing **Case Romane** (Roman Houses; 🕿 06 704 54 544; www.caseromane .it; adult/12-18yr & over 65yr/under 12yr €6/4/ free; 🕙 10am-1pm & 3-6pm Thu-Mon), a frescoed maze of ancient Roman abodes. According to legend, the apostles John and Paul lived here. Entry is to the side of the church, on Clivo di Scaurio.

🄶 CHIESA DI SS QUATTRO CORONATI

🕿 06 704 75 427; Via dei Santissimi Quattro Coronati 20; 🕙 church 6am-8pm Mon-Sat, 6.45am-12.30pm & 3-7.30pm Sun, cloister & oratory of San Silvestro 9.30am-noon & 4.30-6pm Mon-Sat, 9-10.40am & 4-5.45pm Sun; 🚊 Via Labicana

This brooding, fortified 12th-century convent sports a 9th-century bell tower and apse and a soothing 13th-century cloister. The pièces de résistance, however, are solidly coloured 13th-century frescoes starring St Sylvester and Constantine in the oratory of San Silvestro. Ring the bell for a peek.

🎬 REWIND ROME

☎ 06 770 76 627; www.3drewind.com;
Via Capo d'Africa 5; adult/5-12yr €15/8;
🕙 9am-7pm; 🚌 Ⓜ Colosseo

History goes 3-D at Rome's latest virtual-reality drawcard. Especially fun for kids, the tour follows in the footsteps of gladiators from the Ludus Magnus training ground to the Colosseum and its pouncing beasts. While somewhat cheesy, the computer-generated footage of Caput Mundi is worth the fee alone.

🎬 SCALA SANTA & SANCTA SANCTORUM

☎ 06 772 66 41; www.scalasanta.org in Italian; Piazza di San Giovanni in Laterano 14; admission Scala Santa/Sancta Sanctorum free/€3.50; 🕙 Scala Santa 6.15am-noon & 3.30-6.45pm Apr-Sep, 6.15am-noon & 3-6pm Oct-Mar, Sancta Sanctorum 10.30-11.30am & 3.30-4.30pm Apr-Sep, 10.30-11.30am & 3-6pm Oct-Mar; Ⓜ San Giovanni

These 28 wood-protected marble steps are reputedly Pontius Pilate's staircase, scaled by Christ. The steps are so holy that pilgrims climb them on their knees. If you do so, look up at the recently restored 16th-century frescoes, before eyeing-up the 13th-century frescoes and 16th-century gems by Flemish artist Paul Bril in the Sancta Sanctorum, the popes' former private chapel.

🛍 SHOP

🛍 SOUL FOOD Music

☎ 06 704 52 025; Via di San Giovanni in Laterano 192; 🕙 10.30am-1.30pm & 3.30-8pm Tue-Sat; Ⓜ San Giovanni

Soul Food feeds music hunters on a diet of rare vintage vinyl. Flip through the racks and score anything from Hendrix and The Stooges, to electro and low-fi punk. Retro-design T-shirts and offbeat novelties keep pop-trash aficionados grinning.

STAIRWAY TO HEAVEN?

Every year, leagues of Christians put their kneecaps to the test as they climb the Scala Santa (above) to wipe their slates clean of sin. There was no indulgence for Martin Luther, however, who in 1510 decided halfway up the stairs that he didn't believe in the divinity of relics and promptly turned round and walked out. On his return to Germany he further irritated the Catholic Church by starting the Reformation.

He wasn't the only critic. In 1845 Charles Dickens took one look at the stair-climbing Catholics and declared that he'd never seen a more ridiculous and unpleasant sight. The same thought probably crossed the minds of the relic's recent restorers, whose job included cleaning chewing gum off the stairs. That the perpetrators got their stairtop indulgence is highly unlikely.

Stunning 16th-century frescoes help dull the pain in your knees when climbing Scala Santa & Sancta Sanctorum

SUZUGANARU *Fashion*
☎ 06 704 91 719; Via di San Giovanni in Laterano 206; ☽ 3.30-7.30pm Mon, 9.30am-1pm & 3.30-7.30pm Tue-Sat; Ⓜ San Giovanni

Photographer and fashion designer Marcella Manfredini creates whimsical, asymmetrical threads and accessories for idiosyncratic urban princesses. Sharing the racks is a booty of vintage Italian pieces, as well as vintage- and burlesque-inspired creations from Rome-based Slovakian designer Lenka Padysakova. Transcontinental options include hats, bags and fetching wraparound belts by Tomoko Harakawa.

VIA SANNIO *Market*
☽ 8am-1pm Mon-Sat; Ⓜ San Giovanni

Update your wardrobe staples at this buzzing morning market. Expect piles of new and vintage clothing, cheap denim, leather jackets and bargain-priced shoes – patient rummagers are amply rewarded.

EAT

CRAB *Seafood* €€€
☎ 06 772 03 636; Via Capo d'Africa 2; ☽ 8-11.30pm Mon, 1-3pm & 8-11.30pm Tue-Sat, closed 2 weeks Aug; Ⓜ Colosseo

Located in a converted warehouse, just steps from the Colosseum, upmarket Crab serves

NEIGHBOURHOODS

CAELIAN HILL & LATERAN

obscenely good seafood presented with a distinctly Sardinian slant. Be sure not to miss the filling *tagloni al granchio porro* (pasta with juicy tomatoes and wine-soaked crab claws) or the luxe house specialities – Brittany oysters and Catalonian lobster. Sublime.

HOSTARIA ISIDORO
Osteria   €
☎ 06 700 82 66; www.hostariaisidoro .com; Via di San Giovanni in Laterano 134; 12.30-3pm & 7.30-11pm Tue-Sun; M Colosseo
Convivial, no-fuss Isidoro has all the right ingredients: obliging waiters, lip-licking locals and bountiful serves of soul food – golden roast chicken with soothing Gorgonzola and a delicate *penne alle noci* (pasta with walnut sauce).

DRINK

COMING OUT *Gay & Lesbian*
☎ 06 700 98 71; Via di San Giovanni in Laterano 8; 11am-2am; M Colosseo
On warm evenings, with lively crowds on the street and the Colosseum as a backdrop, there are fewer sweeter places to knock back a beer than this intimate, DJ-spun bar. Predominately queer, it's a popular preclubbing stop and a handy spot for a cheap, simple bite too.

GLADIATORI HOTEL TERRACE BAR *Hotel Bar*
☎ 06 775 91 380; Via Labicana 125; 4pm-midnight; M Colosseo
It's a case of Campari meets Colosseum at this gorgeous rooftop hotel bar complete with flower-ringed terrace and 'marry-me' views across to the ancient arena. For maximum effect, head up at sundown for a romantic twilight cocktail.

IL PENTAGRAPPOLO
Wine Bar
☎ 06 709 63 01; Via Celimontana 21B; noon-3pm & 6pm-1am Tue-Thu & Sun, to 2am Fri & Sat; M Colosseo
Mellow, star-vaulted Il Pentagrappolo is the perfect antidote to your Roman sightseeing overload. In a setting of well-groomed Italians, backed by the sounds of a gorgeous grand piano, get your groove back by choosing from a selection of about 15 wines by the glass (or 250 by the bottle), nibbling on moreish bruschetta and cheese platters, and relaxing to live jazz from about 10pm Thursday to Saturday.

PLAY

SKYLINE *Gay Bar*
☎ 06 700 94 31; www.skylineclub.it in Italian; Via Pontremoli 36; admission with Arcigay membership; 10.30pm-4am; M San Giovanni

Lusty Skyline pulls a gay crowd who love the fit-out of bars, video room, cruising areas and cubicles. Monday nights are naked, and second Saturday of the month is Bacchanalian-esque 'sexy night'.

⭐ **VILLA CELIMONTANA** *Park*

🌅 **sunrise-sunset;** 🚌 **Via della Navicella**

Lush pines and palms, a sprinkling of Roman ruins and a 16th-century villa set the scene for blissful chilling at this underrated hilltop park. Home to a modest playground for overactive tots, its greatest claim to fame is the swinging, summer-long **Villa Celimontana Jazz Festival** (www.villacelimontanajazz.com) – also see p24.

>APPIAN WAY

Common corpses were a big no-no in ancient Rome, with residents obliged to bury their dead on tomb-flanked roads outside the city walls. The luckiest ended up on the Appian Way (Via Appia Antica) – a 4th-century BC creation once linking Rome to the Adriatic port of Brindisi, 590km to the southeast.

Dubbed the Regina Viarum (Queen of the Roads), its posse of stately pagan mausoleums turned the cobbled thoroughfare into an afterlife hot spot. Indeed, skyrocketing prices drove the early Christians underground, where they created the area's trademark 300km-odd network of catacombs fit for popes, saints and well-meaning sinners.

At the hands of looting Goths and Normans, funerary finery became evocative ruins, luring Grand Tourists in the 1700s and house-hunting Italian film stars in the 1960s; the latter were seduced by the combo of semibucolic bliss, lavish villas and peep-proof walls.

Illegal development and roaring traffic aside (Sundays are mercifully traffic-free), the Appian Way remains Rome's most photogenic ancient strip. For the perfect introduction, head to Porta San Sebastiano where (if you're lucky) the custodian will treat you to an impressive tower-top view.

APPIAN WAY

👁 SEE

Basilica e Catacombe
di San Sebastiano **1** D3
Catacombe di San
Callisto **2** D3
Catacombe di San Callisto
(2nd entrance) **3** C3
Catacombe di Santa
Domitilla **4** C3
Chiesa del Domine
Quo Vadis? **5** B2
Circo di Massenzio **6** E4
Mausoleo di Cecilia
Metella **7** E4
Porta San Sebastiano **8** B1

🍴 EAT

L'Archeologia **9** D4

⭐ PLAY

Appia Antica Regional Park
Information Point **10** B1

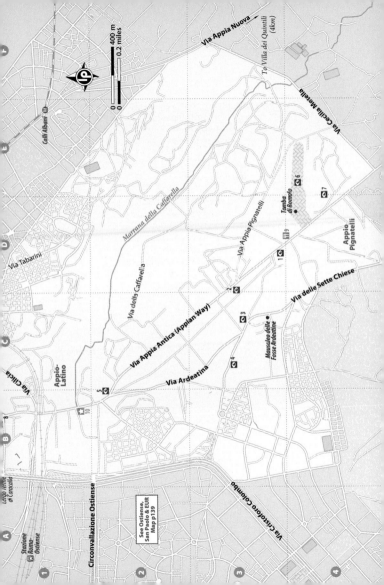

Via Appia Nuova

To Villa dei Quintili (4km)

Via Cecilia Metella

Colli Albani

Marrana della Caffarella

Via Tabarini

Via della Caffarella

Appio Pignatelli

Appio-Latino

Via Glicia

400 m
0.2 miles

0
0

6

7

Tomba
di Romolo

9

1

2

3

Mausoleo delle
Fosse Ardeatine

Via delle Sette Chiese

Via Appia Pignatelli

Via Appia Antica (Appian Way)

4

Via Ardeatina

5

10

See Ostiense,
San Paolo & EUR
Map p139

Circonvallazione Ostiense

Via Cristoforo Colombo

Lago Terme
di Caracalla

Stazione
Roma-
Ostiense

◉ SEE

◉ BASILICA E CATACOMBE DI SAN SEBASTIANO

☎ 06 785 03 50; Via Appia Antica 136; basilica free, catacomb adult/7-15yr/ under 7yr €5/3/free; ☒ 8.30am-noon & 2.30-5.30pm Mon-Sat, closed mid-Nov–mid-Dec; 🚃 Via Appia Antica

Birthplace of the term 'catacomb' (the underground burial site was located 'near the quarry', *kata kymbas* in Greek), the Catacombs of St Sebastian boast three perfectly preserved pagan mausoleums with original 2nd-century frescoes, mosaics and stucco. Above ground, pop into the much-tweaked 4th-century basilica to view one of the arrows used to kill St Sebastian, as well as a marble slab with miraculous imprints of Jesus' footprints. (For the whole story, see Chiesa del Domine Quo Vadis?, right.)

◉ CATACOMBE DI SAN CALLISTO

☎ 06 513 01 51; www.catacombe .roma.it; Via Appia Antica 126; adult/ 6-15yr/under 6yr €8/5/free; ☒ 9am-noon & 2-5pm Thu-Tue, closed Feb; 🚃 Via Appia Antica

Founded in the 2nd century, the mother of Roman catacombs (20km of tunnels, with more to come) is a creepy journey past shadowy sepulchres, papal tombs (16 pontiffs were buried here)

and the crypt of Santa Cecilia. The catacombs in fact became the first official Roman Catholic cemetery in the early 3rd century. When Cecilia's tomb was opened in 1599, centuries after her death, the martyr's body was found perfectly preserved, inspiring Stefano Maderno's sculpture in Basilica di Santa Cecilia in Trastevere (p147).

◉ CATACOMBE DI SANTA DOMITILLA

☎ 06 511 03 42; Via delle Sette Chiese 283; adult/6-15yr/under 6yr €8/5/free; ☒ 9am-noon & 2-5pm Wed-Mon, closed mid-Dec–mid-Jan; 🚃 Via Appia Antica

A faded, untouched fresco of Sts Peter and Paul dating back more than 1600 years is the highlight at these catacombs, which were established on the burial ground of Flavia Domitilla (niece of the emperor Domitian). Among the pagan and Christian wall paintings are around 2000 unopened tombs and the subterranean 4th-century Chiesa di SS Nereus e Achilleus, dedicated to two martyred Roman soldiers.

◉ CHIESA DEL DOMINE QUO VADIS?

Via Appia Antica 51; ☒ 8.30am-12.30pm & 2.30-6.45pm; 🚃 Via Appia Antica

This pint-sized church marks the spot where a fleeing St Peter met a vision of Jesus. When Peter asked 'Domine, quo vadis?' ('Lord, where are you going?'), Jesus replied that

Fausto Zevi
Archaeologist & Professor at La Sapienza University

For a well-rounded classical itinerary… start off with ancient Rome's artistic side at Domus Aurea (p95) and the Palatine (p46), where the frescoes are among the era's finest. Then explore the ancient city's mercantile side at Ostia Antica (p143). For ruins as the Grand Tourists saw them, head to the Appian Way. **Is there room for contemporary architecture in an ancient city?** Certainly. The problem is in creating architecture that understands and respects the history surrounding it. The glass pyramid outside the Louvre works well in its context. Richard Meier's Museo dell'Ara Pacis (p75) does not. **Why not?** It's invasive and oppressive. There's no dialogue with surrounding buildings. The altar itself was taken from its original site and historical context, and now Meier's pavilion has sealed its fate. What's worse, the controversy surrounding the project has reinforced the belief that modern architecture doesn't belong in Rome's historic heart.

he was heading to Rome to be crucified a second time. Taking the hint, Peter headed back into town to meet his own grisly end, which is brilliantly portrayed in Caravaggio's *The Crucifixion of St Peter* in Chiesa di Santa Maria del Popolo (p74). The two holy footprints in the centre aisle of Domine Quo Vadis? are copies of the originals in the Basilica di San Sebastiano (p126), which are said to have belonged to Christ.

☉ CIRCO DI MASSENZIO
☎ 06 780 13 24; Via Appia Antica 153; adult/under 18yr & over 65yr €3/free; ☽ 9am-1.30pm Tue-Sun; ⊟ Via Appia Antica

You can still make out the starting stalls at Rome's best preserved chariot racetrack, a 10,000-seat arena built by Emperor Maxentius around AD 309. The unexcavated ruins of his imperial pad sit above the racetrack's northern end. Nearby, Maxentius built the imposing Tomb of Romulus for his son.

☉ MAUSOLEO DI CECILIA METELLA
☎ 06 780 24 65; Via Appia Antica 161; admission incl Terme di Caracalla & Villa dei Quintili adult/EU 18-24yr/EU under 18yr & over 65yr €6/3/free; ☽ 9am-7.30pm late Mar-Aug, to 7pm Sep, to 6.30pm early-late Oct, to 4.30pm late Oct–mid-Feb, to 5pm mid-Feb–mid-Mar, to 5.30pm mid-late Mar, closed Mon; ⊟ Via Appia Antica

This take-it-or-leave-it drum of a mausoleum – built in the 1st century BC – was turned into a 14th-century fort by the Caetani family, who would bully passing traffic into paying a toll. Beyond the tomb is a picture-perfect section of the actual ancient road, excavated in the mid-19th century.

☉ PORTA SAN SEBASTIANO
☎ 06 704 75 284; Via di Porta San Sebastiano; adult/EU 18-25yr/EU under 18yr & over 65yr €3/1.50/free; ☽ 9am-2pm Tue-Sun; ⊟ Porta San Sebastiano

---

WORTH THE TRIP
Sublimely set on lush green fields, **Villa dei Quintili** (☎ 06 718 24 85; access from Via Appia Nuova 1092; admission incl Mausoleo di Cecilia Metella & Terme di Caracalla adult/EU 18-24yr/EU under 18yr & over 65yr €6/3/free; ☽ 9am-4.30pm Jan–mid-Feb & Nov-Dec, to 5pm mid-Feb–mid-Mar, to 5.30pm mid-end Mar, to 7.15pm Apr-Aug, to 7pm Sep, to 6.30pm Oct, closed Mon) was a 2nd-century luxury abode, built by two brothers who were consuls under Emperor Marcus Aurelius. The villa was, quite literally, to die for: the jealous emperor Commodus had both siblings killed in order to nab the property for himself. Topping the must-sees is the nymphaeum and once-indulgent baths complex, which is complete with pool, *caldarium* (hot room) and *frigidarium* (cold room).

Tread the path of history along Rome's ancient Appian Way (Via Appia Antica)

Rome's best preserved city gate was built in the 5th century as part of the largely intact Aurelian Wall, commissioned by the emperor Aurelian in the 3rd century to keep those pesky barbarians out. The modest indoor museum sheds light on Rome's ancient hulking fence.

EAT
L'ARCHEOLOGIA
Ristorante €€
☎ 06 788 04 94; www.larcheologia.it; Via Appia Antica 139; 🕑 12.30-3pm & 8-11pm Wed-Mon; 🚌 Via Appia Antica
Near the Basilica e Catacombe di San Sebastiano, this baronial-esque dining den – complete with velvet drapes, catacomb wine cellar, and Europe's oldest wisteria in the garden – is a safe bet for authentic regional grub and is a hit with perfectly preened Italian families out for Sunday lunch. The *spaghetti primavera* (spaghetti with zucchini, fresh tomato, basil and prawns) is sublime, and service is refreshingly friendly.

PLAY
⭐ APPIA ANTICA REGIONAL PARK INFORMATION POINT
Bicycle Hire
☎ 06 513 53 16; www.parcoappiaantica.it; Via Appia Antica 58-60; 🕑 9.30am-1.30pm & 2-5.30pm summer, to 4.30pm winter; 🚌 Via Appia Antica
Traffic-free Sundays make the Appian Way perfect peddle fodder, and this tourist information office hires bikes (per hour/day €3/10) for those inclined to two wheels.

>AVENTINE & TESTACCIO

The most southerly of Rome's seven hills, Aventine (Aventino) flanks the mighty ruins of Terme di Caracalla, where ancient Romans came to soak away their stress. The hill itself is best climbed up pedestrian Clivo di Rocca Savelli, which leads up from Tiber-side Via Santa Maria in Cosmedin. Waiting at the top is a beautiful bourgeois blend of Liberty (Italian art nouveau) villas, lush gardens and the soothing austerity of Basilica di Santa Sabina – a rare slice of history in a district attacked by marauding 5th-century Goths. But what Aventine lacks in ancient heavyweights it makes up for in swoon-worthy views, taken through secret piazza-side keyholes or from heavenly scented terraces.

Southwest of the hill, Testaccio swaps grace for grit with its earthy attitude, hardcore AS Roma supporters and rough'n'ready morning market. Battle it out with bargain-hunting *nonne* (grandmas), tuck into tripe, or chow down contemporary art at slaughterhouse-turned-gallery MACRO Future. Once done, work up a sweat on Via di Monte Testaccio, where thumping nightclubs line a hill made of trashed terracotta from Testaccio's long-gone Roman port.

AVENTINE & TESTACCIO

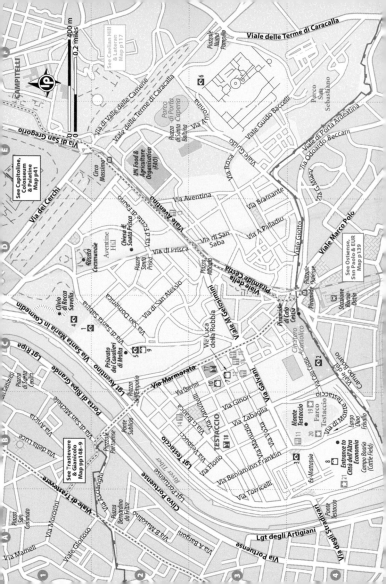

NEIGHBOURHOODS

AVENTINE & TESTACCIO

◉ SEE

◉ BASILICA DI SANTA SABINA

☎ 06 5 79 41; Piazza Pietro d'Illiria 1;
🕑 6.30am-12.45pm & 3-7pm;
🚌 Lungotevere Aventino

Sublimely simple and monumental, this 5th-century basilica boasts original cypress-wood doors featuring one of the oldest crucifixion scenes in existence. Instead of the usual mishmash of plundered ancient pillars, custom-made Corinthian columns line the naves. St Dominic is said to have planted Italy's first orange tree in the serene 13th-century cloister.

◉ CIMITERO ACATTOLICO PER GLI STRANIERI

☎ 06 574 19 00; www.protestant cemetery.it; Via Caio Cestio 5; admission free or by donation €2; 🕑 9am-5pm Mon-Sat, 9am-1pm Sun; Ⓜ Piramide

Percy Bysshe Shelley wrote: 'It might make one in love with death to think that one should be buried in so sweet a place.' And so he was buried, along with fellow romantic poet John Keats, in Rome's shamelessly romantic Protestant cemetery. Wander its mossy paths and stumble across a cast of famous residents, including Italian Communist Party founder, Antonio Gramsci.

◉ MACRO FUTURE

☎ 06 574 26 47; www.macro.roma .museum; Piazza Orazio Giustiniani 4; adult/18-25yr/EU under 18yr & over 65yr €4.50/3.50/free; 🕑 4pm-midnight Tue-Sun; Ⓜ Piramide; ♿

Housed in Rome's ex-slaughterhouse, MACRO's second gallery serves up experimental art in two cavernous industrial halls. Past exhibitors include Ron English, Anish Kapoor and Russia's AES+F Collective. Admission includes MACRO's main gallery (p178), in northern Rome.

◉ PARCO SAVELLO

Via di Santa Sabina; 🕑 dawn-dusk;
🚌 Lungotevere Aventino

Painters, love-struck teens and unfazed felines equally adore this pocket-sized park dubbed the Giardino degli Aranci (Orange Garden) for its sprinkling of lush, scented orange trees. Sit back on the terrace and watch the sun sink over the city to the sounds of church bells, wind and sirens.

◉ PIAZZA DEI CAVALIERI DI MALTA

🚌 Lungotevere Aventino

Taking its name from the Knights of Malta, which has its priory here, this peaceful, cypress-shaded square is famous for its secret keyhole – located at the priory's main entrance. Join the queue of

It's hard to go past the art in MACRO's second gallery, MACRO Future

Peeping Toms and feast your eyes on a fetching Roman surprise.

TERME DI CARACALLA
☎ 06 575 86 26; Viale delle Terme di Caracalla 52; admission incl Mausoleo di Cecilia Metella & Villa dei Quintili adult/ EU 18-24yr/EU under 18yr & over 65yr €6/3/free; ☽ 9am-2pm Mon, 9am-5.30pm Tue-Sun late Mar-Sep, 9am-2pm Mon, 9am-4.30pm Tue-Sun Oct-late Mar; Ⓜ Circo Massimo; ♿

In the 3rd century this was a luxe 10-hectare spa centre boasting a richly decorated pool, hot rooms, *tepidarium* (warm room), gymnasiums, libraries, shops and gardens. Below it all, hundreds of slaves tended to the complex plumb-

ing in 9.5km of tunnels. Soaring ruins and aquatic-themed mosaics evoke its former grandeur, while its finest booty now calls the Vatican Museums (p167) home. For details on Mausoleo di Cecilia Metella and Villa dei Quintili, see p128.

🛍 SHOP
CALZATURE BOCCANERA
Shoes
☎ 06 575 68 04; Via Luca della Robbia 36; ☽ 9.30am-1.30pm & 3.30-7.30pm Tue-Sat, 3.30-7.30pm Mon; 🚌 🚋 Via Marmorata

Tatty Testaccio goes glam at this old-fashioned shoe shop. It's lined with just-off-the-runway men's and women's footwear from

CITTÀ DELL'ALTRA ECONOMIA

Launched in September 2007, Testaccio's **Città dell'Altra Economia** (City of the Other Economy; see below) is Europe's first fair-trade retail, business and culture centre. Located inside the Ex-Mattatoio (former slaughterhouse), it's a sleek combo of restored industrial architecture, contemporary design and feel-good enterprises including shops, a gallery space, **organic bar & restaurant** (☎ 333 418 78 70; 🕙 bar 10am-8pm Tue-Sat, to 7pm Sun, restaurant 8-10.30pm Tue-Fri, 12.30-3pm & 8-10.30pm Sat, 12.30-3pm Sun mid-Sep–Jun, 8-10.30pm Mon-Sat Jul–mid-Sep, closed 2 weeks Aug) and even an ethical bank! It all fronts onto the sprawling emptiness of Campo Boario (Cattle Field), home to the city's annual Fair Trade Festival, usually held in June. Check the website for dates.

On the third Sunday of the month from September to June, it also hosts a day-long organic market and fair. Rotating themes include recyclables and renewable energy. Check www .altradomenica.org (in Italian) for details.

names such as Fendi, Burberry, Prada, D&G and Gucci. There are bags to match and tempting mark-downs at sale time.

🖪 CITTÀ DELL'ALTRA ECONOMIA *Fair Trade*

www.cittadellaltraeconomia.org in Italian; Largo Dino Frisullo; Ⓜ Piramide
There are two retail outlets inside the enlightened Città dell'Altra Economia (City of the Other Economy): **Spazio Bio** (☎ 06 572 89 957; 🕙 10.30am-1.30pm & 2.30-8pm Tue-Sat, to 7pm Sun), stocking organic, fair-trade food and wine; and **Bottega di Commercio Equo e Solidale** (☎ 331 474 53 67; 🕙 10am-8pm Tue-Sat, to 7pm Sun), selling ecofriendly threads, accessories and designer recyclables such as funky lolly-wrapper handbags, milk carton purses and lamps made from classic Italian *caffetiere* (espresso makers). See the boxed text, above, for more.

🖪 IL NEGOZIO BENEDETTINO DELLA BADIA PRIMAZIALE DI SANT'ANSELMO
Food, Cosmetics

☎ 06 5 79 11; Piazza dei Cavalieri di Malta 5; 🕙 10.30am-12.30pm & 3.30-7pm Mon, 9.30am-12.30pm & 3.30-7pm Tue-Thu, 9.30am-1pm & 2.30-7pm Fri-Sun; 🚌 Lungotevere Aventino
In the grounds of the abbey of Sant'Anselmo, which flanks Piazza dei Cavalieri di Malta, this little holy retailer stocks a wide range of products made in abbeys across the world. Look for delights ranging from German friars' beer and Norcia honey, to Praglia cosmetics and wicked Trappisti chocolate bars.

🖪 MERCATO DI TESTACCIO
Market

Piazza Testaccio; 🕙 7.30am-1.30pm Mon-Sat; 🚌 🚋 Via Marmorata

Testaccio's famous morning market packs quite a punch with its earthy old-school attitude coupled with an array of fresh, cheap produce – just imagine crates crammed with mussels, counters piled with cheeses, and stall after stall of wallet-friendly footwear. We suggest you head in early, grab a slab of *pizza rossa* (pizza with tomato) and hunt yourself a bargain.

⊓⊓ EAT

⊓⊓ CHECCHINO DAL 1887
Ristorante €€€

☎ 06 574 63 18; www.checchino-dal -1887.com; Via di Monte Testaccio 30; 🕑 12.30-3pm & 8pm-midnight Tue-Sat, closed Aug; Ⓜ Piramide

A pig's whisker from Rome's former slaughterhouse, this is an elegant choice for classic Roman offal. There's a creamy *rigatoni alla pajata* (pasta with milk-fed veal's intestine) for novices, and tasting menus for the more adventurous. If you ask nicely, you'll be shown the cellar – set inside an artificial Roman mount (see the boxed text, p137).

⊓⊓ DA FELICE
Trattoria €€

☎ 06 574 68 00; Via Mastro Giorgio 29; 🕑 12.30-2.45pm & 8-11.30pm Mon-Sat, 12.30-2.45pm Sun; 🚌 🚈 Via Marmorata

Film director Benigni once wrote an ode to this place (it's hanging on the left-hand wall just inside the entrance). Previously ruled by the notoriously cantankerous Felice, this is now a glammed-up combo of postindustrial chic and schmick-dick diners, but the menu remains true to its roots – whether it's buttery offal offerings or soothing tortellini in broth.

⊓⊓ IL GELATO *Gelateria* €

Viale Aventino 59, 🕑 11am-10.30pm Mon-Sun Mar-late Oct, to midnight Fri & Sat summer, 11am-9.30pm Tue-Sun late Oct-Feb, closed 3 weeks Jan; Ⓜ Circo Massimo

Claudio Torcè is one of Rome's gelato deities and his creamy revelations are proudly seasonal, preservative-free and creative (expect anything from apple strudel to cream of capsicum). The zabaglione *semifreddo* is especially good and best devoured in a waffle *conchiglia* (shell), drizzled with your choice of homemade *caramello* (syrup). Flavours include *caffè* (coffee), *liquirizia* (liquorice), *mandorle tostate* (toasted almonds) and Baileys.

⊓⊓ PIZZERIA REMO *Pizzeria* €

☎ 06 574 62 70; Piazza Santa Maria Liberatrice 44; 🕑 7pm-1am Mon-Sat; 🚌 🚈 Via Marmorata

Though not a place for a romantic tête-à-tête, Remo is one of the city's best-loved pizza peddlers. Tick your choices on a sheet of paper slapped

Get your picnic needs in bulk at Volpetti deli

cheese. Staff are helpful, you can order online and there's a range of ready-to-eat treats.

🍴 VOLPETTI PIÙ *Tavola Calda* €
☎ 06 574 43 06; Via Alessandro Volta 8; 🕙 10.30am-3.30pm & 5.30-9.30pm Mon-Sat; 🚌 🚊 Via Marmorata
One of the few places in Rome where you can stuff yourself silly for less than €20, Volpetti Più is a sumptuous *tavola calda* (buffet); it heaves with pizzas, pastas, soups, vegetables and golden-fried nibbles. Be early or prepare to queue.

🍸 DRINK
🍸 L'OASI DELLA BIRRA
Beer, Wine Bar
☎ 06 574 61 22; Piazza Testaccio 41; 🕙 7.30am-1.30pm & 4.30pm-2am Mon-Sat, 7.30pm-1am Sun; 🚊 🚌 Via Marmorata
Snuggle up in 'The Beer Oasis' cellars and get all indecisive over the 500 brews on offer – from Teutonic heavyweights to local boutique winners. Wine buffs are equally spoilt, and you can soak up the alcohol with bruschetta and cheeses or robust Russian stews.

🍸 LINARI *Café*
☎ 06 578 23 58; Via Nicola Zabaglia 9; 🕙 6.30am-10pm Wed-Mon; 🚌 🚊 Via Marmorata
Despite the shiny makeover, Linari remains local down to its plastic

down by an overstretched waiter and wait for your huge, sizzling, charred-base disc. Expect to queue if you head in after 8.30pm.

🍴 VOLPETTI *Deli* €
☎ 06 574 23 52; www.volpetti.com; Via Marmorata 47; 🕙 8am-2pm & 5-8.15pm Mon-Sat; 🚌 🚊 Via Marmorata
Arguably Rome's best deli, Volpetti stocks everything from spicy Provola cheese to fragrant morning-fresh bread, prosciutto, olive oils, wine, slabs of *torrone* (nougat) and homemade ravioli stuffed with chicory and *taleggio*

pavement chairs and gossiping Testaccio mothers. The now epic counter groans with edible treats, from *pizza al taglio* and schnitzel to salads and perfect pastries. Guzzle a fine espresso and soak up the barside banter.

⭐ PLAY

With a plethora of *discoteche* (nightclubs) lining Via di Monte Testaccio, this is Rome's clubbing heartland. Expect to queue on Saturdays, when suburban party kids head into town to bust a move – both on the dance floor and off.

⭐ AKAB *Nightclub*
☎ 06 572 50 585; www.akabcave.com in Italian; VIa di Monte Testaccio 68-9; admission €15; ⏰ 11pm-4am Tue-Sat, closed late Jun–mid-Sep; Ⓜ Piramide
This eclectic former workshop has an underground cellar, upper floor, garden and whimsical door policy. Expect electro on Tuesdays, retro on Wednesdays, R&B on Thursdays and live local acts on Fridays. Saturdays groove to house.

⭐ METAVERSO *Nightclub*
☎ 06 574 47 12; Via di Monte Testaccio 38; admission €5-7; ⏰ 10.30pm-5am Fri & Sat, closed Jul & Aug; Ⓜ Piramide
The smallest, friendliest place on the Monte Testaccio club strip, Metaverso packs in a cool, alterna-

MONTE TESTACCIO
Wedged between the Ex-Mattatoio and Cimitero Acattolico per gli Stranieri (p132), Monte Testaccio (B4; ☎ 06 06 08; Via Galvani 24; ⏰ by appointment) is Testaccio's 45m-high artificial mount. In ancient times, when the area was a river port, empty terracotta amphorae were discarded in the Tiber. When the waterway became nearly unnavigable, workers changed tack, smashing the amphorae into pieces and stacking them methodically. The result is the grassy hump you see today.

tive crowd with its cheap drinks, vintage film projections, and electronica and hip-hop beats spun by local and global DJs. Monthly Saturday specials include gay-night Phang Off and '60s ode Twiggy.

⭐ VILLAGGIO GLOBALE
Centro Sociale
☎ 347 413 12 05; www.ecn.org/villaggio globale/joomla/in Italian; Via Monte dei Cocci 22; admission varies; ⏰ 10pm-4am mid-Sep–Jun; Ⓜ Piramide
Set in Rome's ex-slaughterhouse, this raw'n'legendary *centro sociale* (social centre; see p199) is loaded with dreadlocks, cheap beer and left-wing, antiracist consciousness. Live gigs and DJ sessions keep the music focused on dancehall, reggae, dubstep, ska and drum'n'bass.

>OSTIENSE, SAN PAOLO & EUR

Packed with postindustrial grit, Ostiense is a hit with hedonists, artists and clued-up investors who know an up-and-coming 'hood when they see one. In the shadow of giant gasometers, clubbers party hard in converted factories, artists exhibit in one-time garages and the district's abandoned wholesale fruit and vegetable markets (ex-Mercati Generali) are marked for a major cultural/retail makeover.

Running north–south through the action, traffic-jammed Via Ostiense is a contradictory cocktail of chintzy *pasticcerie* (patisseries), street-wise Cuban posses, spit-and-sawdust *trattorias* (restaurants) and slinky new-school bars. It's also where you'll find the offbeat brilliance of Centrale Montemartini, where ancient sculpture meets looming machinery.

To the south, pilgrims seek St Paul's blessing in the colossal Basilica di San Paolo Fuori-le-Mura, while further south you'll find Mussolini's Orwellian quarter of EUR (Esposizione Universale Roma; Rome Universal Exhibition). Built for a 1942 World Expo that never happened, it's worth the trek for muscular Fascist monuments and cavernous museum halls filled with quirky Italian collections.

OSTIENSE, SAN PAOLO & EUR

● SEE
Basilica di San Paolo
 Fuori-le-Mura 1 B5
Centrale Montemartini ...2 B3
Museo della Civiltà
 Romana 3 D6
Museo delle Arti e
 Tradizioni Popolari 4 D6
Palazzo della Civiltà
 del Lavoro 5 C6

▥ EAT
Al Ristoro Degli Angeli ...6 C4
Andreotti 7 B2
Doppiozeroo 8 B2
Hostaria Zampagna 9 B4

▤ DRINK
Caffè Letterario 10 B2

★ PLAY
Alpheus 11 A2
Distillerie Clandestine ..12 B4
Goa 13 B4
La Casa del Jazz 14 D2
La Saponeria 15 B4
Rashomon 16 B4
Rising Love 17 B2
Teatro Palladium 18 C4

◉ SEE

◉ BASILICA DI SAN PAOLO FUORI-LE-MURA

☎ 06 541 03 41; Via Ostiense 186; admission church/cloisters free/€3; ⏰ 7am-6.30pm, cloisters 8am-6.15pm Ⓜ San Paolo

Built in the 4th century on the site of St Paul's tomb, and rebuilt 15 centuries later after being razed by fire, this is the world's third-largest church. Admire the triumphal arch's glittering 5th-century mosaics, Arnolfo di Cambio's gothic marble tabernacle and the beautiful Cosmati cloister with its twisted inlaid columns. Around the nave, mosaic portraits depict the popes since St Peter. According to legend, when the portrait

niches run out the world will end. Seven places remain.

◉ CENTRALE MONTEMARTINI

☎ 06 574 80 42; Via Ostiense 106; adult/EU 18-25yr/EU under 18yr & over 65yr €4.50/2.50/free, incl exhibition €8/6/free, incl Capitoline Museums €8.50/6.50/free; ⏰ 9am-7pm Tue-Sun; 🚍 Via Ostiense

Antiquity meets Fritz Lang's Metropolis at the striking outpost of the Capitoline Museums (p42). In an ex-power plant, marble Roman deities are juxtaposed with beastly engines and furnaces in a battle of new gods and old. You'll find the collection's highlights in the Sala Caldaia, among them the youthful *Fanciulla Seduta* and the pensive,

---

GORGEOUS GARBATELLA

Flâneurs shouldn't miss an amble through laid-back **Garbatella** (Map p139, D5; www .rionegarbatella.it; Ⓜ Garbatella), a whimsical suburb just to the east of Ostiense. Featured in the opening scene of Nanni Moretti's film *Caro Diario*, it's a beguiling place of lush communal courtyards, eclectic architecture and technicolour left-wing graffiti.

The district's historic core was developed in the 1920s and 1930s as a garden suburb for the city's working class. Different architects developed different blocks, creating refreshingly heterogeneous streetscapes injected with medieval, Renaissance and baroque accents.

One of Garbatella's most famous architects was Innocenzo Sabbatini, who designed the deliciously deco **Teatro Palladium** (p145) and the mammoth, shiplike **Albergo Rosso** (Red Hostel; Map p139, D3) on Piazza Michele da Carbonara. An exponent of the 'Roman School' of expressionist architecture, Sabbatini created some of Rome's most idiosyncratic buildings between the two world wars.

Not surprisingly, the combination of architectural cool and calming green has turned Garbatella into very fashionable property. Hot or not, it's a mesmerising place, easily reached from Garbatella Metro station by turning right into Via G Pullino and then left 300m later into Via G Ansaldo.

Sculptural hall of fame in Centrale Montemartini

2nd-century BC *Statue of a Muse*, believed by some to be Polimnia.

MUSEO DELLA CIVILTÀ ROMANA

☎ 06 592 60 41; Piazza G Agnelli 10; adult/EU 18-24yr/EU under 18yr & over 65yr €6.50/4.50/free, incl Museo Astronomico & Planetarium €8.50/6.50/free; 🕒 9am-2pm Tue-Sat, 9am-1.30pm Sun; Ⓜ EUR Fermi; ♿

Mussolini's hulking ode to the Roman Empire is a proven kid-pleaser, complete with a giant-scale re-creation of 4th-century Rome, detailed models of the ancient buildings and weaponry, a cross-section of the Colosseum, and casts of the reliefs on the Colonna di Traiano (Trajan's Col-

umn). It's a sprawling place so give yourself plenty of time to snoop through the cavernous halls.

MUSEO DELLE ARTI E TRADIZIONI POPOLARI

☎ 06 592 61 48; www.popolari.arti .beniculturali.it in Italian; Piazza Marconi 8-10; adult/EU 18-24yr/EU under 18yr & over 65yr €4/2/free; 🕒 9am-6pm Tue-Sat, 9am-7.30pm Sun, closed Mon; Ⓜ EUR Fermi

It's likely the idea of a museum dedicated to Italian folk art sounds positively mind-numbing. The Museum of Popular Arts & Traditions, however, is surprisingly engrossing, dishing out hall upon hall of elaborate festive frocks,

White travertine Palazzo della Civiltà del Lavoro

freaky Sicilian marionettes, epic Neapolitan nativity scenes and vintage Catholic votives with a creepy cultish vibe.

PALAZZO DELLA CIVILTÀ DEL LAVORO
Quadratto della Concordia; M EUR Magliana

Dubbed the Square Colosseum due to its superimposed loggias, the Palace of the Workers is EUR's architectural icon – a solid, gleaming office block clad in white travertine. Designed by Giovanni Guerrini, Ernesto Bruno La Padula and Mario Romano (and inaugurated in 1940), its six rows of nine arches honour the project's Fascist commissioner – Benito having six letters, Mussolini having nine.

EAT

AL RISTORO DEGLI ANGELI
Ristorante €€

☎ 06 514 36 020; www.ristorodegli angeli.it; Via Luigi Orlando 2; 8-11.30pm Mon-Sat, closed Aug–mid-Sep; M Garbatella

Al Ristoro's vintage chandelier lights up shelves lined with paintings, homemade preserves, cookbooks and the odd green stiletto (which perfectly matches the owner's green hair). Get snug at this cosy, off-the-radar charmer, and taste-test simple, creative dishes like *cacio e pepe in cialda di parmigiano croccante* (*pecorino* cheese and pepper pasta in a crunchy parmesan crust) before succumbing to the heavenly tiramisu.

ANDREOTTI *Pasticceria* €

☎ 06 575 07 73; Via Ostiense 54; 7.30am-9.30pm; Via Ostiense

Film director and Ostiense local Ferzan Ozpetek is such a fan of the pastries here, he's known to cast them in his films. They're all stars, from the fragrant almond *biscotti* (biscuits) and buttery *crostate* (tarts), to the golden *sfogliatelle romane* (ricotta-filled pastries). There's even a supporting cast of savoury gems such as *frittini* (fried canapés) and cute-as-a-button *bruschettine* (mini bruschetta).

WORTH THE TRIP

Rome's answer to Pompeii, **Scavi Archeologici di Ostia Antica** (Ruins of Ostia Antica; off Map p139, B6; ☎ 06 563 58 099; www.ostiaantica.net; Viale dei Romagnoli 717; adult/concession €6.50/3.25; ⏱ 8.30am-7pm Tue-Sun Apr-Oct, to 6pm Nov-Feb, last tickets 30-60min before closing; Ⓜ Piramide, then suburban train to Ostia Lido; ♿) offers a well-preserved insight into ancient Rome's once-thriving port, an easy 25km southwest of the city. You could happily spend a few hours here, snooping around the ancient restaurants, shops, laundries and houses. Highlights include the impressive mosaics at the Terme di Nettuno and the mosaic-laced merchant guilds' offices on Piazzale delle Corporazioni. In the uncannily hip-looking Thermopolium (bar), note the frescoed pictorial menu above the counter and the alfresco courtyard for patrons. The ticket office sells a handy site map (€2), and there's also a cafeteria/bar (though a picnic is always a good idea). In summer the Roman theatre hosts Cosmophonies (www.cosmophonies .com), a series of concerts focusing on world music and opera.

🍴 DOPPIOZEROO *Bakery, Bar* €

☎ 06 573 01 961; www.doppiozeroo.it;
Via Ostiense 68; ⏱ 7am-10pm Mon, to
2am Tue-Sun; 🚇 Via Ostiense

Sleek urbane interiors and long opening hours keep trendy Romans flocking here, whether it's for morning coffee and pastries, lunchtime *prosecco* (sparkling wine) and pizza (gluttons shouldn't miss the Nutella *pizza bianca*), preclubbing flirtation at the happening *aperitivo* (6pm to 9pm or Sunday brunch (12.30pm to 3.30pm). It closes for one week in August.

🍴 HOSTARIA ZAMPAGNA
Trattoria €

☎ 06 574 23 06; Via Ostiense 179;
⏱ noon-2.30pm & 7-11.30pm Mon-Sat,
12.30-3.30pm Sun; Ⓜ San Paolo
🚇 Via Ostiense

This humble octogenarian has bypassed Via Ostiense's trendification, still dishing out hearty soul food faithful to the city's weekly culinary calendar. Get nostalgic over a bowl of *spaghetti alla carbonara* (spaghetti with an egg, cheese and pancetta sauce), *alla grigia* (with a *pecorino* cheese, pancetta and black-pepper sauce) or *all'amatriciana* (with a tomato, pancetta and chilli-pepper sauce), before getting back to basics with tripe, beef or *involtini* (stuffed rolls of meat).

🍸 DRINK
🍸 CAFFÈ LETTERARIO
Bar, Cultural Centre

☎ 338 802 73 17; www.caffeletterario
roma.it in Italian; Via Ostiense 83;
⏱ 10am-2am Tue-Fri, 4pm-2am Sat &
Sun; 🚇 Via Ostiense

Cars make way for culture at this former garage basement, now a

NEIGHBOURHOODS

OSTIENSE, SAN PAOLO & EUR

cavernous concoction of designer bar, bookshop, art gallery, performance space and nooks with cosy lounges. Grab a beer, eye-up the art and schmooze with the local culture crew. Credit cards not accepted.

PLAY

Like its northern neighbour Testaccio, Ostiense knows how to party. With a backlog of vast warehouse shells and a nearby university campus to boot, we're hardly surprised. Via Libetta and Via degli Argonauti form the district's clubbing hub, where top-notch global DJs dish out anything from new-wave beats to thumping old-school techno.

⭐ ALPHEUS
Live Music, Nightclub
☎ 06 574 78 26; www.alpheus.it in Italian; Via del Commercio 36; admission varies; ⏱ 11pm-4am Fri & Sat Oct-May; Ⓜ Piramide 🚊 Via Ostiense
Mighty Alpheus boasts four halls, mixed crowds and an eclectic music menu spanning live tango, rock and soul, DJ-spun retro, hip-hop and house. Saturday is ever-popular 'Gorgeous I Am' gay night, where techno and handbag come with a side of butt-shaking go-go dancers. Opening hours vary during the week.

⭐ DISTILLERIE CLANDESTINE
Nightclub
☎ 06 573 05 102; www.distillerie clandestine.com in Italian; Via Libetta 13; admission varies; ⏱ 11.30am-4am Thu-Sun Sep-May; Ⓜ Garbatella
One of Rome's umbrella venues, this post-industrial hangout hauls in the hipsters. As well as a restaurant, there's a ship-shaped American bar with what looks like light sabres suspended above it, a designer club that focuses on dance and house, and – gasp – a smoking room.

⭐ GOA *Nightclub*
☎ 06 574 82 77; Via Libetta 13; admission €10-25; ⏱ 11pm-4.30am Oct-May; Ⓜ Garbatella
Rome's clubbing heavyweight pulls the crème of international disc-

---

ROMAN ETIQUETTE: THE ESSENTIALS
> Don't drink to get wasted. Most Italians consider it *molto* trashy.
> Shake hands with strangers and kiss both cheeks when greeting friends.
> Eat pasta with a fork (not a spoon!) and keep your hands on the table, not under it.
> Invited to someone's place for dinner? Take a bottle of wine or flowers or risk making a *brutta figura* (bad impression).
> When visiting churches, shoulders and legs should be covered.

spinners, who whip fashion-literate crowds into a techno-electro frenzy. The night to pick is Thursday, when Europe's finest electronic music DJs man the decks for Ultraheat. Lesbian night Venus Rising (www .venusrising.it in Italian) takes place on the last Sunday of the month.

⭐ LA CASA DEL JAZZ *Live Music*
☎ 06 70 47 31; www.casajazz.it; Viale di Porta Ardeatina 55; admission free–€10; ⏰ 7pm-midnight; Ⓜ Piramide 🚌 Via Cristoforo Colombo

Once a Mafioso's abode, this 1930s villa is now Rome's 'House of Jazz', complete with a 150-seat auditorium, rehearsal rooms, garden, café, restaurant and bookshop (open from 5pm or 7pm on concert nights). Expect anything from Manhattan quartets to celebrated Italian jazz drummer Roberto Gatto.

⭐ LA SAPONERIA *Nightclub*
☎ 06 574 69 99; www.saponeriaclub .it; Via degli Argonauti 20; admission varies; ⏰ 11pm-5am Fri & Sat Oct-May; Ⓜ Garbatella

In a previous life, La Saponeria was a soap factory. These days, it lathers up the punters with guest DJs like up-and-coming Brit Glimpse and Geneva-based electronic meister Lee Van Dowski. Beats span nu-house, nu-funk, minimal techno and dance, with hip-hop and R&B on Saturdays, and the occasional fetish event from Ritual Club (www.ritualtheclub.com).

⭐ RASHOMON
Live Music, Nightclub
☎ 347 340 57 10; www.myspace.com/ rashomonclub; Via degli Argonauti 16; admission varies; ⏰ 11pm-4.30am Thu-Sun Oct-May; Ⓜ Garbatella

Indie, new wave and electronic beats, both live and DJ spun. Past guests to have hit the decks include German electro meister Marek Hemmann, Denmark's Jonas Koop and Holland's genre-busting Legowelt.

⭐ RISING LOVE *Nightclub*
☎ 339 427 06 72; www.risinglove.it in Italian; Via delle Conce 14; ⏰ 11pm-4am Tue-Sun Oct-May; Ⓜ Piramide

For those who love their electronica, techno, funky groove and house, this white-on-white industrial space ticks all the boxes. Local and guest DJs get the crowd rocking, and there are regular one-off nights.

⭐ TEATRO PALLADIUM
Cultural Centre
☎ 06 573 32 768; www.teatro-palladium .it in Italian; Piazza Bartolomeo Romano 8; Ⓜ Garbatella

Set in the now-hip suburb of Garbatella (see the boxed text, p140), this curvaceous 1920s theatre boasts a kick-ass programme of edgy, top-notch performance art, theatre, seminars and music events. It's also a venue for the worldly RomaEuropa festival (p29).

>TRASTEVERE & GIANICOLO

The stuff of postcards, Trastevere wins fans with its lost-in-time laneways, peeling façades and general *allegria* (bonhomie). If you're after buzzing *aperitivo* (happy hour) bars, flirtatious crowds or a late-night book hunt, chances are you'll end up on these cobbled streets. It's less about must-see sights here and more about soaking up the vibe, whether that entails downing beers with Mohican-haired punks at Bar San Calisto, looking for cheap thrills at Porta Portese market or lazy lunching at a hidden trattoria.

Not that Rome's 'left bank' is a cultural slouch The ex-palace of pipe-smoking Queen Christina drips with art treasures; Villa Farnesina boasts fres-coes by Raphael; and Nuovo Sacher is one of Rome's top art-house cinemas.

Sliced in two by Viale di Trastevere, oriented around Piazza Santa Maria di Trastevere, the quarter started life as an ancient mix of vineyards, farms and villas, before turning into a working-class medieval enclave and lat-ter-day real-estate gold mine.

Looking down on the action is lofty Gianicolo (Janiculum), a calming concoction of leafy roads and spectacular city views.

TRASTEVERE & GIANICOLO

👁 SEE

🛍 SHOP

🍴 EAT

🍸 DRINK

⭐ PLAY

Please see over for map

👁 SEE

👁 BASILICA DI SANTA CECILIA IN TRASTEVERE

☎ 06 589 92 89; Piazza di Santa Cecilia; admission church/Cavallini fresco free/€2.50; 🕙 church 9.30am-12.30pm & 4-6.30pm Mon-Sat, 4-6.30pm Sun, fresco 10am-12.30pm Mon-Sat, 11am-12.30pm Sun; 🚌 🚊 Viale di Trastevere

It was here that St Cecilia was (eventually) martyred in 230, after singing songs of praise through various assassination attempts. Below the altar, Stefano Maderno's exquisite statue of the miraculously preserved saint shows exactly how she was found in Catacombe di San Callisto (p126) 13 centuries after her death. **Roman ruins** (admission €2.50; 🕙 9.30am-12.30pm Mon-Sat, 4-6.30pm Sun) lurk underground, while the nun's choir harbours unmissable fragments of Pietro Cavallini's 13th-century fresco *The Last Judgement*.

👁 BASILICA DI SANTA MARIA IN TRASTEVERE

☎ 06 581 48 02; Piazza Santa Maria in Trastevere; 🕙 7.30am-9pm Sep-Jul, 7.30am-1pm & 3-9pm Aug; 🚌 🚊 Viale di Trastevere

This Romanesque ravisher sparkles with glorious 12th-century mosaics in its apse and on the triumphal arch, below which sit six 13th-century mosaics by Pietro Cavallini. The 17th-century wooden ceiling is a Domenichino creation, while some of the Roman columns were snatched from Terme di Caracalla (p133). A beautiful Cosmati paschal candlestick stands on the very spot where a miraculous fountain of oil supposedly sprang in 38 BC.

Be seduced by the architectural curves of Ex Elettro Fonica art gallery (p150)

Via del Gesù

PIGNA

Via Florida

Via dei Falegnami

SANT'ANGELO

Via Catalana

Lgt dei Pierleoni

Piazza Monte Savello

Ponte Fabricio

Piazza di Ponti

Piazza dei Ponziani

Isola Tiberina

Lgt de Cenci

Piazzetta Picinuti

See Centro Storico
Map pp52–3

E

Via Capo di Ferro

Via del Pettinari

Via delle Zoccolette

Via dei Vallati

Lgt delle Zoccolette

River Tiber

Ponte Garibaldi

Piazza Belli

New Internet Point

Tourist Information Point

Via dell'Orologio

Chiesa di San Crisogono

Via della Renella

PARIONE

Corso Vittorio Emanuele II

Via del Monserrato

Via Giulia

REGOLA

Lgt D Sangallo

Lgt dei Tebaldi

Lgt della Farnesina

Ponte Sisto

Lgt del Politeama

Via del Moro

Via della Lungaretta

Piazza Trilussa

Piazza Santa Maria in Trastevere

Ponte G Mazzini

Via della Lungara

12

Via Cosini

Largo Cristina di Svezia

9

Via dei Riari

Via delle Mantellate

Vic della Penitenza

Via di San Francesco di Sales

Orto Botanico

Villa Orto Botanico

Gianicolo (Janiculum)

Piazza San Pietro in Montorio

Via G. Garibaldi

TRASTEVERE

Passeggiata del Gianicolo

Lgt Gianicolense

Via degli Orti d'Alibert

8

Ospedale Bambino Gesù

Via di San Onofrio

6

Passeggiata del Gianicolo

10

Via di San Pancrazio

See Aventine
& Testaccio
Map p131

400 m
0.2 miles

Largo M
Gelsomini

Via Marmorata

TESTACCIO

Via Ginori

Via Zabaglia

Via Galvani

Via Vanvitelli

Via Bianca

Via Vespucci

Via Ghiberti

Via Volta

Via Florio

Via Beniamino Franklin

Via Torricelli

Lgt Testaccio

Largo
Ascianghi

Ponte
Sublicio

Via di San Michele

Via Anicia

Via della Luce

Piazza
Mastai

Via San Francesco a Ripa

Via Natale del Grande

Piazza San
Cosimato

Via Mameli

Via Dandolo

Via Morosini

Via di Porta di Ripa Grande

Lgt Ripa

Piazza
di Santa
Cecilia

Piazza de'
Mercanti

Via di Santa Maria in Cosmedin

Lgt Aventino

Via di Santa Sabina

Via di San Alessio

Via Melania

Via Pollione

Piazza di
San Francesco d'Assisi

Via Ascianghi

Piazza
Bernardino
da Febre

Via B Musolino

Via degli Orti Trastevere

Via A Bargoni

Via N Parboni

Via I Nievo

Via E Benaglia

Viale di Trastevere

Circo Portuense

Lgt Portuense

Via M Carcani

Via Portuense

Via Sacchi

Via E Cairoli

Via Glandelli

Via Nicola Fabrizi

Via Trenta Aprile

Via G Medici

Via P Roselli

Via Mercanthi

Via Giacinto Carini

Via G Rossetti

Via M Quadrio

Via F Torre

Via G B Nicolini

Via Francesco
D Guerazi

Via Felice Cavallotti

Via A Alessandro Poerio

Via T Francesco dell'Ongaro

Via E Bandiera

Via Anton Giulio Barili

Via Pisacane

Villa
Sciarra

To Villa Doria
Pamphilj (400m)

To Stazione
Trastevere (300m);
Teatro India (800m);
Città del Gusto (1km)

To Villa
Medici

☺ CHIESA DI SAN FRANCESCO D'ASSISI A RIPA

☎ 06 581 90 20; Piazza San Francesco d'Assisi 88; ☼ 7am-1pm & 4-7.30pm Mon-Sat, 7am-noon & 4-7pm Sun; ☒ ☒ Viale di Trastevere

Think the *Ecstasy of St Teresa* in Chiesa di Santa Maria della Vittoria (p86) is risqué? See Bernini turn up the heat with his even more sexually ambiguous *Blessed Ludovica Albertoni* (1674). It sizzles away in the fourth chapel on the left. The church itself sits on the site of a hospice that was visited by St Francis of Assisi in 1219.

☺ CHIESA DI SAN PIETRO IN MONTORIO & TEMPIETTO DI BRAMANTE

☎ 06 581 39 40; Piazza San Pietro in Montorio 2; ☼ church 8.30am-noon Mon-Sun, also 3-4pm Mon-Fri, tempietto 9.30am-12.30pm & 4-6pm Tue-Sun Apr-Sep, 9.30am-12.30pm & 2-4pm Tue-Sat Oct-Mar; ☒ Lungotevere della Farnesina

An architectural Kinder Surprise, Bramante's perfectly proportioned Tempietto (Little Temple) is tucked away in the courtyard of Chiesa di San Pietro in Montorio, reputedly the site of St Peter's crucifixion. Lauded as the first great building of the High Renaissance, it was completed in 1508, with Bernini adding the staircase in 1628. Bernini also contributed a chapel (the second on the left) in the church.

EDICOLA NOTTE

Blink and you might miss it! Measuring only 1m wide and 7m long, **Edicola Notte** (www.edicolanotte.com in Italian; Vicolo del Cinque 23; ☼ 8pm-2am) is Rome's tiniest art gallery. Established by Chinese-Malay artist and expat HH Lim, it's a peek-from-the-street affair, lit up each night for voyeuristic passers-by. And before you start making size jokes, remember, it's what you do with it that counts – past exhibitors include art world heavies such as Jannis Kounellis, Yan Pei Ming and Yang Jiechang.

☺ EX ELETTRO FONICA

☎ 06 647 60 163; www.exelettrofonica .com in Italian; Vicolo Sant'Onofrio 10-11; admission free; ☼ 4-8pm Tue-Sat, closed Aug; ☒ Lungotevere Gianicolense

That architects Federico Bistolfi and Alessandra Belia once worked for architectural wild child Zaha Hadid is obvious in the arresting design of this radio workshop turned art gallery. A curvaceous spectacle where walls become floors, it's an appropriate backdrop for the work of dynamic, new-gen artists from Italy and beyond.

☺ FONDAZIONE VOLUME!

☎ 06 689 24 31; Via San Francesco di Sales 86-8; admission free; ☼ 5-7.30pm Tue-Sat; ☒ Lungotevere della Farnesina; ♿

Head to this former glass factory for experimental, site-specific installations from A-list local and global artists. Past exhibitors include Jannis Kounellis, Sol Lewitt, Bernhard Rudiger and Nahum Tave – each in turn has transformed the tiny space into completely different realities.

GALLERIA LORCAN O'NEILL
☎ 06 688 92 980; www.lorcanoneill.com; Via degli Orti d'Alibert 1E; admission free; 🕒 noon-8pm Mon-Fri, 2-8pm Sat; 🚊 Lungotevere Gianicolense
Kick-started by a London art dealer and set in a converted stable, this is one of Rome's most respected private galleries. It was also one of the first to bring edgy international names to the city – think Tracey Emin, Max Rental, Matvey Levenstein, as well as local talent such as Luigi Ontani and Pietro Ruffo.

GALLERIA NAZIONALE D'ARTE ANTICA DI PALAZZO CORSINI
☎ 06 688 02 323; www.galleriaborghese.it; Via della Lungara 10; adult/EU 18-25yr/EU under 18yr & over 65yr €4/2/free; 🕒 9am-7.30pm Tue-Sun; 🚊 Lungotevere della Farnesina
Once home to reveller Queen Christina of Sweden, whose richly frescoed bedroom witnessed a steady stream of male and female

lovers, 16th-century Palazzo Corsini houses part of Italy's national art collection (the rest is in Palazzo Barberini; p87). Scan the walls for Van Dyck's *Madonna della Paglia* (Madonna of the Straw), Rubens' St Sebastian and Caravaggio's *San Giovanni Battista* (St John the Baptist). Don't miss the Bologna school brilliance waiting in room 7.

GIANICOLO
Piazza Giuseppe Garibaldi; 🚌 Via del Gianicolo; ♿
It was here in 1849 that Giuseppe Garibaldi and his makeshift army fought pope-backing French troops in one of the fiercest battles in the struggle for Italian unification. Although a cannon is still fired from it every day at noon, Rome's highest hill is now better known for great views, pony rides and Neapolitan puppet shows at weekends.

ORTO BOTANICO
☎ 06 499 17 107; Largo Cristina di Svezia 24; adult/6-11yr & over 60yr €4/2; 🕒 9am-5.30pm Mon-Sat early Oct-Mar, to 6.30pm Mon-Sat Apr-early Oct; 🚌 Lungotevere della Farnesina
Established in 1883, Rome's botanical gardens are a soothing antidote to the capital's urban excess. Chill out with splash-happy ducks; check out the

CROSS-TOWN CRUISING

Hop on (and off) bus 3 for a cool cruise around town. From Stazione Trastevere, it's a quick trip to Sunday-market favourite Porta Portese (p154). When you're haggled out, head east across the Tiber to shop responsibly at Testaccio's Città dell'Altra Economia (p134) and drop in on Keats and Shelley at Cimitero Acattolico per gli Stranieri (p132). Back on board, salute imperial icons Circo Massimo (p43) and the Colosseum (p44) before a spiritual stopover at colossal Basilica di San Giovanni in Laterano (p118). Further on, take a boho bite at Rouge (p111) before a magical stroll through Quartiere Coppedè (p180). Bus to the end of the line for modernist musing at Galleria Nazionale d'Arte Moderna (p175) or uncomplicated chilling in Villa Borghese (p180).

healing Giardino dei Semplici (a garden with 300 species of medicinal plants); smell your way through the Giardino degli Aromi (labelled in Braille); or simply fall for the dreamy city views.

☯ VILLA FARNESINA
☎ 06 680 27 268; Via della Lungara 230; adult/14-18yr/under 14yr & over 65yr €5/4/free; ☾ 9am-1pm Mon-Sat; 🚌 Lungotevere della Farnesina
This luxurious 16th-century pad was designed by Sienese architect Baldassare Peruzzi who, along with Sebastiano del Piombo and the great Raphael, smothered the place in frescoes. While Raphael painted the *Triumph of Galatea,* he did little more than design the celebrated *Cupid and Psyche;* it was executed by his assistants while he dallied with his mistress from a nearby bakery.

⬜ SHOP

⬜ ANTICA CACIARA TRASTEVERINA *Food, Wine*
☎ 06 581 28 15; Via San Francesco a Ripa 140; ☾ 7am-8pm Mon-Sat; 🚌 🚊 Viale di Trastevere
The fresh ricotta is a prized possession at this century-old deli, and usually snapped up by lunch. If you're too late, take solace in the famous *pecorino romano* or the *burrata pugliese* (a creamy cheese from the Puglia region), or simply lust after the fragrant hams, bread, *baccalà* (salted cod), peppers, Sicilian anchovies and local wines.

⬜ BIBLI *Books*
☎ 06 588 40 97; www.bibli.it in Italian; Via dei Fienaroli 28; ☾ 5.30pm-midnight Mon, 11am-midnight Tue-Sun; 🚌 🚊 Viale di Trastevere
Intelligentsia types flock here to stock their bookshelves, hobnob

at the regular readings and launches, and discuss plots and characters over cake at the in-house café. There's a limited selection of books in English. *Aperitivo* is served from 7.30pm to 10.30pm, and brunch at weekends from 12.30pm to 3.30pm for particularly peckish bookworms.

JOSEPH DEBACH *Shoes*
☎ 348 781 93 58; www.josephdebach .com in Italian; Vicolo del Cinque 19; ⏱ 5-11pm Sat-Thu winter, 4pm-midnight Sat-Thu summer; 🚊 Piazza Trilussa
Shoes with teeth and tongues, covered in cartoon collage or funked-up with an abacus wedge heel? Created by Libyan-born designer Joseph Debach, these outrageous numbers are more about 'wow' than 'wear', as *calzatura* (footwear) is transformed into cutting-edge culture.

LA CRAVATTA SU MISURA
Accessories
☎ 06 890 16 941; www.lacravattasu misura.it in Italian; Via Santa Cecilia 12; ⏱ 3.30-7.30pm Mon, 10am-2pm & 3.30-7.30pm Tue-Sat; 🚊 🚊 Viale di Trastevere
A chic little shop with ties draped over the wooden furniture and rolls of fine Italian silks and English wools lined up out the back, La Cravatta makes exquisite neckwear to customer specifications. At a push staff will have your new favourite ready in a few hours.

On the lookout for bargains amid the array of wares at Porta Portese (p154)

NEIGHBOURHOODS

TRASTEVERE & GIANICOLO

🖸 PORTA PORTESE *Market*
🕙 7am-1pm Sun; 🚍 🚊 Viale di Trastevere

Locals joke that if you have something stolen during the week, you can buy it back here on Sunday. Rome's biggest, busiest and best-known flea market has thousands of stalls pushing everything from cheap jeans, shoes and bags to Romanian pop CDs, Peruvian ponchos and the odd kitchen sink. Keep your valuables safe and don't forget to haggle.

🖸 ROMA-STORE *Perfume*
☎ 06 581 87 89; Via della Lungaretta 63; 🕙 10am-8pm; 🚍 🚊 Viale di Trastevere

A shop without a sign is usually a good… sign. This enchanting perfume shop is no exception; it's crammed full of deliciously enticing bottles of scent and lotions. Get fresh with in-the-know brands such as Serge Lutens, Laboratorio Olfattivo, E Coudray and État Libre, or go retro-Britannia with Floris London.

🖸 SCALA QUATTORDICI
Fashion
☎ 06 588 35 80; Via della Scala 13-14; 🕙 4-8pm Mon, 10am-1.30pm & 4-8pm Tue-Sat; 🚍 🚊 Viale di Trastevere

Make yourself over à la Audrey Hepburn at this classic Trastevere boutique. It's filled with haughty attitude, rolls of luscious fabrics and exquisite hand-stitched off-the-peg and tailor-made outfits.

🖸 TEMPORARY LOVE
Fashion, Accessories
☎ 06 583 34 772; www.temporarylove .net; Via di San Calisto 9; 🕙 11am-8pm Tue-Sun; 🚍 🚊 Viale di Trastevere

The coolest new kid on the block, boutique-cum-gallery Temporary Love collaborates with edgy artists to create limited-edition men's and women's bags and threads, from funky graphic T-shirts to hand-painted totes. There are five collections/exhibitions a year, and past collaborators include France's Serge Uberti and local street-art hero Sten.

🍴 EAT

One of your best bets for authentic Roman grub (and a few exotic extras), Trastevere is crammed with atmospheric trattorias, elegantly retro restaurants and a brilliant new-school rebel in Glass Hostaria. As a general rule, steer clear of 'tourist menus' and follow the nose of a local.

🍴 BIR & FUD
Trattoria, Beer Bar   € €
☎ 06 589 40 16; www.birefud.blogspot .com; Via Benedetta 23; 🕙 6.30pm-12.30am Sun-Thu, to 2am Fri & Sat, closed Aug; 🚍 Piazza Trilussa

CITTÀ DEL GUSTO

Foodies shouldn't miss a trip to **Città del Gusto** (City of Taste; ☎ 06 55 11 21; www.gam berorosso.it; Via Enrico Fermi 161; 🚊 Viale Guglielmo Marconi), a multistorey shrine to gastronomy run by Italy's premier food organisation, Gambero Rosso. Buy cookbooks in the **shop** (🕙 9am-1pm Mon-Fri); watch top chefs in action in the culinary 'theatre'; take a cooking course (three hours, €65 to €90, in Italian); or get wine savvy at one of the tasting sessions. Flaunt your newly acquired expertise at the **wine bar** (☎ 06 551 12 264; 🕙 9am-4.30pm Mon, 9am-midnight Tue-Fri, 7.30pm-midnight Sat), which serves breakfast (from 9am Monday to Friday), a lunch buffet (1pm to 2.30pm Monday to Friday, €12), *aperitivo* (from 6.30pm Tuesday to Friday, from 7.30pm Saturday, €10) and dinner (from 8pm Tuesday to Saturday).

Boutique Italian beers and top-notch, simple flavours define this lively offspring of Pizzarium (p171). Join the fans for staples like *supplì* (deep-fried rice balls) and bubbling thin-crust pizza, dished out by clued-up staff who'll find you the perfect brew to wash it all down with.

🍴 DA AUGUSTO *Trattoria* €
☎ 06 580 37 98; Piazza de' Renzi 15;
🕙 12.30-3pm & 8-11pm, closed Aug;
🚊 🚋 Viale di Trastevere
Plonk yourself at one of the tables for a quintessentially Roman experience involving gruff waitresses rattling off the specials with seasoned nonchalance, gruffer *casalinghe* (housewives) yelling out to neighbours across the piazza, and cheap, smashing staples such as *rigatoni all'amatriciana* (pasta with a tomato, pancetta and chilli-pepper sauce) and Friday's *baccalà* (salted cod with tomato,

onion and black pepper) served with crunchy *casareccio* bread.

🍴 DA LUCIA *Trattoria* €
☎ 06 580 36 01; Vicolo del Mattonato 2;
🕙 12.30-3pm & 7.30-11pm Tue-Sun,
closed 2 weeks Aug; 🚊 🚋 Viale di
Trastevere
Eat beneath fluttering neighbourhood knickers at this terrific trattoria that heaves with hungry locals and tourists. Located on a cobbled backstreet that's classic Trastevere, it serves up a cavalcade of Roman specialities including *trippa all romana* (tripe with tomato sauce) and *pollo con peperoni* (chicken with capsicum), as well as gutbusting antipasti.

🍴 DAR POETA *Pizzeria* €
☎ 06 588 05 16; Vicolo del Bologna 46;
🕙 from 6.30pm; 🚊 Piazza Trilussa
Expect to queue at this Michelin-listed pizza peddler, tucked down a cute Trastevere side street. It's

famed for its light, slow-rising dough and new-school creative toppings (apple and Grand Marnier pizza, anyone?). There's a decadent ricotta and Nutella calzone, great bruschetta and fresh, righteous salads for carb-conscious diners.

🍴 FORNO LA RENELLA
Pizza al Taglio   €

☎ 06 581 72 65; Via del Moro 15-16; 🕙 9am-9pm; 🚃 Piazza Trilussa

The wood-fired ovens at this historic Trastevere bakery have been firing for decades, producing a lip-smacking daily batch of pizza, bread and biscuits. Pizza toppings (and fillings) vary seasonally, pleasing fans that span skinheads with bulldogs to chihuahua-clutching pensioners.

🍴 GLASS HOSTARIA
Ristorante   € €

☎ 06 583 35 903; www.glasshostaria .it; Vicolo del Cinque 58; 🕙 8-11.30pm Tue-Sun; 🚃 Piazza Trilussa

While we love the sleek Andrea Lupacchini–designed interiors, the real star here is Cristina Bowerman's scandalously good mod-Italian nosh. Nibble on *guanciale* (pig's cheek) and red-onion marmalade bread, then swoon over textured gems such as pistachio-encrusted scallops with fresh pancetta and lemongrass

sauce. The tasting menus (€55 and €70) are optimal, while two gracious sommeliers can help you pick the perfect drop.

🍴 JAIPUR *Indian*   €

☎ 06 580 39 92; www.ristorantejaipur .it in Italian; Via di San Francesco a Ripa 56; 🕙 7pm-midnight Mon, noon-3pm & 7pm-midnight Tue-Sun; 🚃 🚋 Viale di Trastevere

A lifeline for curry lovers, don't let the gaudy fit-out freak you out – the Indian grub here is some of Rome's best. The focus is on northern Indian cooking, with a large selection of tandoori dishes and *murghs* (chicken-based dishes), as well as tasty herbivorous options.

🍴 LA FONTE DELLA SALUTE
Gelateria   €

☎ 06 589 74 71; Via Cardinale Marmaggi 2-6; 🕙 10am-1am; 🚃 🚋 Viale di Trastevere

Okay, maybe it's not the 'fountain of health' it purports to be, but you can always opt for the yummy soy and yoghurt-based gelati. In any case, the fruit-flavoured sorbets are so delicious they're bound to give you a salubrious glow.

🍴 LA GENSOLA *Ristorante*   € €

☎ 06 581 63 12; Piazza della Gensola 15; 🕙 1-3pm & 8pm-midnight, closed Sun mid-May–mid-Sep; 🚃 🚋 Viale di Trastevere

Watching Italians swoon over their food is a reassuring sign, and a common sight at this simple yet stylish Sicilian smasher. The star turn is the seafood, prepared simply and skilfully in dishes such as linguine with fresh anchovies and *pecorino* cheese and fried *zuccherini* (tiny fish) with fresh mint. Waiters are attentive, and just a little quirky.

🍴 PANATTONI *Pizzeria* €
☎ 06 580 09 19; **Viale di Trastevere 53;** ⏰ **6.30pm-2am Thu-Tue;** 🚌 🚃 **Viale di Trastevere**
It might be dubbed *l'obitorio* (the morgue) for the marble table tops, but there's nothing sedate about this raucous, retro spectacle of mid-century signage, swift no-nonsense waiters, passing rattling trams and loud locals scoffing bubbling pizzas and golden-fried *supplì*. Topping it off is the luscious tiramisu.

🍴 PARIS *Ristorante* €€
☎ 06 581 53 78; **Piazza San Calisto 7;** ⏰ **noon-3pm & 7.30-11pm Tue-Sat, 7.30-11pm Mon & Sun, closed Sun winter & 1 week Aug;** 🚌 **Piazza Trilussa**
The best place outside of the Ghetto to tuck into Jewish-Roman food, Paris rolls out classics like *fritto misto con baccalà* (deep-fried vegetables with salted cod) and *carciofi alla giudia* (Jewish-style artichokes). Mainstream Roman regulars include a just-right

Slow down the pace with a streetside alfresco meal at one of Trastevere's atmospheric nosh spots

rigatoni alla carbonara (pasta with egg and bacon sauce).

🍴 SISINI *Pizza al Taglio*   €
Via di San Francesco a Ripa 137; 🕑 **9am-10pm Mon-Sat, closed Aug;** 🚌 🚊 **Viale di Trastevere**

Locals know where to come for the best *pizza al taglio* (pizza by the slice) in Trastevere, and you'll need to jostle with them to make it to the counter. Simple varieties reign supreme – try the Margherita (tomatoes, basil and mozzarella) or *zucchine* (zucchini) and you'll see what we mean – although the *supplì* and potato croquettes run a close second.

🍴 VALZANI *Pasticceria*   €
☎ **06 580 37 92; Via del Moro 37;** 🕑 **10am-8pm Wed-Sun, 2-8pm Mon & Tue, closed Jul & Aug;** 🚌 🚊 **Piazza Sonnino**

Eighty-something Signora Valzani still rules the roost at this fragrant *pasticceria* (pastry shop) that opened in 1925 and is famed for its Sacher torte (fans include local film director Nanni Moretti). Those after an instant sugar high shouldn't miss the chocolate-covered *mostaccioli* (grape-must biscuits), Roman *torrone* (nougat), yuletide *pangiallo* cake (honey, nuts, dried fruit) and the heavenly *cannoli siciliani,* a ricotta-filled pastry studded with candied orange.

🍸 DRINK

After dark, Trastevere heaves with merrymakers, who make good use of the neighbourhood's stock of packed bars, pubs and cafés. Most of the action takes place on the eastern side of Viale di Trastevere, around Piazza Santa Maria in Trastevere, Piazza Trilussa and the streets off Piazza de'Renzi and Piazza Sant'Egidio.

🍸 BAR LE CINQUE *Bar*
Vicolo del Cinque 5; 🕑 **6am-2am Mon-Sat, 6pm-2am Sun;** 🚌 🚊 **Piazza Sonnino**

There's no sign outside, and it looks like an ordinary, old-school bar, but this is a Trastevere favourite, never short of a small crowd clustered around outside, here for the cute location and the easy-going vibe.

🍸 BAR SAN CALISTO *Bar*
☎ **06 583 58 69; Piazza San Calisto 3-5;** 🕑 **6am-2am Mon-Sat;** 🚊 🚊 **Viale di Trastevere**

Tough, tatty and never dull, this stuck-in-time bar packs in a motley crew, from students, punks and dealers, to moody matriarchs and card-playing *nonni* (grandpas). Arty types adore its shortcomings, not to mention the dirt-cheap prices and legendary chocolate: drunk hot with cream in winter and licked as gelato in summer.

☐ FRENI E FRIZIONI *Bar*
☎ 06 583 34 210; www.freniefrizioni
.com in Italian; Via del Politeama 4-6;
🕑 6.30pm-2am; 🚊 Piazza Trilussa

Once a garage (the name means 'brakes and clutches'), this is now one of Rome's coolest bars. It's a designer-grunge concoction of concrete floors, funky furniture, chandeliers and spritz-loving arty types. The gut-filling *aperitivo* is a bargain (beer/cocktails €6 to €10, from 7pm to 10.30pm), and tables can be booked in advance if you insist on sipping seated.

☐ IL BARETTO *Bar*
☎ 06 583 65 422; Via Garibaldi 27;
🕑 7am-2am Mon-Sat, 5pm-2am Sun;
🚊 🚉 Piazza Sonnino

Venture a little way up the Gianicolo, up a steep flight of steps from Trastevere. Trust us, it's worth it. Waiting for you is this truly hip cocktail bar, its huge plate-glass windows overlooking the district. *Aperitivo* is served from 7pm to 10pm and the garden terrace makes for perfect alfresco posing. Add meaty basslines and a vintage-meets-pop-art aesthetic, and it becomes clear why we're smitten.

☐ LA MESCITA AT FERRARA
Enoteca
☎ 06 583 33 920; Piazza Trilussa 41;
🕑 wine bar 6pm-2am, restaurant & osteria 7.30-11.30pm; 🚊 Piazza Trilussa

Though it incorporates an upmarket restaurant and breathe-easy *osteria* (focusing on pan-Italian and traditional local dishes respectively), Ferrara's real drawcard is its snug wine bar, La Mescita. You might need the staff's help to navigate the 1200-label wine list, with circa 35 elegant drops by the glass. Relieve the exhaustion with the scrumptious selection of *aperitivo* snacks.

☐ LETTERE CAFFÈ
Café, Cultural Centre
☎ 06 645 61 916; www.letterecaffe.org in Italian; Via San Francesco a Ripa 100-1;
🕑 6.30pm-2am; 🚊 Piazza Trilussa

Culture vultures call into Lettere to flick through books, schmooze over drinks and catch the eclectic, arty line-up. Expect poetry slams on Mondays, electronic beats on Wednesdays, and anything from Patty Smith tribute bands to live impromptu painting gigs anytime in between. Scan the website for gigs.

☐ LIBRERIA DEL CINEMA
Café
☎ 06 581 77 24; www.libreriadel
cinema.roma.it in Italian; Via dei Fienaroli 31; 🕑 café 5-10pm Sun-Fri, to 11pm Sat, bookshop 3-10pm Mon, 11am-10pm Tue-Fri & Sun, 11am-11pm Sat; 🚊 🚉 Viale di Trastevere

Ponder Pasolini over peppermint tea at this intimate café,

SPOON IT LIKE TOTTI

In 2007, AS Roma captain Francesco Totti bagged the European Golden Boot as the highest goal scorer across all European divisions. The following year, he scored the *Pallone d'Argento* (Silver Ball) for his sportsmanship. Romans couldn't help gloating about their favourite son, not once lured away from his beloved hometown by lucrative foreign contracts. Then again, when you earn €6 million per season, there's no rush to pack.

Born in 1976, Totti first played for AS Roma at 16, a club whose left-leaning roots made it the darling of historically working-class Testaccio and Trastevere. In January 2008, he scored his 200th goal with the club in a 4-0 win against Torino. Comparisons to David Beckham are somewhat inevitable. Like Posh's squeeze, Totti is simultaneously worshipped for his looks and skills, and derided for perceived intellectual shortcomings. In 2005, after scoring at the Rome Derby, he slipped the football up his shirt and simulated labour with the help of some other players – a tribute to his pregnant wife, TV starlet Ilary Blassi.

set snugly inside a hip cinema bookshop. In an atmosphere filled with the chatter of local directors, actors and writers, the bookshop itself boasts an arty selection of DVDs, as well as a busy cultural calendar. Check the website for upcoming screenings, readings and discussions.

▼ OMBRE ROSSE *Wine Bar*
☎ 06 588 41 55; Piazza Sant'Egidio 12; 🕑 8am-2am; 🚊 Piazza Trilussa
Warm wooden interiors, a piazza-side location and cosmopolitan crowds lend much-loved Ombre Rosse effortless continental cool. There's a particularly fine selection of rums and whiskies, monthly art exhibitions and weekly live jazz/blues/acoustic acts (from 9.30pm on Thursdays).

⭐ PLAY

⭐ BIG MAMA *Live Music*
☎ 06 581 25 51; www.bigmama.it; Vicolo di San Francesco a Ripa 18; annual/monthly membership €13/8; 🕑 9pm-1.30am Tue-Sun Oct–mid-Jun; 🚊 Piazza Trilussa
The best place to wallow in the Eternal City blues, this cramped basement pulls in top musicians from Italy and beyond. Jams also span soul and jazz to funk and rock'n'roll gospel. Tables can be booked online or over the phone.

⭐ NUOVO SACHER *Cinema*
☎ 06 581 81 16; www.sacherfilm.eu in Italian; Largo Ascianghi 1; 🚊 🚋 Viale di Trastevere
That this retro cinema appears in Nanni Moretti's film *Il Caim-*

ano (The Caiman; 2006) is no coincidence. The Italian director owns the joint and oversees its clued-up art-house line-up. If it's a Nema-ye Nazdik release you're after, chances are you'll find it here. Films are usually screened in their original language on Mondays, while summer screenings take place in the courtyard beside the cinema.

⭐ TEATRO INDIA *Theatre*
☎ 06 688 04 601; www.teatrodiroma
.net in Italian; Lungotevere dei Papare-
schi; 🚌 Via Enrico Fermi
Boasting a fetching postindustrial setting, the younger sister of the Teatro Argentina (p71) churns out sharp experimental theatre (which makes for a refreshing change in Rome). Expect any-thing from Pasolini's *The Divine Mimesis* to new works by Saverio La Ruina.

⭐ VILLA DORIA PAMPHILJ
Park
🕐 dawn-dusk; 🚌 Via di San Pancrazio
Laid out by Alessandro Algardi in the mid-16th century, this is Rome's largest park. Romantic and rolling, it's an ideal spot for recuperating beside a baroque fountain, feeding the ducks in the lake, or strolling along the picture-perfect walkways under parasol pines. It's also a great place for kids.

>VATICAN CITY & PRATI

Home to some of the world's longest queues, Vatican City (Città del Vaticano) is also its tiniest sovereign state. A mere 0.44 sq km, it comes complete with in-house currency, postage, newspaper, radio station, camply garbed Swiss Guards and toy-town railway station. It might sound cute, but it's anything but quaint. Bombastic St Peter's is the world's second-largest basilica, and the biggest, richest and most magnificent church in Italy. Crafted by the deities of Renaissance and baroque architecture, it can easily pull 20,000 visitors a day. Next door, the Vatican Museums can make a hardened art buff weep.

To the north, Madonnas give way to middle-class tendencies. The ordered streets of Prati house dishy wine bars and restaurants, retail-ripe Via Cola di Rienzo, kooky Cinema Azzurro Scipioni and swinging jazz club Alexanderplatz.

The peaceful Borgo district, wedged between the Vatican and hulking Castel Sant'Angelo, is where awestruck pilgrims crashed in the Middle Ages. Stroll down Borgo Pio for shop-hopping cardinals, Catholic kitsch and the odd vintage neighbourhood bar.

VATICAN CITY & PRATI

◉ SEE
Castel Sant'Angelo	1	E5
St Peter's Basilica	2	B5
St Peter's Square	3	C5
Vatican Gardens	4	B5
Vatican Museums	5	C5

⌂ SHOP
Centro Russia Ecumenica Il Messaggio dell'Icona	6	D5
Furla	7	D4
Outlet Gente	8	D4

🍴 EAT
Castroni	9	E4
Castroni	10	C4
Del Frate	11	D3
Dino & Tony	12	C3
Dolce Maniera	13	C3
L'Arcangelo	14	F4
Osteria dell'Angelo	15	C2
Pizzarium	16	A4
Settembrini	17	E1
Shanti	18	D3

🍸 DRINK
Art Studio Café	19	E3
Gran Caffè Esperia	20	G5
Latteria Borgo Pio	21	D5

★ PLAY
Alexanderplatz	22	B3
Baan Thai	23	D4
Cinema Azzurro Scipioni	24	D3
Fonclea	25	D4

Please see over for map

SEE

CASTEL SANT'ANGELO

☎ 06 681 91 11; Lungotevere Castello 50; adult/EU 18-24yr €5/2.50, extra €2 for exhibitions; ⏱ 9am-7pm Tue-Sun; 🚌 Piazza Pia; ♿

Originally a white-marble marvel topped with cypress trees, Hadrian's 2nd-century mausoleum was rebranded a papal fortress in the 6th century (with a passageway to the Vatican added in 1277). It was through its arrow slits that Pope Clement VII watched his city burn during the 1527 Sack of Rome. Its upper floors boast sumptuous Renaissance interiors, while the terrace (immortalised in Puccini's opera *Tosca*) offers aria-worthy views. Down below, Ponte Sant'Angelo (Bridge of Sant'Angelo) was commissioned by Hadrian in AD 136 and lined with Bernini's elegant angels 15 centuries later.

ST PETER'S BASILICA

☎ 06 698 81 662; www.stpetersbasilica .org; Piazza San Pietro; ⏱ 7am-7pm Apr-Sep, to 6pm Oct-Mar, mass 8.30am, 10am, 11am, noon & 5pm Mon-Sat, 11.30am, 12.15pm, 1pm, 4pm & 5.45pm Sun & holidays, vespers 5pm Sun; 🚌 Via della Conciliazione or Piazza del Risorgimento Ⓜ Ottaviano-San Pietro

You don't need to be religious to be bowled over by this architectural

Capture a bird's-eye view from the dome of St Peter's Basilica

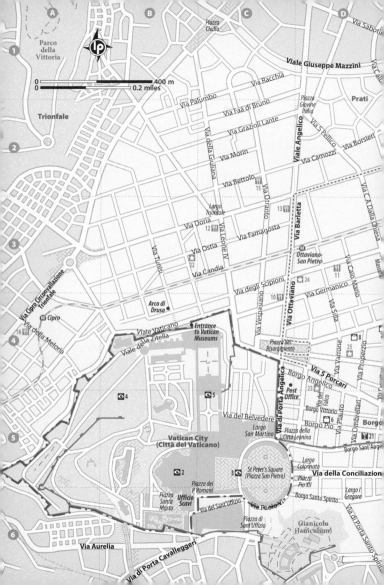

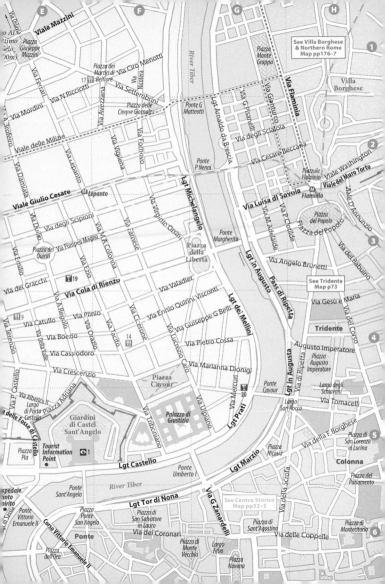

Elisabetta Lulli
Restoration artist

I restore… Anything from Renaissance frescoes and baroque façades to ancient mosaics, both on-site and in museums such as the Capitoline Museums (p42). **Major causes of damage…** Include mould and previous restorations where harsh chemicals were applied. Since the establishment of the Instituto Centrale per il Restauro (Central Institute of Restoration) in the 1950s, the substances we use are compatible with the original materials. **My favourite project…** Was working on Chiesa di San Carlo alle Quattro Fontane (p86). Recovering the building's original surfaces and colours was wonderful. **Don't miss…** The Sistine Chapel in Vatican Museums (opposite). There are so many artists represented there – not just Michelangelo. The frescoes in Basilica di San Clemente (p118) are also personal favourites. **For a lesser-known treat…** Go and see the late-Roman mosaics at Chiesa di Santa Costanza (p175). The church itself is a well-preserved example of Roman architecture and very atmospheric.

overstatement – you just need to be appropriately clad (no shorts, miniskirts or bare shoulders). The basilica's portico features a mosaic (c 1298) by Giotto from the original 4th-century building, while the red porphyry disc inside the main door marks the spot where Charlemagne and later Holy Roman Emperors were crowned by the pope. To the right of the high altar, believers wear down the foot of a bronze St Peter (reputedly a 13th-century work by Arnolfo di Cambio), while those *sans* vertigo hit Michelangelo's majestic **dome** (with/without lift €7/5; ⏰ 8am-6pm Apr-Sep, 8am 5pm Oct-Mar) for heavenly bird's-eye views.

🄲 ST PETER'S SQUARE

🚌 Via della Conciliazione or Piazza del Risorgimento Ⓜ Ottaviano-San Pietro

From above, Piazza San Pietro looks like a giant keyhole. The square's creator, Bernini, described the double colonnade as 'the motherly arms of the church'. He'd planned for the square to gob-smack pilgrims as they emerged from the tangle of medieval streets, an effect spoilt when Mussolini bulldozed Via della Conciliazione through the area. Caligula shipped in the central obelisk from Heliopolis, and it was later used by Christian-culling Nero as a turning post at his chariot-racing circus.

🄲 VATICAN GARDENS

fax 06 698 84 019; www.biglietteri amusei.vatican.va/musei/tickets; Città del Vaticano; adult/concession €31/25; ⏰ tour times vary, see website; 🚌 Piazza del Risorgimento Ⓜ Ottaviano-San Pietro

Book online at least a week ahead to secure a guided snoop around the Vatican's backyard. It's a soothing spectacle, complete with flower-filled French parterre, formal Italian garden, English wood and grottoes. There's even a kitchen garden, although you can forget about pressing the papal tomatoes.

🄲 VATICAN MUSEUMS

☎ 06 698 84 676; www.vatican.va; Viale Vaticano; adult/6-18yr & student under 27yr/under 6yr €15/8/free, last

Kitsch religious icons make great souvenirs

Sun of month free; 🕙 9am-6pm (last admission 4pm) Mon-Sat, 9am-2pm (last admission 12.30pm) last Sun of month; 🚌 Piazza del Risorgimento Ⓜ Ottaviano-San Pietro; ♿
Save time by purchasing tickets online (www.biglietteriamusei .vatican.va; €4 booking fee per ticket) to the Vatican's astounding art collection. For a whistle-stop tour, check out Stanze di Raffaello, the Pinacoteca, Gallerie delle Carte Geografiche and the Sistine Chapel. Hire the useful audioguide (€7) or consider prebooking a two-hour

guided tour (☎ enquiries 06 698 83 145; visiteguidatesingoli.musei@scv.va; www .biglietteriamusei.vatican.va; adult/concession €31/25; 🕙 Mon-Sat, see website for times) of the collection and Sistine Chapel. From April to October (August excepted), the collection is also open from 7pm to 11pm (last admission 9.30pm) on numerous Fridays. Online bookings are mandatory.

🛍 SHOP

🛍 CENTRO RUSSIA ECUMENICA IL MESSAGGIO DELL'ICONA Souvenirs
☎ 06 689 66 37; Borgo Pio 141;
🕙 9.30am-7pm Mon-Sat, 10am-5pm Sun; 🚌 Piazza del Risorgimento
One person's holy icon is another's religious kitsch. Either way, the glittery collection of Byzantine-style icons and prayer cards make great original souvenirs, whether you're buying for God-fearing *nonna* or postmodern pals.

🛍 FURLA Accessories
☎ 06 687 45 05; www.furla.com; Via Cola di Rienzo 226; 🕙 10am-2pm & 4-8pm Mon, 10am-8pm Tue-Sat;
Ⓜ Ottaviano-San Pietro
Furla makes for an affordable Fendi stand-in. Simple, savvy designs are sexed-up with a brilliant array of colours and finishes, and you can mix and match with

Furla shades and stilettoes. Other branches can be found in Tridente (p77) and Monti (p98).

OUTLET GENTE
Fashion, Accessories

☎ 06 689 26 72; Via Cola di Rienzo 246; 🕒 10am-7.30pm Tue-Sat, 11am-2pm & 3.30-7.30pm Mon & Sun; Ⓜ Ottaviano-San Pietro

If your credit card doesn't cut it at the main Gente store (p78), try your luck in its basement outlet, where anything from Prada loafers to Miu Miu threads are subject to democratic mark-downs of up to 50%.

EAT

AL SETTIMO GELO
Gelateria   €

☎ 06 372 55 67; Via Vodice 21a; 🕒 10am-9.30pm Tue-Sat, 10am-1.30pm & 3.30-9.30pm Sun, closed Jan-early Feb; 🚇 Piazza Giuseppe Mazzini

The name's a play on '7th heaven' and it's not a far-fetched title for one of Rome's finest gelaterie, fixated on top-notch ingredients. Jaded palates shouldn't miss the Greek ice cream with cardamom, made to a vintage Afghan recipe.

CASTRONI *Deli*   €

☎ 06 687 43 83; Via Cola di Rienzo 196; 🕒 8am-8pm Mon-Sat; Ⓜ Ottaviano-San Pietro

An Aladdin's cave for gluttonous gourmands, Castroni's seemingly infinite sweep of shelves prop up everything from artichoke pâté and jaw-busting blocks of chocolate to hard-to-find foreigners such as Twinings tea. The bar makes a mean espresso, and you can also sample delights at the nearby Via Ottaviano 55 branch, or further afield on Via Nazionale (see p101).

DEL FRATE *Enoteca*   € €

☎ 06 323 64 37; Via degli Scipioni 118; 🕒 1-3pm & 6.30pm-12.30am Mon-Fri, 6.30pm-1.30am Sat, closed 2 weeks Aug; Ⓜ Ottaviano-San Pietro

A hit with vino-versed locals, slick and spick Del Frate mixes cellar classics with fabulous seasonal nosh. The *crudo* (raw) dishes are especially good (opt for the tuna tartare), while the wicked hot-chocolate pie will leave you craving confession.

DINO & TONY *Trattoria*   €

☎ 06 397 33 284; Via Leone IV 60; 🕒 12.30-3pm & 7.30-11.30pm Mon-Sat, closed Aug; Ⓜ Ottaviano-San Pietro

While Tony stirs the pots, tenor-toned Dino delivers songs, punchlines and mammoth serves of simple Roman soul food. The *pasta alla grigia* (pasta with a *pecorino* cheese, pancetta and black-pepper sauce) is legendary,

Castroni's foodie den encourages covetousness of the gourmet kind (p169)

while the heaving antipasto platter (think prosciutto, croquettes, rocket-laced pizza and vegetables au gratin) is a belt-busting feast. Top it off with Dino & Tony's trademark *granita di caffè* (coffee with shaved ice and whipped cream). Note that credit cards are not accepted.

🍴 DOLCE MANIERA
Pasticceria   €

☎ 06 375 17 518; Via Barletta 27; 🕙 24hr; Ⓜ Ottaviano-San Pietro
Day or night, this buzzing basement bakery keeps the munchies at bay with its diet-defying snacks.

Devour filthy-fresh *panini* (sandwiches), slabs of pizza, pastries, cakes and obscenely cheap *cornetti* (Italian croissants) in their every variation.

🍴 L'ARCANGELO
Ristorante   €€

☎ 06 321 09 92; Via Giuseppe Gioachino Belli 59-61; 🕙 1-2.30pm & 8-11.30pm Mon-Fri, 8-11.30pm Sat Sep-Jul; Ⓜ Lepanto 🚌 Via Cicerone
Local foodies are quick to recommend this elegant gem, where Italian classics undergo perfect makeovers – think anchovy tart, borage and dried fruits, or hazel-

COMMANDMENTS ON WHEELS

In June 2007 the Vatican released a 36-page document entitled *Guidelines for the Pastoral Care of the Road*. Complete with a set of 10 commandments for mortal motorists, it warns against showing off in one's car, using it as an occasion for sinning or abusing it as an expression of power and domination. Considering the Italian penchant for looking good, back-seat shenanigans and cutting off other drivers, we can only pray that the Lord has a very forgiving streak.

nut mousse with grappa-infused *gianduia* chocolate.

☎ OSTERIA DELL'ANGELO
Trattoria €

☎ 06 372 94 70; Via Giovanni Bettolo 24;
🕑 8.30-11pm Mon & Sat, 12.30-2.30pm
& 8.30-11pm Tue-Fri, closed 2 weeks Aug;
Ⓜ Ottaviano-San Pietro

Ex-rugby player Angelo and his fresh-from-the-scrum staff do a brilliant open grill and a massive set menu (€25 to €30). Dishes include robust pastas, salad and mains spanning rabbit to tripe. Best of all, bread, wine and water are included in the price. No credit cards.

☎ PIZZARIUM *Pizza al Taglio* €

☎ 06 397 45 416; Via della Meloria 43;
🕑 11am-9pm Mon-Sat; Ⓜ Cipro-Musei Vaticani

Without a doubt, Rome's best pizza by the slice (even foodie authority Il Gambero Rosso agrees). Served on a chopping board, its fluffy dough and perfect crust are topped with intensely flavoured produce. Eat standing up. A selection of hard-to-find beers completes the revelation.

☎ SETTEMBRINI
Wine Bar, Ristorante €€

☎ 06 323 26 17; Via Luigi Settembrini 25; 🕑 12.30pm-1am Mon-Fri, 6pm-1am Sat; 🚌 Piazza Giuseppe Mazzini

Media types from the nearby RAI television offices adore this slinky wine bar/restaurant; its contemporary lines make a suitable backdrop for celebrity bitching. Fuelling the conversation is a sassy Euro wine list, new-wave rustic dishes, and a five-course degustation menu paired with five different wines.

☎ SHANTI *Indian* €

☎ 06 324 49 22; Via Fabio Massimo 68;
🕑 12.30-3pm & 7pm-midnight Mon-Sun; Ⓜ Ottaviano-San Pietro

Thank Krishna for Shanti, one of Rome's best bets for subcontinental grub. Eastern exotica, soft lighting and oh-so-sweet waiters perfectly pair delicately spiced numbers such as *shanty kofta* (vegetable croquettes), tandoori and dhal; best savoured with a heavenly rosewater lassi.

DRINK

ART STUDIO CAFÉ *Café*
☎ 06 326 09 104; www.artstudiocafe .com; Via dei Gracchi 187a; 🕙 7.30am-9.30pm Mon-Sat; M Ottaviano-San Pietro

Prati's yummy-mummies love this arty café, with its in-house mosaic school for those who like to get creative over bergamot tea. Sign-up or simply sip, sup and snap-up ready-made crafts off the shelves.

GRAN CAFFÈ ESPERIA *Café*
☎ 06 321 10 016; Lungotevere dei Mellini 1; 🕙 6.40am-9pm Mon-Sun May-Sep, to 9.30pm Oct-Apr; 🚍 Piazza Cavour

Everyone loves a revamped art nouveau café, especially Prati's pressed and preened bourgeoisie, who flock here for perfect *caffè* and pastries, or a glass of bubbly sipped at one of the 'look-at-me' pavement tables.

LATTERIA BORGO PIO *Bar*
☎ 06 688 03 955; Via Borgo Pio 48; 🕙 7am-9pm Mon-Sat Apr-Jul, to 8pm Sep-Mar, closed Aug; 🚍 Piazza del Risorgimento

The marble bar at this veteran *cremeria* (a dying breed of bar selling farm-fresh milk) has been propping up espresso-guzzling, *cornetto*-munching locals since 1912 (the wooden fridge is even older). Catch up on local gossip beside the poker machine, or kick back with the paper and *panini* on the postcard-worthy street.

PLAY

ALEXANDERPLATZ
Live Music
☎ 06 397 42 171; www.alexanderplatz .it; Via Ostia 9; admission with monthly membership €10; 🕙 8pm-1.30am Mon-Sun, closed Aug; M Ottaviano-San Pietro

Rome's top jazz club lines up sterling local and foreign acts (regulars include George Coleman and Lionel Hampton). Gigs kick off around 10pm, and you'll need to book a table if you fancy dining with your wining. From June to September, the club goes alfresco for the Villa Celimontana Jazz Festival (p24).

BAAN THAI *Massage*
☎ 06 688 09 459; www.baanthai.it; Borgo Angelico 22a; from €35; 🕙 10am-10pm Mon-Sun; 🚍 Piazza del Risorgimento

A perfect post-Vatican reward, this soothing massage centre blends Thai-chic interiors, heavenly scented oils and gracious masseurs. Treatments include a body-melting Ayurvedic massage (€60 for an hour), and it's always best to book if you're dropping by Friday to Sunday.

⭐ CINEMA AZZURRO SCIPIONI
Cinema
☎ 06 397 37 161; www.azzurroscipioni .com in Italian; Via degli Scipioni 82; tickets €5; Ⓜ Ottaviano-San Pietro
Italian film-maker Silvano Agosti opened his little two-screen affair after dreaming that Charlie Chaplin told him to do so. Think that's quirky? Did we mention the airline seats? The 'in-flight' entertainment spans foreign and local art house to immortal Hollywood classics.

⭐ FONCLEA *Live Music*
☎ 06 689 63 02; www.fonclea.it in Italian; Via Crescenzio 82a; admission free Sun-Thu, €6 Fri & Sat; 🕑 7pm-2am Sep-May; 🚌 Piazza del Risorgimento
The best place for a night out in the Borgo, Fonclea is a great little pub for live music – it usually hosts cover bands playing anything from jazz to soul, funk to rock. From June to August Fonclea moves outdoors. Phone for the location.

>VILLA BORGHESE & NORTHERN ROME

Before Rome's promotion to national capital in 1871, the area north and northeast of Tridente was a verdant tonic of vineyards, monasteries and noble family pads. The postunification building boom bulldozed the bliss, with Villa Borghese one of its few escapees.

Laid out by leading landscape designers, including Scotland's Jacob More, its 59 hectares are just the spot for a little personal urban renewal. It's also a fine spot for a cultural assignation, with residents that include the Museo Carlo Bilotti, the Casa del Cinema and the art-buff mecca Museo e Galleria Borghese.

Running along the park's western flank, ancient Via Flaminia heads north towards cultural hot spots MAXXI and Auditorium Parco della Musica, love-struck Ponte Milvio and roaring Stadio Olimpico. To the east, Rome's suburban sprawl serves up an eclectic bag of gems, from contemporary art hub MACRO, to early Christian mosaics, storybook streets and subterranean frescoes.

VILLA BORGHESE & NORTHERN ROME

👁 SEE
Basilica di Sant'Agnese
Fuori-le-Mura **1** H4
Catacombe di Priscilla ...**2** G3
Chiesa di Santa
Costanza ....(see 1)
Explora - Museo dei
Bambini di Roma **3** C5
Galleria Nazionale
d'Arte Moderna **4** D5
Galleria Traghetto **5** F6
Hybrida
Contemporanea .... (see 9)
Il Sole **6** G5
MACRO (Museo d'Arte
Contemporanea
di Roma) **7** F5

MAXXI (Museo
Nazionale delle Arti
del XXI Secolo) **8** B3
Mondo Bizzarro **9** F5
Museo Carlo Bilotti **10** D5
Museo e Galleria
Borghese **11** E5
Museo Nazionale Etrusco
di Villa Giulia **12** D4
Oredaria **13** F5
Ponte Milvio **14** B2
Quartiere Coppedè **15** F4

🛍 SHOP
Notebook ....(see 18)

🍴 EAT
Red **16** C3

🍸 DRINK
Casina Valadier **17** D6

⭐ PLAY
Auditorium Parco della
Musica **18** C3
Casa del Cinema **19** E6
Silvano Toti Globe
Theatre **20** D5
Stadio Olimpico **21** A2
Teatro Olimpico **22** B3

Please see over for map

◉ SEE

◉ BASILICA DI SANT'AGNESE FUORI-LE-MURA & CHIESA DI SANTA COSTANZA

☎ 06 861 08 40; www.santagnese .net in Italian; Via Nomentana 349; catacombs adult/7-15yr €8/5; ⏲ basilica 7.30am-noon & 4-7.30pm, mausoleum & catacombs 9am-noon & 4-6pm, last tour 5.30pm, catacombs closed Sun morning & late Oct-late Nov; 🚌 Via Nomentana

Constantine dedicated the 4th-century Basilica di Sant'Agnese to fireproof St Agnes – depicted in the glittering 7th-century apse mosaic withstanding flames, and buried in the crowd-free catacombs below. Across the convent courtyard, the circular Chiesa di Santa Costanza was built as a mausoleum for Constantine's daughters, Constance and Helen. Considered one of the finest architectural works of late Roman antiquity, its 4th-century mosaics are reputedly Christendom's oldest surviving. Note that the catacombs are closed in November.

◉ CATACOMBE DI PRISCILLA

☎ 06 862 06 272; Via Salaria 430; admission €8; ⏲ 8.30am-noon & 2.30-5pm Tue-Sun, closed 3 weeks Aug; 🚌 Via Salaria

No antipodean drag queens here, just some of ancient Rome's most fascinating funerary frescoes. Subterranean treasures include an

1800-year-old image of the Madonna and Child (considered to be the world's oldest known picture of Mary), and the fascinating Cappella Greca funerary chapel, with its beautiful 3rd-century biblical scenes and stucco decoration.

◉ EXPLORA – MUSEO DEI BAMBINI DI ROMA

☎ 06 361 37 76; www.mdbr.it; Via Flaminia 82; adult/3-12yr/under 3yr €6/7/ free; ⏲ visits depart 10am, noon, 3pm & 5pm Tue-Sun Sep-Jul, noon, 3pm & 5pm Aug; Ⓜ Flaminio

Kids can explore their inner adult at Explora. Set up as a miniature town, the museum comes complete with a hospital outpatient department and a mini-size TV studio. It's a hands-on, feet-on, full-on experience that your nippers will love. And it runs on solar power. Visits are limited to 1¾ hours, with bookings advisable on weekdays and essential on weekends.

◉ GALLERIA NAZIONALE D'ARTE MODERNA

☎ 06 322 98 221; www.gnam.arti .beniculturali.it; Viale delle Belle Arti 131, disabled entrance Via Antonio Gramsci 73; adult/EU 18-25yr/EU under 18yr & over 65yr €10/8/free; ⏲ 8.30am-7.30pm Tue-Sun; 🚌 Viale delle Belle Arti; ♿

Oft-overlooked, GNAM is one of Rome's coolest art museums, packed with a brilliant collection

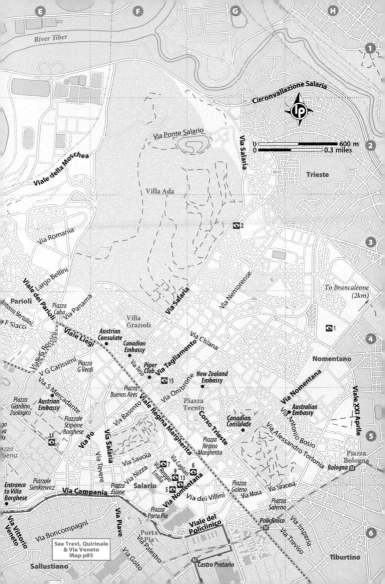

of mostly Italian painting and sculpture from the 19th and 20th centuries. Highlights include works by Canova, Modigliani and the *macchiaioli* (Italy's 'impressionists'). There are also works by pre-surrealist de Chirico; futurists Boccioni and Balla; Transavanguardia icons Clemente, Cucchi and Paladino; and canvas-ripping Lucio Fontana. International stars include Degas, Cezanne, Duchamp and Klimt. There's a gorgeous garden-party café for a charming cultural epilogue.

◉ MACRO (MUSEO D'ARTE CONTEMPORANEA DI ROMA)

☎ 06 671 070 400; www.macro.roma .museum; adult/EU 18-25yr/EU under 18yr & over 65yr €4.50/3/free; 🕙 9am-7pm Tue-Sun; 🚊 Via Nizza

Now flaunting a bold, cutting-edge wing (hip bar included) by French architect Odile Decq, MACRO showcases prime modern art from Italy and beyond. Permanent highlights include work by post-WWII Italian great Achille Perilli, as well as Nuova Scuola Romana artists from the Pastificio Cerere (see the boxed text, p108). Admission to MACRO also covers entry to its Testaccio outpost, MACRO Future (p132).

◉ MAXXI (MUSEO NAZIONALE DELLE ARTI DEL XXI SECOLO)

☎ 06 321 01 81; www.maxxi.beni culturali.it; Via Guido Reni 4A; adult/under 14yr €11/free; 🕙 11am-7pm Tue & Wed-Sun, 11am-10pm Thu; 🚌 🚊 Via Flaminia

Impressive views come with the contemporary art at MAXXI

Zaha Hadid's much anticipated museum of contemporary art and architecture is as much a destination for its monumental minimalism as it is for its exhibitions. Glide through the 'Space Odyssey' interiors for permanent works from icons like Anish Kapoor and temporary shows spanning rationalist architecture to Turkish video installations.

⊙ MUSEO CARLO BILOTTI

☎ 06 853 57 446; www.museocarlobilotti .it; Viale Fiorello La Guardia; adult/child €4.50/2.50, supplement for special exhibitions €1.50; ۞ 9am-7pm Tue-Sun; 🚇 Porta Pinciana

Drop into Villa Borghese's Orangery to eye-up a small-yet-superb collection of art amassed by late Italo-American cosmetics tycoon, Carlo Bilotti. Paintings range from a Warhol portrait of Bilotti's wife and late daughter, to 18 works by Italian great Giorgio de Chirico. Temporary shows bump up the booty, with one recent exhibition showcasing photographic art by Helmut Newton and Robert Mapplethorpe.

⊙ MUSEO E GALLERIA BORGHESE

☎ 06 3 28 10; www.ticketeria.it; Piazzale del Museo Borghese; adult/EU 18-25yr/EU under 18yr & over 65yr €8.50/5.25/free; ۞ 9am-7.30pm Tue-Sun; 🚇 Via Pinciana

If you only have the time (or the inclination) for one art gallery in Rome, make it this one. Housing the 'queen of all private art collections', it's a perfectly digestible introduction to Renaissance and baroque art. Visitors are admitted at two-hour intervals (9am, 11am, 1pm, 3pm and 5pm) for a maximum two-hour visit, so after you've picked up your prebooked ticket you'll have to wait for your allocated entry time. The quietest times to visit are 9am and 5pm, and prebooking is necessary. Book three days ahead to avoid disappointment.

⊙ MUSEO NAZIONALE ETRUSCO DI VILLA GIULIA

☎ 06 82 46 20; www.ticketeria.lt; Piazzale di Villa Giulia 9; adult/EU 18-25yr/EU under 18yr & over 65yr €4/2/free; ۞ 8.30am-7.30pm Tue-Sun; 🚇 Viale delle Belle Arti

Classicists will drool over what is Italy's finest collection of pre-Roman booty, housed in a 16th-century summer house built for Pope Julius III. Among the prized possessions are the touchingly intimate 6th-century BC Etruscan *Sarcofago degli Sposi;* a polychrome terracotta statue of *Apollo of Veio;* and the recently acquired 2500-year-old *Euphronius Krater,* considered one of the finest examples of Hellenic pottery in the world.

📷 PONTE MILVIO

🚌 **Ponte Milvio**

It's only natural that a bridge now famous for drawing love-struck teens (see the boxed text, below) should have a history racked with angst. In 312, Emperor Constantine defeated Maxentius here – a pivotal moment in Europe's conversion to Christianity. In 1849 Giuseppe Garibaldi's troops blew up the original 109 BC structure to halt the French. The bridge was rebuilt the following year.

📷 QUARTIERE COPPEDÈ

🚌 🚋 **Viale Regina Margherita**

If Gaudí and the Grimm Brothers had gone into town planning together, suburbia would probably look like this. Best entered from the corner of Via Tagliamento and Via Dora, this compact quarter is a mesmerising mishmash of Tuscan turrets, Liberty sculptures, Moor-ish arches, Gothic gargoyles, frescoed façades, and palm-fringed gardens – all designed by little-known Florentine architect Gino Coppedè in the 1920s. At its heart is whimsical Piazza Mincio; its Fontana delle Rane (Fountain of the Frogs) is inspired by the more famous Fontana delle Tartarughe (Fountain of the Turtles; p55).

📷 VILLA BORGHESE

Entrances at Porta Pinciana, Piazzale Flaminio & Pincio (above Piazza del Popolo); ⏰ **dawn-dusk;** 🚌 **Porta Pinciana**

Rome's answer to New York's Central Park, Villa Borghese is a central spot to catch your breath. The oh-so-proper English-style Giardino del Lago is a late-18th-century creation, as is Piazza di Siena (an amphitheatre used for Rome's top equestrian event in May). At the park's western end, the Pincio Hill gardens offer stunning views

---

LOVE IS A BRIDGE

In Federico Moccia's 2006 teen novel *Ho voglia di te* (I Want You), the protagonist, Step, invents a legend whereby lovers seal their undying love by locking a chain around the third lamppost on Ponte Milvio (above) and throwing the key into the Tiber below.

One film adaptation later and fiction turned to phenomenon as lovesick Italian teens began flocking to the bridge, padlocks at the ready. Within months, three lampposts had collapsed under the weight of locks, prompting then-mayor Walter Veltroni to install specially designated posts for the padlocks instead – a move his right-wing opponent condemned as 'anti-romance' (no laughing matter in love-struck Italy).

Years on, the (modified) tradition continues, complete with padlock- and pen-flogging vendors and a virtual version at www.lucchettipontemilvio.com (in Italian) for environmentally responsible lovebirds.

Find your inner romantic on the lake at Villa Borghese

across Rome, while bike hire (€4 per hour) is available at several locations, including on Viale delle Belle Arti near the Galleria Nazionale d'Arte Moderna (p175).

🛍 SHOP

🏠 **NOTEBOOK** *Books, Music*
☎ **06 806 93 461; Viale Pietro de Coubertin 30;** ⏰ **10am-8pm, to 11.30pm on concert nights;** 🚊 **Viale Tiziano**
This sprawling shop at Auditorium Parco della Musica (p182) offers up a hefty collection of art, film, music, design and travel books (mostly in Italian). It also stocks a range of CDs, DVDs and Auditorium merchandise to satisfy the most smitten of culture

vultures. To get the lowdown on upcoming literary events, jump onto the Auditorium Parco della Musica website (www.auditorium .com) and do a keyword search for 'bookshop'.

🍽 EAT

🍽 **RED** *Ristorante, Bar* €€
☎ **06 806 91 630; Viale Pietro de Coubertin 12-16;** ⏰ **10.30am-2am Mon-Sun, happy hour 6.30-9pm;** 🚊 **Viale Tiziano**
Part of the Auditorium Parco della Musica (p182) performing arts centre, we love this designer show-off for its Philippe Starck furniture, metro-glam crowd and refreshing Med-twist dishes (think giant prawns with balsamic

vinegar). Less impressive is the stingy one-drink-equals-one-serve-only *aperitivo* (happy hour) rule, so pile that plate high with dishy options such as marinated eggplant and fluffy vegetarian couscous, or opt for à la carte.

DRINK

Drinking is a cultural experience on these northern streets: Galleria Nazionale d'Arte Moderna (p175), Auditorium Parco della Musica (right) and Casa del Cinema (right) boast decent in-house cafés, and at the time of writing drinking spots were being proposed for MACRO (p178) and MAXXI (p178).

☆ CASINA VALADIER
Ristorante, Garden Bar

☎ 06 699 22 090; www.casinavaladier .it; Piazza Bucarest; ☼ outdoor bar varies, usually 11am-7pm Sat & Sun May–mid-Oct (weather permitting), restaurant 1-3pm & 8-11pm Tue-Sat, 12.30-3pm Sun; Ⓜ Flaminia

This chichi restaurant (housed in a beautifully restored neoclassical lodge with a sterling panorama of Rome) is perfect for a romantic rendezvous, and its lush, citrus-sprinkled garden is perfect for lazy, sun-soaked sipping. So slip on those shades and toast to the view with a flute of pink *prosecco* (sparkling wine).

☆ PLAY

☆ AUDITORIUM PARCO DELLA MUSICA *Cultural Centre*

☎ 06 802 41 281, box office 199 109 783; www.auditorium.com; Viale Pietro de Coubertin; 🚌 Viale Tiziano 🚋 Via Flaminia

Rome's new cultural heart is a thumping mix of music gigs, art exhibitions, literary events, noshing and culturally savvy shopping. Catch anything from the Israeli Philharmonic Orchestra to a Steve Reich retrospective, or simply explore the Renzo Piano architecture on 50-minute **guided tours** (adult/under 26yr & student/over 65yr €9/5/7; ☼ hourly 11.30am-5.30pm Sat & Sun), in Italian. Tours in English should be booked one week ahead.

☆ CASA DEL CINEMA *Film Centre*

☎ 06 42 36 01; www.casadelcinema.it; Largo Marcello Mastroianni 1; ☼ gallery 3-7pm Mon-Fri, bookshop noon-8pm Tue-Sun, DVD library 4-8.30pm Wed-Sun (last entry 6.30pm); 🚌 Via Pinciana

Set in the grounds of Villa Borghese, the House of Cinema boasts a film-themed exhibition space, three screening rooms showcasing anything from local indie flicks to Irish retrospectives, café/bar **Cinecaffè** (☎ 06 420 16 224; ☼ 9am-8pm Mon-Sun) and 2500-plus DVDs, which you can view for *nada* on the in-house computers.

ROME'S 'LITTLE CHELSEA'

If you're heading to MACRO (p178), check out the southern end of Via Reggio Emilia. The block between Via Alessandra and Via Nomentana is the heart of Rome's unofficial 'Little Chelsea' – a reference to Manhattan's gallery-crammed district. While the claim may be a little ambitious, the handful of top-notch private galleries includes pop surrealism-meets-erotica gallery/bookshop **Mondo Bizzarro** (☎ 06 442 47 451; www.mondobizzarro.net; Via Reggio Emilia 32; ⏰ 11.30am-7.30pm Mon-Sat) and **Hybrida Contemporanea** (☎ 06 997 06 573; www.hybridacontemporanea.it; Via Reggio Emilia 32/A; ⏰ 10am-8pm Tue-Sat); the latter curated by photographer/artist Marcello di Donato. Other worthy stops include **Oredaria** (☎ 06 976 01 689; www.oredaria.it; Via Reggio Emilia 22-24; ⏰ 10am-1pm & 4-7.30pm Tue-Sat) and historic Venetian dealer **Galleria Traghetto** (☎ 06 442 91 074; www.galleriatraghetto.it in Italian; Via Reggio Emilia 25; ⏰ 2.30-7.30pm Tue-Sat). Around the corner, **Il Sole** (☎ 06 440 49 40; www.galleriailsole.it; Via Nomentana 169; ⏰ 3.30-7.30pm Thu & Fri, 10am-1pm Sat) is another outlet for contemporary talent.

⭐ SILVANO TOTI GLOBE THEATRE *Theatre*
☎ 06 06 08; www.globetheatreroma.com; Largo Aqua Felix; 🚌 Piazzale Brasile

Romeo and Juliet were Italian, so it makes perfect sense to catch their sweet nothings in the native tongue. Do so in Rome's replica of London's Globe Theatre, serving up seasons of Shakespeare (in Italian) each June to September. Scan the website for upcoming shows and box office times.

⭐ STADIO OLIMPICO *Stadium*
☎ 06 3 68 51; Viale del Foro Italico; Ⓜ Ottaviano-San Pietro & 🚌 32

Weekend football at the Olympic stadium is as Roman as offal, and from September to March you can cheer or jeer one of Rome's two teams – AS Roma and SS Lazio –

most Sundays. Tickets (€15 to €65) are sold through www.listicket.it and at the many Roma and Lazio club stores around town. And remember: no photo ID, no entry to the stadium.

⭐ TEATRO OLIMPICO
Live Music
☎ 06 320 17 52; www.teatroolimpico.it in Italian; Piazza Gentile da Fabriano 17; 🚌 Viale del Vignola

While the star attraction here is the season of chamber music by the **Accademia Filarmonica Romana** (www.filarmonicaromana.org in Italian), Rome's Olympic Theatre is known to let loose with the odd contemporary gig, whether it's the bin-smashing Stomp dance group or Hollywood choreographer Daniel Ezralow. Check the website for upcoming shows.

>SNAPSHOTS

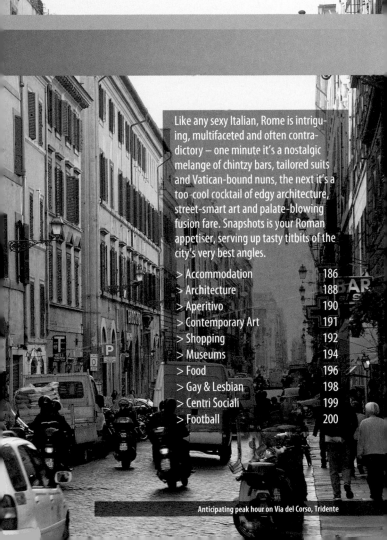

Like any sexy Italian, Rome is intriguing, multifaceted and often contradictory — one minute it's a nostalgic melange of chintzy bars, tailored suits and Vatican-bound nuns, the next it's a too-cool cocktail of edgy architecture, street-smart art and palate-blowing fusion fare. Snapshots is your Roman appetiser, serving up tasty titbits of the city's very best angles.

Anticipating peak hour on Via del Corso, Tridente

ACCOMMODATION

From art deco dens and Ferragamo-designed pads, to calming convents and just-like-*nonna* (grandma) *pensioni* (small hotels or guesthouses), slumber comes in all shapes and styles in Rome. When choosing a place to crash, it's worth considering which neighbourhood it calls home.

For the full Roman experience, it's hard to beat the *centro storico* (historic city centre). This is the city's heart, home to icons such as Piazza Navona and the Pantheon, countless restaurants and bars, and nightlife hot spot Campo de' Fiori. It's right in the action, which also means prices are generally higher and the streets a lot noisier.

An easy walk across the Tiber, Trastevere is equally gorgeous. Its cobbled laneways are sprinkled with options ranging from converted cloisters to minimalist hotels. It's also swamped with party people, especially in the summer, when bar-lined streets heave with happy hedonists – good news for party people, bad news for light sleepers. A good compromise is the Prati district: just north of the Vatican, it's easy on the eye, well connected to the *centro storico,* but relatively peaceful at night.

Elegant Tridente, *paradiso* for serious shopaholics, is crammed with an army of A-list designer boutiques, restaurants and celeb-loved hotels. Those wanting to be near (but not on top of) the action should consider staying on Caelian Hill. Immediately south of the Colosseum, it's within walking distance of the major ancient icons, and home to a small but savvy number of nosh spots and drinking dens.

Wedged between Rome's ancient hub and its clubbing heartland of Testaccio and Ostiense is the leafy, moneyed neighbourhood of Aventine, home to mainly upmarket accommodation choices but a sound option if you want the best of both worlds.

 Hotels & Hostels

Need a place to stay? Find and book it at lonelyplanet .com. Numerous properties are featured for Rome – each personally visited, thoroughly reviewed and happily recommended by a Lonely Planet author. From hostels to high-end hotels, we've hunted out the places that will bring you unique and special experiences. Read independent reviews by authors and other travellers, and get practical information including amenities, maps and photos. Then reserve your room simply and securely via Hotels & Hostels – our online booking service. It's all at lonelyplanet.com/hotels.

At the other end of the scale is raffish, multicultural Esquiline. This is where you'll find Rome's main train station, airport buses and the bulk of the hostels and budget *pensioni*. It's not the most idyllic location (women on their own may feel especially uncomfortable after dark); however, the area has been spruced up in recent years and competition between hotels has forced many places to lift their game, so it's not impossible to find a gem. It's also relatively convenient if you plan to party in student hub San Lorenzo or bohemian Il Pigneto.

When it comes to prices, expect to pay roughly between €40 and €150 for a double room in a one-star hotel; €60 to €150 in a two-star; €80 to €300 in a three-star; €200 to €400 in a four-star; and upwards of €300 in a five-star. The star rating system only relates to a hotel's facilities, not to its level of service, comfort or atmosphere, so always get the lowdown from independent hotel reviews (see the boxed text, left). Booking ahead is also a good idea, especially if you're heading there from April to June, in September, October or at Christmas. When reserving a room, make sure you ask for a *camera matrimoniale* if you're after a double bed or a *camera doppia* if you want twin beds. A room with air-con is a sound investment in July and August when the city sizzles.

If you arrive without a booking, try the free **hotel reservation service** (☎ 06 699 10 00; ⏱ 7am-10.30pm) opposite platform 21 at Stazione Termini (Map p93, D2). If you can, try to research the hotel suggested before committing. Alternatively, head to the Enjoy Rome (p218) tourist office. Online B&B booking agencies include www.b-b.rm.it, www.bbitalia.it and www.cross-pollinate.com. For hostels, log onto www.ostellionline.org (in Italian).

BEST FOR...
> Gay-friendly hospitality: 58 Le Real de Luxe (www.lerealdeluxe.com)
> Budget slumming: The Beehive (www.the-beehive.com)
> Idiosyncratic rooms: Casa Howard (www.casahoward.com)
> Celebrity spotting: Hotel De Russie (www.hotelderussie.it)
> Intimate chic: Daphne Inn (www.daphne-rome.com)

BEST FOR FABULOUS VIEWS
> Hotel Forum (www.hotelforumrome.it)
> Hotel Scalinata di Spagna (www.hotelscalinata.com)
> Portrait Suites (www.portraitsuites.com)
> Albergo Abruzzi (www.hotelabruzzi.it)
> Hotel Sant'Anselmo (www.aventinohotels.com)

ARCHITECTURE

For buffs of the built world, Rome is a proverbial candy shop – a glorious three-millennium mash-up of architectural hits (and misses). A Renaissance *palazzo* (palace) perches on a Roman theatre at Area Archeologica del Teatro di Marcello e del Portico d'Ottavia (p51); a 12th-century basilica sits slap-bang on a 4th-century church at Basilica di San Clemente (p118); and ancient columns bear the Romanesque Basilica di Santa Maria in Trastevere (p147).

Styles interweave with seasoned ease, whether it's Renaissance and baroque at Chiesa del Gesù (p51), mock-Mannerism and Liberty in Quartiere Coppedè (p180) or Fascism and Roman imperialism at Palazzo della Civiltà del Lavoro (p142).

Thankfully, Rome has *finally* decided not to rest on its architectural laurels. Recent additions read like a who's who of world architects: Italy's Renzo Piano designed the acoustically magnificent Auditorium Parco della Musica (p182); Britain's Zaha Hadid created MAXXI (p178); France's Odile Decq whipped up brewery-turned-gallery MACRO (p178); and New York modernist Richard Meier served up Museo dell'Ara Pacis (p75). Upcoming projects include Santiago Calatrava's fan-shaped Sports City/Tor Vergata University project in the city's east, the Rem Koolhaas–inspired *mercati generali* (wholesale markets) redevelopment and Massimiliano Fuksas' space-age convention centre in EUR.

Even Rome's iconic ruins echo modern sensibilities: the colossal Terme di Caracalla (p133) was a prototype day spa; the Mercati di Traiano (p45) boasted 150 ancient shops, bars and offices; and the Colosseum (p44) featured a complex pulley system to lift its four-legged victims onto its blood-thirsty stage, rock-star style. And then there's the Pantheon (p57): this was ancient Rome's best-preserved building and the planet's largest cast-concrete construction right up until the 20th century.

And while the Renaissance gave the city gems such as the Michelangelo-domed St Peter's Basilica (p163) and Bramante's bite-sized Tempietto (p150), Rome's finest moment came in the 17th and 18th centuries. The age of baroque redefined the city's historic hub with a tour de force of theatrical masterpieces, with works such as Bernini's flamboyant Fontana dei Quattro Fiumi (Fountain of the Four Rivers) in Piazza Navona (p58), Borromini's revolutionary Chiesa di San Carlo alle Quattro Fontane (p86) and Nicola Salvi's photogenic Trevi Fountain (p88) transforming what had become an urban has-been into Europe's show-stopping diva.

BEST FOR...
> Ancient ingenuity: Pantheon (p57)
> Jaw-dropping grandeur: St Peter's Basilica (p163)
> Enchanting eclecticism: Quartiere Coppedè (p180)
> Fascist pastiche: Palazzo della Civiltà del Lavoro (p142)
> Rooftop panorama: Il Vittoriano (p45)

BEST CONTEMPORARY ICONS
> Auditorium Parco della Musica (p182)
> MACRO (p178)
> MAXXI (p178)
> Museo dell'Ara Pacis (p75)

BEST FOR FRESCOED CEILINGS
> Vatican Museums (p167)
> Palazzo Farnese (p57)
> Palazzo Barberini (p87)
> Villa Farnesina (p152)
> Chiesa del Gesù (p51)

BEST MEDIEVAL MARVELS
> Chiesa di Santa Prassede (p95)
> Basilica di San Clemente (p118)
> Basilica di Santa Maria in Trastevere (p147)
> Basilica di Santa Sabina (p132)
> Basilica di Santa Cecilia in Trastevere (p147)

Top left A solemn parade of statuary leads the way to St Peter's Basilica (p163)

APERITIVO

Hit many of the capital's bars (and several restaurants) from 6.30pm to 9.30pm and prepare for miniature foodie feasts – think buffet spreads of crunchy cod fritters, olive-stuffed pastries, bite-sized frittata, lush salads, minibruschetta and bowls of spicy couscous.

Welcome to happy hour, Italian-style. Kick-started in the northern cities of Milan and Turin, *l'ora d'aperitivo* has become a nightly ritual for fresh-faced Roman denizens. We don't blame them. The buffets are often free with your drink, or yours for a specified drink-n-*aperitivo* charge. In the warmer months, crowds spill out onto the streets, sipping Negronis (apéritif made of gin, Campari and sweet vermouth), crunching crostini and eagerly awaiting the next dish straight out from the kitchen.

Morsels aside, some venues offer serious feeds, with giant bowls of pasta and steaming risotto. Suddenly you're full and dinner has been sorted for under €10. Not a bad *affare* (deal). If you're an *aperitivo* size queen, don't miss the themed buffets at trendy Fluid (p68), or the Med-Arabesque spreads at arty Freni e Frizioni (p159) or sister venue Société Lutèce (p69). Other *aperitivo* hubs include Doppiozeroo (p143), Obikà (p66) and La Mescita at Ferrara (p159); the latter serving anything from fresh mussels to whole slabs of *pecorino romano* cheese. On Sundays, ever-eclectic Micca Club (p105) combines *aperitivo* with a funky vintage flea market. And while it may be tempting to pile that plate sky high, don't forget: this is the land of *la bella figura,* where looking cool is good, and canapé landslides are not. Do like the locals do and stuff yourself silly *discreetly*.

Above Enjoy *aperitivo* beneath the chandeliers at Freni e Frizioni (p159)

CONTEMPORARY ART

Revved by culture-vulture mayor Walter Veltroni, Rome hurled itself into the new millennium with an ever-expanding modern art scene. The opening of high-profile Gagosian Gallery (p87) in 2007, alongside the launch of two major art fairs in 2008, gave the city impetus in its dream to topple Turin's status as Italy's contemporary art heavyweight. Fast forward to today and a combination of funding cuts from current mayor Gianni Alemanno, fallout from the recent global financial crisis and the delayed opening of a pared-back MAXXI (p178) have somewhat marred the momentum.

Despite the continuing exodus of emerging artists to cheaper and more dynamic pastures, young-blood galleries like Ex Elettro Fonica (p150) and Condotto C (see the boxed text, p98) provide a much-needed stage for daring new talent. Complementing them is a selection of established commercial gallery hubs, including Tridente's historic Via Margutta (Map p73, C3) and suburban Via Reggio Emilia (see the boxed text, p183). The latter strip is also home to MACRO (p178), one-time brewery and now one of Rome's pre-eminent modern-art museums. Its sister venue, MACRO Future (p132), delivers anything from pop surrealist retrospectives to multisensory installations in a spectacular slaughter-house setting. MACRO Future has also become a hub for international photography festival FotoGrafia (p28) and Rome's major contemporary art fair, The Road to Contemporary Art (www.romacontemporary.it).

Across town to gritty San Lorenzo, the post-industrial motif continues at former pasta factory Pastificio Cerere (see the boxed text, p108), Rome's most historic modern-art incubator.

For up-to-date info on exhibitions around Rome, pick up a free copy of *Arte e Roma* or *Vedere a Roma* from galleries, or scan www.exibart.com (in Italian).

BEST FOR MODERN ART
> MAXXI (p178)
> MACRO (p178)
> Palazzo delle Esposizioni (p97)
> MACRO Future (p132)
> Galleria Nazionale d'Arte Moderna (p175)

BEST OF THE REST
> Pastificio Cerere (p108)
> Museo Carlo Bilotti (p179)
> Galleria Lorcan O'Neill (p151)
> Fondazione Volume! (p150)
> Ex Elettro Fonica (p150)

SHOPPING

Retail in Rome is refreshingly real. Boutiques cram medieval streets, wine stores are family heirlooms, and artisan studios hide down secret laneways. Chains do exist – a quick saunter down Via del Corso (Map p73, B2) confirms it – but they play second fiddle. A single shopping fix might involve monk-made aphrodisiacs from Ai Monasteri (p59), a vintage Lazio drop from Trimani (p104) and deconstructed kimonos from Antichi Kimono (p59).

Antiques aficionados have several streets to drool over, including Via Margutta (Map p73, C3), Via Giulia (Map pp52–3, B5), Via dei Banchi Vecchi (Map pp52–3, B4) and Via dei Coronari (Map pp52–3, B3), the latter being famous for its antiques fair (p29).

For eclectic jewellery, pop into the *centro storico's* Tempi Moderni (p62), explore Via del Pellegrino (Map pp52–3, C5) or head across town to Fabio Piccioni (p98) or La Grande Officina (p109). Indeed, San Lorenzo harbours brilliant handmade booty, from surrealist bags at Claudio Sanó (p108) and edgy couture at Myriam B (p109) to Jap-Med ceramics at Le Terre di AT (p109) and Grué chocolate at Said (p110). For a more centrally located sugar fix, don't miss Confetteria Moriondo & Gariglio (p61), whose historic red and blue gift boxes were designed to commemorate the engagement and wedding of Italy's last king Umberto II to Maria José of Belgium in 1930.

Foodies who can't stop at cocoa can fill that extra suitcase at Volpetti (p136), fair-trade neighbour Spazio Bio at Città dell'Altra Economia (p134), sprawling Castroni (p169) and Buccone (p77), although it's worth finding out what you're allowed to take home through customs first.

Those plotting a head-turning strut into the arrivals hall shouldn't miss Rome's posse of innovative fashion boutiques. Admittedly upstaged by the glamour and big business of Milan, Italy's capital is hardly a fashion faux pas. Valentino ditched Paris for Rome to celebrate his 45 years as a frock star in 2007, recalling the heady 1950s and '60s when Rome was Italy's style queen. Back then, Hollywood royals such as Audrey Hepburn and Ava Gardner flocked to ateliers such as Sorelle Fontana – creators of Anita Ekberg's Trevi-soaked gown in Fellini's *La Dolce Vita* – for a little Roman reinvention.

Via dei Condotti (Map p73, C4) and its surrounding streets still heave with fashion heavyweights as well as lesser-known, art-laced staples My Cup of Tea (p78) and Bomba (p77).

And while label-loving mortals hunt down cut-priced couture across the Tiber at Outlet Gente (p169), those after edgier local threads skip the mainstream predictability of high-street strips Via del Corso and Via Nazionale (Map p93, A2) for the *centro storico's* Via del Governo Vecchio (Map pp52–3, C4) – home to ever-inspiring Arsenale (p60) and a score of new and retro independent gems. Guys looking beyond Armani suits and Diesel trainers will find solace on the streets of Monti, where unisex Super (p99), Contesta Rock Hair (p98) and Abito (p97) counterbalance the Roman penchant for preppy chic and 'trash 'n' flash' with their fresh, original threads.

To check out Rome's edgiest and most experimental fashion talent, don't miss events organised by The Hysterics (www.myspace.com/the hystericsfashionshow in Italian), which include the occasional Vintage Market and MoodZ party at Circolo degli Artisti (p113).

It's worth remembering that non-EU residents who spend more than €155 at shops displaying a Europe Tax Free sticker can grab a tax-free rebate (ask in store). Italian law requires you hold onto all *ricevute* (receipts).

The best shopping tip, however, is to hit the city during the *saldi* (sales), which run from early January to mid-February and from July to early September. For general shopping hours, see the Directory (p214).

BEST FOR...
> Stocking the pantry: Castroni (p169)
> Street-cool bags: Temporary Love (p154)
> Smelling sweet: Roma-Store (p154)
> The person who's got it all: Claudio Sanò (p108)
> Market haggling: Porta Portese (p154)

BEST FOR SAVVY SOUVENIRS
> Alinari (p76)
> Nardecchia (p61)
> Retro (p62)
> Bookàbar (p97)
> Le Terre di AT (p109)

Above Fashion cognoscenti scrutinise what's hot along Via dei Condotti, Tridente

MUSEUMS

Museums in Rome pack a mighty punch. Quite frankly, the sheer breadth and depth of cultural treasure in this city is almost embarrassing. Collections have most bases covered, from Etruscan bling at Museo Nazionale Etrusco di Villa Giulia (p179) to mafia pistols at Museo Criminologico (p56), to ill-fated English scribes at the Keats-Shelley House (p74). And as if it all wasn't overwhelming enough, the Italian Culture Ministry has been on a mission to reclaim a swathe of looted ancient artefacts sold to major international institutions. In 2007, Los Angeles' Getty Museum returned 40 items in return for long-term loans of other objects. In February 2010, an Italian court ruled one of the Getty's most prized possessions, an ancient Hellenic statue called *Victorious Youth,* be seized and returned to Italy – a decision the Getty vowed to appeal in Italy's highest court.

Topping Rome's museum hit list are the renowned Museo e Galleria Borghese (p179), Vatican Museums (p167) and Capitoline Museums (p42). They are crammed to their elegant rafters with ancient sculpted heroes and villains, fabulous frescoes and must-see masterpieces, both Renaissance and baroque. The brilliance keeps coming at Palazzo Barberini – Galleria Nazionale d'Arte Antica (p87), which hosts salon after salon of works from the likes of Guido Reni, Caravaggio and Bernini – not forgetting Holbein's famous portrait of Henry VIII.

Equally mesmerising are the Galleria Doria Pamphilj (p55) and Galleria Colonna (p88), where anything from Velázquez to Guercino await in private aristocratic pads. If that's still not enough mid-millennium art, don't miss frescoed palace Villa Farnesina (p152) and the neighbouring Palazzo Corsini (p151), former abode of Swedish party princess Queen Christina and current home to canvases by Van Dyck, Rubens and Fra Angelico.

Ancient treasure is equally abundant. Eye-up the beautiful 1st-century bronze *Erma di Canefora* at the Palatine (p46) or luscious Roman mosaics at Museo Nazionale Romano: Palazzo Massimo alle Terme (p96); stumble across underground frescoes at Catacombe di Priscilla (p175) or classical buttocks beneath baroque frescoed ceilings at Museo Nazionale Romano: Palazzo Altemps (p57). For an even more striking contrast, don't miss Centrale Montemartini (p140), where Roman busts, mosaics and tombs are set against brooding machinery. Originally a temporary storage solution for the Capitoline Museums, the museum is now one of the most atmospheric spots to spend a few cultured hours.

Then there are the lesser-known gems, such as the Museo Nazionale d'Arte Orientale (p95), with its collection of precious Eastern exotica; the offbeat Museo delle Arti e Tradizioni Popolari (p141); and the tucked-away Raccolta Teatrale del Burcardo (p51), Rome's cute-and-compact theatre museum.

If you plan on hitting several museums and sights, it's worth considering one of the various discount cards available (see p215). Many museums and galleries offer free admission to visitors under 18 and over 65 years, and discounted admission for EU citizens aged between 18 and 25. Some also offer reduced entry to accredited teachers and journalists, so it's always worth asking – and always worth carrying official photo ID.

Many museums and archaeological sites close their ticket office up to 75 minutes before closing time, so don't leave your visit to the last hour. Both Museo e Galleria Borghese and Domus Aurea (p95) require that you book tickets in advance. Several other museums and sights can be prebooked for a fee of €1.50 via **Pierreci** (☎ 06 399 67 700; www.pierreci.it) or **Ticketeria** (☎ 06 3 28 10; www.ticketeria.it), although this isn't normally necessary.

Most importantly, Rome's state-owned museums are closed on Mondays, so keep this in mind when planning your itinerary.

BEST FOR ANCIENT BOOTY
> Capitoline Museums (p42)
> Vatican Museums (p167)
> Museo Nazionale Romano: Palazzo Massimo alle Terme (p96)
> Museo Nazionale Romano: Palazzo Altemps (p57)
> Museo Nazionale Etrusco di Villa Giulia (p179)

BEST CLASSICAL SITES
> Palatine (p46)
> Colosseum (p44)
> Mercati di Traiano & Museo dei Fori Imperiali (p45)
> Terme di Caracalla (p133)
> Scavi Archeologici di Ostia Antica (p143)

BEST FOR...
> Subterranean surprises: Basilica e Catacombe di San Sebastiano (p126)
> Dramatic contrasts: Centrale Montemartini (p140)
> Renaissance and baroque masterpieces: Museo e Galleria Borghese (p179)
> East meets West: Museo Nazionale d'Arte Orientale (p95)
> Insight into modern Italy: Galleria Nazionale d'Arte Moderna (p175)

BEST FOR CHILDREN
> Explora – Museo dei Bambini di Roma (p175)
> Museo della Civiltà Romana (p141)
> Museo delle Arti e Tradizioni Popolari (p141)
> Capuchin Cemetery (p86)
> Catacombe di San Callisto (p126)

FOOD

Taste buds are spoilt rotten in Rome. Even the simplest snack can turn into a revelation, whether you're downing a slice of slow-food pizza from Pizzarium (p171) or a whisky-flavoured gelato from Il Gelato di San Crispino (p91). The secret is an obsession with top-notch ingredients and fresh, seasonal produce; whatever's on sale at the market that morning determines the day's menu. The surrounding Lazio region is the city's veritable larder, straining the vendors' stalls with everything from plump winter artichokes to succulent summer figs.

Roman grub is essentially earthy and rustic, featuring peasant staples such as *baccalà* (salted cod) and *guanciale* (pig's cheek), and revealing regional influences from neighbouring Abruzzo, Molise and Tuscany. This is the home of *spaghetti alla carbonara* (spaghetti with an egg, *pecorino* cheese and *guanciale* sauce) and *bucatini all'amatriciana* (pasta with a tomato, pancetta and chilli-pepper sauce), as well as comforting classics such as *pasta con ceci* (pasta with chickpeas), *spaghetti alla grigia* (pasta with piquant *pecorino* cheese, pancetta and black pepper) and *stracciatella* (soothing chicken soup with whisked egg and Parmesan). It's also where you'll savour deep-fried Jewish-Roman delicacies such as *fiori di zucca* (zucchini flowers) stuffed with mozzarella and anchovies and *carciofi alla giudia* (artichokes), as well as hearty offal offerings inspired by the city's former slaughterhouse (see p17).

And while old-school flavours are alive and kicking, new-school chefs are sexing them up with increasingly edgy, creative twists – think sesame-crusted salted cod with vanilla sauce, or tempura brain served with eggplant *caponata* (relish) and smoked garlic sauce. Two of the finest creators of contemporary Italian nosh are Francesco Apreda of Imàgo (p81) and Cristina Bowerman of Glass Hostaria (p156), chefs whose Italo-fusion fare has helped push Rome's dining scene beyond the predictable and provincial. Alongside other designer darlings such as Trattoria (p66), Obikà (p66) and Settembrini (p171), their restaurants are challenging the once-too-common fact that designer Roman nosh spots look better than they taste.

Not that the humble, gingham-tableclothed trattoria (or its smaller version, the *osteria*) is on its way out. Locals know all too well that some of the best meals in Rome are often the cheapest, served by gruff waiters in naff-looking boltholes, where vintage cooks have perfected their specialised repertoire over decades of kneading and stirring.

To eat like the locals, down a quick cappuccino and *cornetto* (Italian croissant) at a bar for *colazione* (breakfast), and follow it with a long, lazy *pranzo* (lunch), usually eaten about 1.30pm. Lunch is the day's main meal, with many smaller businesses shutting shop for several hours for some chilled-out midday munching. *Cena* (dinner) is usually a lighter affair, although demanding work schedules are slowly turning this around. And while most restaurants open for dinner at around 7.30pm, locals usually don't hit the tables until 8.30pm or 9pm. It's always a good idea to book ahead at very popular places (the day before is usually safe, two days prior for weekends), and a must at foodie favourites Colline Emiliane (p90), Da Gino (p64), Agata e Romeo (p101) and Imàgo. Note that many restaurants close for at least a week in August, so it's best to call ahead.

And while a full Italian meal consists of an antipasto, a *primo platto* (first course), a *secondo piatto* (second course) with an *insalata* (salad) or *contorno* (vegetable side dish), *dolci* (sweet), fruit, coffee and *digestivo* (liqueur), most Romans mix and match so ordering a *primo* followed by an *insalata* won't leave you blushing. Best of all, the often extensive choice of antipasti, pasta dishes, pizzas, salads and sides means that vegetarians won't go hungry, although it's worth asking if dishes are *senza carne o pesce* (without meat or fish). For completely stress-free vego/vegan dining, don't miss fine-dining Arancia Blu (p109) and Margutta RistorArte (p81).

BEST FOR MOD-ITALIAN SENSATIONS
> Imàgo (p81)
> Glass Hostaria (p156)
> Il Convivio Troiano (p65)
> Trattoria (p66)
> Ristorante Pastificio San Lorenzo (p111)

BEST FOR...
> Perfect pizza: Da Baffetto (p63)
> Abundant *aperitivo*: Freni e Frizioni (p159)
> Roman soul food: Da Gino (p64)
> Creative vegetarian: Arancia Blu (p109)
> Dreamy gelato: Il Gelato di San Crispino (p65 & p91)

Above The day market at Campo de' Fiori (p51) stocks the shelves of everyone from *mamma* to head chefs at top restaurants

GAY & LESBIAN

Despite the increasing visibility of (some may argue stereotyped) gays in the Italian media, Rome is yet to achieve the queer-friendly fabulousness of capitals like London, Berlin and Madrid. Topping the list of local party poopers is the Vatican, whose staunch conservatism regarding gay rights continues to keep civil unions at bay. A spate of highly publicised homophobic attacks in 2009 did little to help the city's GLBTI image.

Conservative elements aside, the winds of change are blowing. Italy's capital is home to Europe's first openly transgender parliamentarian (Vladimir Luxuria); the mammoth, summer-long Gay Village (see the boxed text, p29); as well as the 2011 edition of EuroPride (www.europride.info).

An excellent resource for visitors is GLBTI bookshop Libreria Babele (p215), which stocks gig-listing street press *AUT* (in Italian) and *Pride*. Useful online resources include www.gay.it (mostly in Italian) and www.mario mieli.org (in Italian), the latter belonging to the city's main socio-political GLBTI association, Circolo Mario Mieli di Cultura Omosessuale (p215). Like its younger rival, the Di'Gay Project (www.digayproject.org), the organisation spins out everything from cultural events to club nights. It also produces the handy *Gay Map of Rome,* available free in queer venues across town.

Of Rome's numerous saunas, Europa Multiclub (p215) is arguably the best. Saunas, and also several clubs, insist patrons have an Arcigay Uno Club Card, available from those venues requiring it.

Above Flying the flag in celebration during Gay Pride festivities

CENTRI SOCIALI

Wouldn't be seen dead in a squat? Think again. In Rome organised squats trade needles and fleas for cutting-edge art and music. Dubbed *centri sociali* (social centres), these hubs of counterculture were kick-started in the 1970s, when anti-establishment types wanted their own places to play punk, plan protests and just hang out. In the 1980s, *centri sociali* gave birth to Italy's hip-hop and rap-music scenes, with politicised local groups Assalti Frontali and Onda Rossa Posse getting their break in squats such as the legendary Forte Prenestino (see the boxed text, p113).

While the early days saw regular police hassle, most *centri sociali* have been around long enough to fit into the establishment – to the dismay of many old-schoolers. Brancaleone (see the boxed text, p113) draws top international DJs, while Villaggio Globale (p137) has hosted the likes of Massive Attack and reggae royal Macka B. Less fortunate of late is experimental arts incubator Rialtosantambrogio (p71), seized by police several times in 2009 for alleged noise and building safety breeches. Mid-2010, the centre's future was on the line, with plans to move it from its real-estate goldmine address.

Despite the 'mainstreaming', these grungy hangouts still dish out Rome's most alternative (and often cheapest) entertainment. On any night, you could be attending a Charles Bukowski poetry slam, eyeing up an indie fashion show or working up a sweat to cult French DJ Miss Kittin. To find out what's on, check the venues' websites, scan *Trovaroma* (Thursday insert in newspaper *La Repubblica*) and *Roma C'e'* on Wednesday, and see listings in free fortnightly minimag *Zero* (www.zero.eu), available from bars and clubs.

Above Villaggio Globale (p137) funks it up with big-name indie and hip-hop bands in Rome's former slaughterhouse

FOOTBALL

Forget St Peter's Basilica. Rome's true centre of worship is the Stadio Olimpico (p183). From September to May, the faithful flock here to venerate their cashed-up, goal-scoring deities with a fervour of biblical proportions. In Italy football verges on obsession. When the national team scored the World Cup in 2006, half a million fans flocked to the Circo Massimo to watch pin-up captain Fabio Cannavaro flaunt the trophy.

The victory had been a leap of faith for Italians, rocked only months earlier by a match-fixing scandal involving Juventus team manager Luciano Moggi. Further soul-searching occurred in 2007 after a spate of stadium clashes across Italy led to tougher security measures, including named tickets and photo-ID checks at stadium entry points.

When it comes to loyalties, Rome is fiercely divided by its two premiere-league rivals: Lazio (the *biancazzuri* – white and blues; www.sslazio.it in Italian) and AS Roma (the *gialloross* – yellow and reds; www.asroma.it in Italian). While Lazio fans have an unfortunate reputation for racism and right-wing sympathies, *romanisti* (Roma supporters) celebrate their working-class, Roman-Jewish roots, as well as their celebrity captain Francesco Totti (see the boxed text, p160), Italy's highest-paid player. His chipping technique, called *er cucchiaio* (spoon) in Roman dialect, is the stuff of legend.

To cheer him on, join the *romanisti* in Stadio Olimpico's *curva sud* (southern stand). To jinx him, join Lazio fans in the *curva nord* (northern stand).

Above Football fans wave scarves in support of AS Roma at Stadio Olimpico (p183)

>BACKGROUND

Eye to eye with Emperor Constantine at the Capitoline Museums (p42)

BACKGROUND

HISTORY

SHE-WOLVES, TWINS & TANTRUMS

According to legend, Romulus and Remus were the fruit of a steamy encounter between vestal virgin Rhea Silva and Mars, the god of war. Set adrift on the Tiber to escape King Amulius' death warrant, the infant twins were discovered on the banks below the Palatine (p46) by a clucky she-wolf, who suckled them until a shepherd found and raised them. When Amulius captured the unruly Remus, brother Romulus set him free, knocking off the king and paving the way for a city of their own. But the brotherly goodwill was short-lived: bickering over the new city walls drove Romulus to murder his brother and take full credit for the founding of Rome on 21 April 753 BC.

Most historians have a more prosaic take on the city's birth, which involved an amalgamation of Etruscan, Latin and Sabine settlements on the Palatine, Esquiline and Quirinal hills.

RISE & FALL OF AN EMPIRE

The deposition of the Etruscans' seventh (and final) king, Tarquin the Proud, heralded the birth of the Roman Republic in 509 BC. Replacing royalty was the Senate, comprising elders from the city's premium fami-lies whose unofficial motto was 'divide and conquer'. The Etruscans were assimilated, surrounding tribes allied and Rome's influence spread. The Appian Way (Via Appia Antica; p22) became Rome's first superhighway, and a thriving port was established in Ostia (see the boxed text, p143) in 380 BC to stock the burgeoning city. After booting out the Greeks from southern Italy in 272 BC and defeating the Carthaginians in the Punic Wars (264–146 BC), Rome finally emerged as the Mediterranean's superpower.

Equally power-hungry was rising military star Julius Caesar, who defied Roman law by 'crossing the Rubicon' border and wresting power in AD 49. Five years later, he was assassinated near Largo di Torre Argentina (Map pp52–3, E5). After almost two decades of civil war, Caesar's height-challenged nephew, Octavian (using the title Augustus; r 27 BC–AD 14), defeated Mark Antony and his Egyptian lover Queen Cleopatra VII to become Rome's first emperor, thereafter leading Rome into a period of stability and success. Writers such as Virgil, Ovid, Horace and Tibillus boosted the city's cultural kudos; buildings were restored; and monuments such as the Ara Pacis Augustae (Altar of Peace; p75) were erected. As the emperor himself so modestly put it: 'I found Rome brick, I left it marble.'

But if Augustus set new standards of artistic achievement, his successors reached new depths of depravity. Tiberius (r 14–37) threw his enemies off the cliffs of Capri; Caligula (r 37–41) dressed up as deities; and Nero (r 54–68) blamed the great fire of AD 64 on the city's Christians, leading to the persecution of thousands, including St Peter and St Paul. Sounder rule under Trajan (r 98–117) and Hadrian (r 117–38) was followed by more upheaval – Barbarian invasions led Emperor Aurelian (r 270–75) to build the still-standing Aurelian wall, while the joint abdication of Maximian and Diocletian in 305 left the sprawling empire to Galerius in the east and Constantius in the west. Inspired by a vision of the cross, Constantius' son Constantine (r 306–37) defeated his own rival Maxentius on Ponte Milvio (p180) in 312, becoming Rome's first Christian leader and commissioning the city's first Christian basilica, San Giovanni in Laterano (p118). When Constantine shifted his power base to Byzantium (modern Istanbul) in 330, however, Rome's *cuput mundi* (capital of the world) days were over.

POPES, ARTISTS & REINVENTIONS

By the 6th century, Barbarian, Goth and Vandal attacks had left the city in ruins and a population of 1.5 million had shrunk to a measly 80,000. Ready at the rescue was Pope Gregory the Great (r 590–604), who restored infrastructure, negotiated with invaders, built basilicas and pulled in the pilgrims. When Pope Leo III (r 795–816) allied with the Franks and crowned Charlemagne Holy Roman Emperor in 800, Rome's starring role on the Christian stage was set. The papacy had by now become a lavish prize for Europe's power brokers, with the French temporarily taking control and moving the papal court to Avignon from 1309 to 1379. When the papacy returned in the form of Pope Gregory XI in 1377, Rome was once more a city tattered by vicious feuding between powerful rival families such as the Colonna and the Orsini.

Rome's much-needed revamp arrived with the Renaissance, when a succession of ambitious 15th- and 16th-century pontiffs commissioned artistic greats to turn the has-been backwater into an enviable capital. Michelangelo (1475–1564) frescoed the Sistine Chapel in the Vatican Museums (p167); Bramante (1445–1514) redesigned St Peter's Basilica

BACKGROUND

(p163); and Caravaggio (1571–1610) brought his trademark chiaroscuro to Chiesa di San Luigi dei Francesi (p54).

It wasn't all plain sailing. In 1527 Pope Clement VII (r 1523–34) took refuge in the Castel Sant'Angelo (p163) as Charles V's Spanish troops ransacked Rome. Remarkably, the papacy survived and a new generation of over-the-top churches such as Chiesa del Gesù (p51) gave the proverbial finger to Martin Luther's burgeoning Reformation.

Less inspiring was the Counter-Reformation's persecution of intellectuals and free-thinkers, among them Galileo Galilei (1564–1642) and Dominican monk Giordano Bruno (1548–1600) – the latter was burnt at the stake in Campo de' Fiori (p51). Rome's Jews faired little better under Pope Paul IV (1475–1559), his *Cum nimis absurdum* canon forcing them to live in the dank Ghetto until Italy's unification in 1870.

Ironically, out of the repressive Roman Inquisition the baroque age burst onto the scene in the 17th century. Bombastic fountains, churches and sculptures sprouted across the city, among them Bernini's sexually charged *Blessed Ludovica Albertoni* in Chiesa di San Francesco d'Assisi a Ripa (p150) and Borromini's masterpiece Chiesa di San Carlo alle Quattro Fontane (p86).

The 18th-century rage for all things classical turned Rome into a Grand Tour stopover, with thousands of rosy-cheeked Brits and northern Continentals heading in to wax lyrical amid the ruins. Among them were poets Byron, Shelley and Keats and German wordsmith Goethe, who stopped by to write his 1817 travelogue, *Italian Journey*. While Wagner took tea at Caffè Greco (p82), the city's young and beautiful lingered on the Spanish Steps (p76) in the hope of being picked up as artists' models.

FASCIST DAYS

One man who would have had little success on the steps is Benito Mussolini (1883–1945). Exploiting the unemployment and high inflation following WWI, the stout socialist-turned-Fascist won complete control of Italy by late 1925. Fancying himself a modern-day Augustus, *il duce* (the leader) forced Rome through an extreme makeover, bulldozing the Via dei Fori Imperiali right through the city's ancient heartland, commissioning monumental sports complex Foro Italico and developing the austere showpiece suburb of EUR (p138). To keep the church onside, he signed the Lateran Pact in 1929, declaring Catholicism Italy's sole religion and giving the Vatican independent status.

Mussolini's own prayers for a glorious burial alongside his ancient Roman idol at Mausoleo di Augusto fell on deaf ears. Defeated by the Allies, the executed dictator was hung upside down and stoned In Milan's Piazza Loreto in 1945. The following year, the monarchy was ditched by referendum and Italy's blue-bloods were forced into exile (allowed to return as private citizens and magazine fodder in 2003).

CONTEMPORARY COMEBACKS

The opening scene of Federico Fellini's film *La Dolce Vita* (1960) exemplifies the halcyon days of Rome in the late 1950s and 1960s – an era marked by urban expansion, growing middle-class wealth and a taste for internationalism. In 1957 the Treaty of Rome was signed in the Sala degli Orazi e Curiazi at the Capitoline Museums (p42), founding the European Economic Community (EEC). Three years later, the Olympic Games were held at the Stadio Olimpico (p183).

Although blighted by student and worker revolts (and the odd spot of terrorism), the 1970s and '80s were marked by an economic growth that was sorely undone in the '90s by rising unemployment, a floundering lira and major government corruption scandals.

A seasoned comeback kid, the city of Rome smartened up its act for the Jubilee Year celebrations in 2000, restoring monuments, revamping museums and commissioning cutting-edge architectural showpieces. Five years later, a gob-smacking 4 million poured into the capital in a single week to mourn the death of the people's pope, John Paul II.

FURTHER READING

Complex and contradictory, Rome is worth its weight in books. To dig deeper into its psyche, flip open the following titles:

> *The Oxford History of the Roman World* (2001) John Boardman, Jasper Griffin and Oswyn Murray (eds) – fascinating essays on literature, arts and politics.
> *Rome: The Biography of a City* (1998) Christopher Hibbert – an overview of the city's history.
> *The Fall of the Roman Empire* (2005) Peter Heather – a fresh interpretation of the empire's last 100 years.
> *Roman Tales* (1954) Alberto Moravia – 61 short stories about struggling working-class Roman characters by one of the 20th century's greatest Italian scribes.
> *Food of Love* (2004) Anthony Capella – a light-hearted comedy of errors set in Trastevere, with a scrumptious foodie flavour.

GOVERNMENT & POLITICS

The resignation of Rome's left-wing mayor Walter Veltroni in February 2008 ended one of the city's most high-profile and celebrated political terms. A jazz-obsessed cinephile (and the Italian voice of Major Turkey Lurkey in Disney's 2005 animation feature *Chicken Little*), Veltroni had a passion for the arts and star-studded celebrations, heralding a series of major cultural initiatives. Soon after his election win in 2001, €5 million was allocated for the development of La Casa del Jazz (p145). In 2004 Veltroni inaugurated the Casa del Cinema (p182), before convincing Nicole Kidman to help launch Rome's inaugural international film festival in 2006. A year later, the city rolled out a series of VIP-studded events to celebrate designer Valentino's 45 years in fashion.

With Veltroni focused on nabbing the nation's top job – an ultimately unsuccessful venture – Rome's mayoral shoes were filled by tough-talking, right-wing Gianni Alemanno, member of Silvio Berlusconi's Il Popolo della Libertà party. Alemanno's electoral victory in April 2008 was overshadowed by his past. The Bari-born politician is an ex-MSI (*Movimento Sociale Italiano;* Italian Social Movement) activist and member of the AN (*Alleanza Nazionale;* National Alliance), and news of his mayoral win drew Fascist salutes from far-right supporters – a PR nightmare Alemanno was quick to distance himself from. Indeed, since taking office, he has had to walk an ideological tightrope as he tries to position himself as a mayor for everyone. The results have been mixed. Infuriating Rome's Jewish community in September 2008 by refusing to condemn Fascism as 'absolute evil', Alemanno won praise two months later for leading a group of 250 schoolchildren to Auschwitz and urging them never to forget the tragedy of the Holocaust.

ROME LIFE

Many Romans lament that their famous gregariousness has been sorely tested by euro-era price hikes, flagging infrastructure, maddening traffic (400,000 scooters alone) and choking pollution. High rents see 70% of Romans aged between 20 and 30 still living at 'hotel *mamma*', while a 2007 study revealed traces of cocaine and cannabis in Rome's less-than-fresh air.

Grazie a Dio (thank God) it's not all doom and gloom. On becoming mayor in 2008, Alemanno inherited a vast urban renewal plan from his predecessor Walter Veltroni. During his time in opposition, Alemanno had often spoken out against the plan but as mayor he has backed the ambitious programme, which calls for the construction of 100,000 new houses and flats, 14 new transport corridors (including four Metro lines), the creation of 19 parks and a substantial redevelopment of the capital's run-down suburbs.

In March 2009, Alemanno unveiled his own proposals for a massive redevelopment project in Rome's southern and eastern suburbs, with plans including an aqueduct in EUR, a much-needed revamp of the Ostia seafront and the construction of a Disney-style Ancient Roman theme park. This last proposal provoked a predictable uproar, with critics saying it would be better to spend money restoring the real Colosseum rather than building a kitsch facsimile, and advocates hailing the prospect of new jobs and a tourism boost.

Greater environmental consciousness has seen city authorities tackle Romans' penchant for cars with extended traffic restrictions and the introduction of gradually more popular car- and bike-sharing schemes. And greater security consciousness saw Alemanno launch a 24-hour CCTV monitoring centre in March 2010, aimed at streamlining video surveillance of the entire city, from museums to bus lanes. By mid-2010, Rome's army of CCTV cameras numbered 5000 – an increase of 3700 since March the same year.

FILM

There was a certain irony when fire swept through Rome's Cinecittà studios in August 2007. Once the heart of a booming local film industry, its partial destruction felt like a smouldering statement on the current state of Italy's underfunded, underinspiring film scene. Quentin Tarantino's appraisal at the 2007 Cannes film festival was less poetic: 'New Italian cinema is just depressing. Recent Italian films I've seen all seem the same. All they talk about is boys growing up, or girls growing up, or couples in crisis, or holidays for the mentally disabled.' Among the many *offesi* (offended) was the perma-tanned Sophia Loren, who

TOP FIVE FILMS SET IN ROME
> *Ladri di Biciclette* (1948) Vittorio de Sica
> *Roman Holiday* (1953) William Wyler
> *La Dolce Vita* (1960) Federico Fellini
> *Caro Diario* (1993) Nanni Moretti
> *Saturno Contro* (2006) Ferzan Ozpetek

replied: 'How dare he talk about Italian cinema when he doesn't know anything about American cinema?'

Wounded pride aside, recent Italian offerings are a far cry from the days of neorealist masterpieces such as Roberto Rossellini's *Roma Città Aperta* (Rome Open City; 1945) and Vittorio de Sica's *Ladri di Biciclette* (Bicycle Thieves; 1948), or the cutting-edge cool of Fellini's *Roma* (1972). And while modern Roman directors include award-winning Nanni Moretti, Roberto Benigni and Turkish-born Ferzan Ozpetek, the local scene is still waiting for a brash world icon to rival Spain's Pedro Almodovar.

Not that Rome is dry of 21st-century celluloid standouts. Recent contenders include Ozpetek's coming-out comedy *Mine Vaganti* (Loose Cannons; 2010), Matteo Garrone's Cannes prize-winner *Gomorra* (Gomorrah; 2008), Emanuele Crialese's trans-Atlantic epic *Nuovomondo* (Golden Door; 2006) and Saverio Costanzo's Israeli/Palestinian-themed *Private* (2004).

DIRECTORY

TRANSPORT

ARRIVAL & DEPARTURE

AIR

Rome is served by most of the world's major international airlines, the majority of which use Rome's main international airport, Leonardo da Vinci (commonly known as Fiumicino). Low-cost carriers and charter flights mainly fly into the city's much smaller second airport, Ciampino.

Leonardo da Vinci (Fiumicino) Airport

Rome's major airport, **Leonardo da Vinci** (☎ 06 6 59 51; www.adr.it) is 30km southwest of the city centre. It's divided into five terminals: Terminals A and AA (domestic flights), Terminal B (international flights to Schengen countries), Terminal C (all other international flights) and Terminal 5 (flights to the USA and Israel).

The Leonardo Express train offers the easiest connection to/from Fiumicino. Express services depart from Platform 25 at Stazione Termini (Map p93, D2) every 30 minutes from 5.52am to 10.52pm. From Fiumicino, trains run between 6.35am and 11.35pm. Journey time is 30 minutes each way. Single tickets cost €11 from station ticket machines and €12 from the stand on the platform (under 12 years for free).

To reach Stazione Termini from the airport, don't take trains marked Orte or Fara Sabina. These slower trains stop at Rome's Trastevere, Ostiense and Tiburtina stations only. If you require these stations, services run every 15 minutes (hourly on Sundays and public holidays) from 5.57am to 10.57pm, and from Tiburtina from 5.06am until 10.36pm. Journey time is 30 minutes to Ostiense and 45

CLIMATE CHANGE & TRAVEL

Travel – especially air travel – is a significant contributor to global climate change. At Lonely Planet, we believe that all who travel have a responsibility to limit their personal impact. As a result, we have teamed with Rough Guides and other concerned industry partners to support Climate Care, which allows people to offset the greenhouse gases they are responsible for with contributions to energy-saving projects and other climate-friendly initiatives in the developing world. Lonely Planet offsets all staff and author travel.

For more information, turn to the responsible travel pages on www.lonelyplanet.com. For details on offsetting your carbon emissions and a carbon calculator, go to www.climatecare.org.

minutes to Tiburtina. Tickets cost €5.50. Purchase tickets from vending machines in the arrivals hall and train station, from ticket offices and from *tabacchi* (newsagents).

Cotral (☎ 800 15 00 08; www .cotralspa.it in Italian) runs eight daily buses from Stazione Tiburtina via Stazione Termini to Fiumicino, including night services at 12.30am, 1.15am, 2.30am and 3.45am, returning at 1.15am, 2.15am, 3.30am and 5am. Tickets, available on the bus, cost €4.50. Neither Stazione Termini nor Stazione Tiburtina is a particularly safe area to hang around at night.

If you want to take a cab, use only licensed taxis, coloured white with a taxi sign on the roof and an identifying number on the doors. The set fare to Rome's *centro storico* (historic city centre) is €40, which is valid for up to four passengers and includes luggage. Expect a journey time of at least 45 minutes.

All major car-hire companies are represented at Fiumicino.

Ciampino Airport

If you're heading into Rome on budget carriers like Easyjet or Ryanair, chances are you'll be landing at **Ciampino** (☎ 06 6 59 51; www.adr.it), located 15km southeast of the city centre.

Your best bet to and from the airport is the **Terravision** (☎ 06 454 41 345; www.terravision.eu) coach service. Buses depart from Via Marsala outside Stazione Termini roughly every 20 to 40 minutes between 4.30am and 9.20pm and from Ciampino between 8.15am and 12.15am. Buy tickets (single/return €4/8) for the 45-minute journey from Terracafè at Stazione Termini or at Ciampino.

Alternatively, **SIT** (☎ 06 591 68 26; www.sitbusshuttle.com) covers the same route, with regular departures from Stazione Termini between 4.30am and 9.30pm, and from Ciampino between 7.45am and 11.15pm. Single tickets, available on the bus, cost €8 from Termini, €6 from Ciampino.

Schiaffini (☎ 800 700 805; www .schiaffini.com) runs up to 20 daily services to and from Via Giovanni Giolitti outside Termini. Buy tickets from sellers outside the bus (€4.50) or on board (€6.50).

By taxi the set rate to or from Ciampino is €30 and journey time is 50 minutes. Take licensed taxis only – coloured white, with a rooftop taxi sign and an identification number on the doors.

TRAIN

Stazione Termini (Map p93, D2) is Rome's main train and transport hub, with regular services connecting the capital to other European destinations, major Italian cities and many smaller towns. The station's helpful but busy **informa-**

GREENER WAYS TO ROME

Cheap flights might be the quickest way to Rome from other European hubs, but it's worth considering the train. Not only will it reduce your carbon footprint, it'll make the journey as much of an event as the destination itself. Catch the 12.30pm Eurostar from London's St Pancras station, and you'll have time for a quick drink in Paris before catching the overnight Paris–Rome Palatino service. Enjoy a three-course meal, sleep off a bottle of wine and wake up to Italian landscapes. Best of all, you'll step off in the centre of Rome. While advanced bookings can offer discounted fares, €310 for London to Rome one way is realistic for a bunk in a six-berth couchette. Check www.seat61.com/Italy.htm for details and booking links.

tion office (⏱ 7am-9.45pm) is located opposite platform 5, although it's often quicker to get information online at www.trenitalia.com or by calling ☎ 89 20 21 (in Italian).

GETTING AROUND

The best way to get around (and enjoy) Rome's relatively compact *centro storico* is on foot. The city's two Metro lines (A and B) are of limited value to visitors, bypassing much of the historic hub. More extensive is the city's bus network, which, like the city's modest tram network, is run by **ATAC** (☎ 06 5 70 03, toll-free 800 431 784; www.atac.roma.it). The website features a journey planner and downloadable transport maps. In this book, the nearest Metro, bus or tram is noted after the Ⓜ , 🚌 or 🚋 in each listing.

TRAVEL PASSES

Public transport tickets are valid on all modes of public transit, except on trains to Fiumicino. BIT (*biglietto integrato a tempo*; €1) is a single ticket valid for 75 minutes and one Metro ride; BIG (*biglietto integrato giornaliero*; €4) is a daily ticket; BTI (*biglietto turistico integrato*; €11) is a three-day ticket; CIS (*carta integrate settimanale*; €16) is a weekly ticket; and *abbonamento mensile* tickets (€30) cover a month. If you intend exploring neighbourhoods beyond the *centro storico* (which you should), you're usually better off buying a day or multiday pass, rather than single-trip tickets.

Purchase tickets at *tabacchi*, at newsstands and from vending machines before boarding buses, trams and trains. Validate them at the Metro gate or in the machines onboard buses and trams.

Note that the Roma Pass (p215) comes with a three-day travel pass.

BUS

The main bus station is in front of Stazione Termini (Map p93, C1),

RECOMMENDED MODES OF TRANSPORT

	Piazza Navona	Colosseum	Spanish Steps	Auditorium Parco della Musica
Piazza Navona	n/a	🚌 15min	walk 20min	walk 30min, 🚌 15min & walk 5min
Colosseum	🚌 15min	n/a	🚌 20min	M 18min, 🚌 15min & walk 5min
Spanish Steps	walk 20min	🚌 20min	n/a	M 2min, 🚌 15min & walk 5min
Auditorium Parco della Musica	walk 5min, 🚌 15min & walk 30min	walk 5min, 🚌 15min & M 18min	walk 5min, 🚌 15min & M 2min	n/a
Vatican City	🚌 15min & walk 5min	🚌 20min	walk 15min & M 8min	walk 15min, 🚌 20min & walk 5min
Trastevere	walk 25min	walk 30min	🚌 25min	🚌 20min, 🚌 20min & walk 5min
Stazione Termini	🚌 20min & walk 5min	M 6min	M 10min	M 10min, 🚌 15min & walk 5min
Piazzale Ostiense	🚌 30min	M 6min	M 20min	M 18min, 🚌 15min & walk 5min
San Lorenzo	walk 15min, 🚌 20min & walk 5min	🚌 20min	walk 15min & M 10min	🚌 30min

where there's an **information booth** (🕒 7.30am-8pm). Other hubs are at Largo di Torre Argentina (Map pp52–3, E5), Piazza Venezia (Map p41, C1) and Piazza di San Silvestro (Map p85, A3). Buses generally run from about 5.30am to midnight.

Two of the most useful routes are 64 (Termini–Centro Storico– St Peter's) and 40 Express (same route, quicker, less crowds). Both

are notorious for pickpockets, so be on guard.

Other handy routes include the H (Termini–Trastevere), 3 (Stazione Trastevere–Testaccio–San Giovanni–San Lorenzo–Villa Borghese (northern entrance), and 105 (Termini–Piazza Vittorio Emanuele II–Il Pigneto).

More than 20 lines operate all-night services, running every 15 minutes Friday and Saturday,

Vatican City	Trastevere	Stazione Termini	Piazzale Ostiense	San Lorenzo
walk 5min & 🚌 10min	walk 25min	walk 5min & 🚌 20min	🚌 30min	walk 2min & 🚌 30min
🚌 20min	walk 30min	Ⓜ 6min	Ⓜ 6min	🚌 20min
Ⓜ 8min & walk 15min	🚌 25min	Ⓜ 10min	Ⓜ 20min	Ⓜ 20min
walk 5min, 🚊 20min & walk 15min	walk 5min, 🚊 20min & 🚌 20min	walk 5min, 🚊 15min & Ⓜ 10min	walk 5min, 🚊 15min & Ⓜ 18min	🚊 30min
n/a	🚌 20min	walk 15min & Ⓜ 16min	walk 15min & Ⓜ 25min	🚌 40min
🚌 20min	n/a	🚌 20min	🚊 20min	🚌 30min
Ⓜ 16min & walk 15min	🚌 20min	n/a	Ⓜ 8min	🚌 15min
Ⓜ 25min & walk 15min	🚊 20min	Ⓜ 8min	n/a	🚌 20min
🚌 40min	🚌 30min	🚌 15min	🚌 20min	n/a

and every 30 minutes Sunday to Thursday. Services are marked by an N after the number.

METRO

With Termini their only interchange point, Linea A (Line A; red) and Linea B (Line B; blue) traverse the city in an X-shape, missing most of the areas of interest to visitors. Trains run approximately every three to 10 minutes between 5.30am and 11.30pm (one hour later on Saturdays).

Tickets can be bought at station vending machines and are valid on city buses and trams.

TRAM

The most useful tram routes for visitors are line 8, which connects Largo di Torre Argentina (Map pp52–3, E5) to Trastevere and beyond; line 2, which links Piazzale

Flaminio (Map p73, A1; just north of Piazza del Popolo) to MAXXI (p178) and Auditorium Parco della Musica (p182); and line 19, connecting Il Pigneto and San Lorenzo to Quartiere Coppedè (p180) and GNAM (p175).

TRAIN
Unless you're travelling beyond the main metropolitan area to sites such as Ostia Antica (see the boxed text, p143), you shouldn't need to use Rome's suburban train network.

TAXI
Use only licensed taxis (coloured white with a taxi sign on the roof and an identifying number on the doors) and always go with the metered fare, never an arranged price (the set fares to and from the airports excepted). In town (within the ring road) flag fall is €2.80 (Sundays/10pm to 7am €4/5.80), then it's €0.92 per kilometre.

Hailing cabs doesn't usually work. Use a taxi rank or book one over the phone – be aware that the meter starts running as soon as you book. For bookings, try the following:
La Capitale (☎ 06 49 94)
Radio Taxi (☎ 06 35 70)
Samarcanda (☎ 06 55 51)

PRACTICALITIES
BUSINESS HOURS
Banks generally open from 8.30am to 1.30pm and from 2.45pm to 4.30pm on weekdays. Some central branches also open from 8.30am to 12.30pm on Saturdays.

Most shops in central Rome open between 9am and 7.30pm (or 9.30am and 8pm) Monday to Saturday. Some larger shops and supermarkets also trade on Sundays, typically from 11am to to 7pm. Many smaller, family-run shops open from 9am to 1pm and 3.30pm to 7.30pm (or 4pm to 8pm) Monday to Saturday. That said, it is not uncommon for shops to close earlier if business is slow on a particular day.

Many food shops close on Thursday afternoons in winter and Saturday afternoons in summer, while other shops may be closed Monday mornings.

Most restaurants operate from noon to 3pm and 7.30pm to 11pm (later in summer). Bars and cafés usually open from 7.30am to 8pm, although some remain open until 1am or 2am. *Discoteche* (clubs) usually open at about 10pm, although there won't be a crowd before midnight.

Opening hours for the major sites vary enormously. Many of the big archaeological drawcards open from 9am until an hour before sunset. Major museums tend to open from 9.30am to 7pm. Note that last admission to museums is generally one hour before the stated closing time, and that most state-run museums are closed on Mondays. Individual opening hours are given for each listing in this book.

DISCOUNTS

Discount cards can be purchased at any of the museums or monuments listed. The Roma Pass is also available at tourist information kiosks. Look for the following discount cards:

Appia Antica Card (adult/EU 18-24yr €6/3, valid 7 days) covers the Terme di Caracalla, Mausoleo di Cecilia Metella and Villa dei Quintili.

Archaeologia Card (adult/EU 18-25yr €23.50/13.50 plus €2 for special exhibitions, valid 7 days) covers all four Museo Nazionale Romano venues, as well as the Colosseum, Palatine, Roman Forum, Terme di Caracalla, Mausoleo di Cecilia Metella and Villa dei Quintili.

Museo Nazionale Romano Card (adult/ EU 18-24yr €7/3 plus €3 for special exhibitions, valid 3 days) provides entrance to all venues of Museo Nazionale Romano – Crypta Balbi, Palazzo Altemps, Palazzo Massimo alle Terme and Terme di Diocleziano.

Roma Pass (www.romapass.it; €25, valid 3 days) includes free admission to two museums or sights (from a list of 38), reduced entry to extra sights and events, and unlimited public transport. If you use it for more-expensive

sights such as Capitoline Museums, it's real value for money.

GAY & LESBIAN TRAVELLERS

In addition to the gay and lesbian venues listed in the individual neighbourhood chapters of this book, check out the following resources and venues:

Circolo Mario Mieli di Cultura Omosessuale (Map p139, B6; ☎ 06 541 39 85; www.mariomieli.it in Italian; Via Ffeso 2A) Rome's main GLBT (gay, lesbian, bisexual and transgender) organisation. Churns out film nights and fun one-off club nights at Muccassassina (see the boxed text, p113), as well as the handy *Gay Map of Rome*, available free in queer venues across town.

Europa Multiclub (Map p85, D1; ☎ 06 482 36 50; www.qaysaune.it; Via Aurellana 40) Of the city's three saunas, this is the best in town. Note that saunas insist you have an Arcigay Uno Club Card (€15), available from the venues.

Libreria Babele (Map pp52-3, B4; ☎ 06 687 66 28; www.libreriababele.it in Italian; Via dei Banchi Vecchi 116) GLBT bookshop that stocks gig-listing street press such as *AUT* (in Italian) and monthly magazine *Pride*. Check the bookshop's website for queer cultural events.

HOLIDAYS

New Year's Day 1 January
Epiphany 6 January
Easter Monday March/April
Liberation Day 25 April
Labour Day 1 May
Feast of SS Peter & Paul 29 June
Ferragosto (Feast of the Assumption) 15 August

All Saints' Day 1 November
Christmas Day 25 December
Santo Stefano (Boxing Day) 26 December

INTERNET

Free wi-fi hot spots cover much of central Rome, including major parks and piazzas. It's free (for an hour a day) but you need to register and to do this you'll need an Italian mobile-phone number. If you've got one, open your browser, fill in the registration form and validate the account with a quick phone call (from the mobile whose number you've provided).

Internet cafés are also plentiful but you'll need to show official photo ID. Try the following:

Internet Café (Map p93, B3; ☎ 06 478 23 051; Via Cavour 213; ⏱ 11am-1am Mon-Fri, 3pm-1am Sat & Sun, closed late Dec-early Jan) Rates are per hour (€2 to €2.90) and vary according to the time of day; they're cheapest before 4pm.

New Internet Point (Map pp148-9, E4; ☎ 06 583 33 316; Piazza Sonnino 27; ⏱ 8.30am-10pm) Across the road from the tourist information point. Rate is €4 per hour.

Yex Internet Point (Map pp52-3, D5; Piazza Sant'Andrea della Valle 1; ⏱ 10am-10pm) Close to Piazza Navona. All terminals have webcams. The rate is €4.80 per hour.

INTERNET RESOURCES

Dolce Vita Blog (www.blogdolcevita.com) Italy-wide blog covering festivals, events, Italian design, holiday hot spots, and offbeat news.

In Rome Now (www.inromenow.com) Run by two American expats, with loads of information, from what's on and the weather, to insider tips and a blog.
Lonely Planet (www.lonelyplanet.com) Information, links and resources.
Pierreci (www.pierreci.it) Book tickets online to the Colosseum and other major sights.
Roma C'è (www.romace.it in Italian) Savvy, user-friendly info about the week's hottest cultural happenings.
Roma Style (www.romastyle.info in Italian) Up-to-date info on Rome's alternative music and culture scene.
Roma Turismo (www.romaturismo.it) Rome Tourist Board's comprehensive website, listing official accommodation options, upcoming events and more.
Rome Review (www.romereview.com) Heaps of reviews, as well as listings of films screening in English and podcasts.

LANGUAGE
BASICS

Hello. (morning/ afternoon and evening)	Buongiorno./ Buonasera.
Goodbye.	Arrivederci.
How are you?	Come sta?
I'm fine, thanks.	Bene, grazie.
Excuse me.	Mi scusi./ Permesso.
Yes.	Sì.
No.	No.
Thanks.	Grazie.
You're welcome.	Prego.
Do you speak English?	Parla inglese?
I don't understand.	Non capisco.
How much is this?	Quanto costa?
That's too expensive.	È troppo caro.

EATING & DRINKING

That was delicious!	*Era squisito!*
I'm a vegetarian.	*Sono vegetariano/a. (m/f)*
Please bring the bill.	*Il conto, per favore.*

EMERGENCIES

I'm sick.	*Sono ammalato/a. (m/f)*
Help!	*Aiuto!*
Call the police!	*Chiama la polizia!*
Call an ambulance!	*Chiama un'ambulanza!*

TALK THE TALK

Good for you!	*Bella pe' tte!*
You crack me up (you make me laugh)!	*Sei un tajo!*
See you later.	*Se beccamo.*
There's no way/possibility. (lit: There's no tripe for cats.)	*Non c'è trippa pe' gatti.*
Gosh!	*Ammazza!*
Stop it!	*Accanna!*
Cupola of St Peter's Basilica.	*Er Cuppolone.*

MONEY

Rome isn't a bargain destination. Two top-notch museums, an all-day travel pass, a cheap lunch, a couple of coffees and a decent restaurant dinner can easily set you back €80 a day, on top of your hotel bill. Add a few cocktails and a little retail therapy, and watch the figure soar. Seasoned budget travellers might get by on €40 per day, excluding accommodation expenses. Public transport is relatively cheap, and many museums are free to EU citizens under 18 and over 65 years and discounted to EU citizens aged between 18 and 24 years. It's also worth considering the various discounts (p215) available.

For currency exchange rates, see the inside front cover.

TELEPHONE

Italy uses the GSM 900/1800 cellular system, compatible with phones from the UK, Europe, Australia and most of Asia, and dual-band GSM 1900/900 phones from North America and Japan. Public phones are plentiful in Rome, although most only accept *schede telefoniche* (phone cards). Cards cost €5, €10 and €20 and can be bought from *tabacchi*, as well as some newsstands and bars. Some phones accept major credit cards. For international calls, it's better value to buy one of a range of long-distance phone cards from *tabacchi*.

COUNTRY & CITY CODES

Italy's country code is ☎ 39, and the Rome area code is ☎ 06. Do not omit the 0 if calling Rome from abroad. To call abroad from Italy, dial ☎ 00 before the country code.

USEFUL NUMBERS
Local directory enquiries (☎ 89 24 12)
International directory enquiries (☎ 41 76)
Reverse-charge (collect) (☎ 170)

TIPPING
In restaurants where a service fee is not included, it's customary to leave a 10% tip. Rounding your taxi fare to the nearest euro will suffice, and don't forget to drop about €4 into the porter's hand at A-list hotels.

TOURIST INFORMATION
Comune di Roma runs a free **multilingual tourist infoline** (☎ 06 06 08; www.060608.com; ☿ 9am-9pm) providing information on events, hotels, transport etc, as well as booking museum, exhibition and concert tickets. Maps and other information are available at its tourist information points:

Fiumicino Airport (Terminal C, International Arrivals; ☿ 9am-6.30pm)

Monti & Esquiline (Map p93) Stazione Termini (D2; ☿ 8am-8.30pm) In the hall running parallel to platform 24; Via Nazionale (B2; ☿ 9.30am-7pm)

Piazza Navona (Map pp52-3, D3; ☿ 9.30am-7pm)

Trastevere (Map pp148-9, E4; Piazza Sonnino; ☿ 9.30am-7pm)

Trevi (Map p85, A4; Via Marco Minghetti; ☿ 9.30am-7pm)

The **Rome Tourist Board** (APT; ☎ 06 06 08; www.turismoroma.it; Terminal B, International Arrivals, Fiumicino Airport; ☿ 9am-6.30pm) has loads of information on accommodation, itineraries and activities.

Enjoy Rome (Map p93, D1; ☎ 06 445 18 43; www.enjoyrome.com; Via Marghera 8A; ☿ 8.30am-7pm Mon-Fri, 8.30am-2pm Sat Apr-Sep, 9am-5.30pm Mon-Fri, 8.30am-2pm Sat Oct-Mar) is a private tourist office that books accommodation and arranges guided tours.

TRAVELLERS WITH DISABILITIES
Infamous for blocked (or nonexistent) pavements, tiny lifts, unruly traffic and cobbled streets, Rome isn't exactly a breeze for travellers with disabilities. Admittedly, improvements are being made: newer buses and trams generally accommodate wheelchairs, most museums now have ramps, and all Metro Line B stations (except Termini, Circo Massimo, Colosseo, Cavour and EUR Magliana) are wheelchair accessible. Metro Line A is pretty much off limits, but wheelchair-friendly bus 590 follows the same route.

If travelling by train, the **Sala Blu Assistenza Disabili** (Map p93, C2; ☎ 06 488 17 26; ☿ 7am-9pm) next to platform 1 at Stazione Termini can give information on user-friendly trains and help with transport at the station.

When booking a taxi, make sure you request one suitable for *sedie a rotelle* (wheelchairs).

>INDEX

See also separate subindexes for See (p227), Shop (p229), Eat (p230), Drink (p231) and Play (p231).

000 map pages

000 map pages

000 map pages